Never Say No to a Rock Star

In the Studio with Dylan, Sinatra, Jagger, and More

by Glenn Berger

schaffner
press

TUCSON, ARIZONA

Cover and Interior Design: James Kiehle
Author Photo (current): Joshua Silk
Author Photo (A&R Studios): Brad Davis

Excerpt from Lyrics to "Harpo's Blues" by Phoebe Snow, Copyright © 1974, granted by Permission of the Estate of Phoebe Laub.

Other parts of this book have appeared previously in different form in the following online publications:

  Literal Latte ("Oddballs and Angels: Phoebe Snow");
  Esquire ("Bob Dylan's *Blood on the Tracks:* The Untold Story");
  SOS ("Phil Ramone and the Secrets of Vocal Production")

For permissions and copyright information, contact the publisher:
Attn. Permissions, Schaffner Press, POB 41567, Tucson, AZ 85717.
No part of this book may be excerpted or reprinted without the publisher's written consent, except in brief excerpts for review purposes only.

Library of Congress Cataloging-in-Publication Data

Names: Berger, Glenn, 1955-
Title: Never say no to a rock star : in the studio with Dylan, Sinatra,
  Jagger, and more / by Glenn Berger.
Description: First paperback edition. | Tucson, AZ : Schaffner Press, [2016]
Identifiers: LCCN 2016017682| ISBN 9781943156085 (pbk.) | ISBN
9781943156108
  (epub) | ISBN 9781943156092 (pdf)
Subjects: LCSH: Berger, Glenn, 1955- | Sound recording executives and
  producers--United States--Biography.
Classification: LCC ML429.B33 A3 2016 | DDC 781.49092 [B] --dc23
LC record available at https://lccn.loc.gov/2016017682

Dedicated to Milton Brooks, aka "Broadway Max," and the rest of the staff at A&R Studios.

Table of Contents

Foreword
by Judy Collins

Glenn Berger's new book, "Never Say No To A Rock Star," is such a great view of the entire recording experience, the people, the music, the personalities, the tension, the magic—the food! The scenes feel totally real. Glenn captures the excitement of making music and gives the reader a true feeling of being a part of the drive and fantasy, the magic and insanity, the moments of sheer exasperation and sheer wonder. It was always a pleasure to work with Glenn in the midst of the madness as well as the moments of bliss when it all came together. He reminds me in his book of the time of my recording "Send in the Clowns," which was created with the help of Arif Mardin, Phil Ramone, and Jonathan Tunick, three of the most amazing geniuses in the business. I loved that Glenn was there, with his delight and wonder at the center of it all, where everyone wanted to be, in those mostly closed sessions. They were historic, melodic, frantic, delicious and full of contrast— from the sublime to the ridiculous. Glenn takes the reader to the universe of the great A&R Studios in New York where some of the most memorable music of the past century was made. Congratulations, Glenn, you tell it the way it was. And I loved reliving it with you.

—Judy Collins, Grammy Award-winning
singer/songwriter and author

Never Say No to a Rock Star

Prelude

"It Was All Me"

One of my psychotherapy clients, despite years of earnest work on himself, still ached with loneliness. Stephen had been living a noble life. He had been sober for decades. He cared for his mother with Alzheimer's and his developmentally-disabled brother. He'd been training to be a therapist like myself.

But this upstanding life wasn't enough for the ultimate breakthrough. Stephen couldn't find someone to love. Unable to show all of himself, he shied away from his more tender feelings, even with me, his therapist, whom he had known for years. He knew that he would have to make himself vulnerable in front of another human being if he wanted an intimate relationship. If he had any chance of getting to that raw, open place, it had to begin with me, one of the few people in the world he trusted.

Stephen regularly listened to his most beloved music while driving in his car. Recently, he found himself overwhelmed with emotion while listening to his favorite songs. The chords and melodies broke him open in a way that he couldn't close back up. He figured that if he brought in these recordings, and we listened to them together, maybe he would have no choice but to let me see his heart.

I welcomed Stephen into my sanctuary at our next session. I was in my usual shrink uniform. One of the lesser reasons I became a therapist after years in the music biz was because I was starting to look like one. Bald, bespectacled, short, and Jewish, in my navy blazer and fine chocolate corduroys, in my respectable mid-fifties, I could have been a 21st century, New York, ex-hipster version of Sigmund himself; no one would have suspected the life I once led.

Stephen came into my office with his favorite songs programmed on his iPhone. We set up the I-dock. He sat opposite me in the identical chairs I use in my office. His party-boy looks had faded a bit with age, with his knowing smile, wide nose, little goatee and cropped white hair. He hailed from South Georgia, a part of the country so different than my own that he could have just as well been from Mongolia. But, strangely, we related to each other on many levels, our deep appreciation of certain kinds of music being one of them. I sat with my notebook on my lap, ready to note any revelation Stephen might have. He reached over to the screen of his smart device.

The song began.

I closed my eyes. I couldn't help moving my head to the loping easy rock-gospel groove.

The female background singers took it up and sang, "Don't trouble the waters," and a voice totally recognizable to me answered in call and response.

It was Aretha Franklin. She was my favorite singer of all time. Hailing from a gospel upbringing, she began her recording career with a stint as a conventional easy listening act in the early '60s. Then she was liberated into the heights of R&B heaven by the sage impresario, Ahmet Ertegun, who founded, and, with his brother Nesuhi, ran Atlantic Records in the 1940s. They turned the world on to American Rhythm and Blues. By the 1960s, with the influence of the likes of producers Arif Mardin and Jerry Wexler, Atlantic represented the New York soul sound at its funkiest and classiest.

Her hits for that label in the late '60s, like "Chain of Fools," "Rock Steady," "Respect," and "(You Make Me Feel Like a) Natural Woman," will remain soulful till the saints come marching in. No one could move you and groove you like Ree.

And here she was singing, "I know that, if you only believe."

After the intro, the song took its time to get going. With organ, bass and drums behind, Aretha played a languid, funky verse on the Fender Rhodes electric piano.

Then the moan of an electric guitar told us it was time for the entrance of the Queen of Soul.

She took it up and launched into the first verse of her rendition of "Bridge Over Troubled Waters." By increments she took it higher, and by the time she sang the hook line the second time, she was opening up to the heavens, she was finding that place inside where nothing is held back. She was pure. Everything that Stephen — and I — wanted to be.

With my eyes still closed, I swayed, overtaken by the rhythm and the sound. I snapped back for a second and opened my eyes to check on Stephen. I could see he was feeling it deep. I closed mine again, and Aretha's voice hit me in the center of my being.

Then something unexpected happened. Rich, strong, caramel-colored emotion started coming up from my depths. It was rising from my core, lifting higher. All of a sudden the heat was in my chest, and then my throat, and then my face. Losing all self-control, tears burst out my eyes, rolling down my cheeks. It was a feeling I could find no name for — not pain, not sadness, exactly — something I didn't comprehend.

Just when I thought I could take no more, and Miss Franklin couldn't get any deeper, she sang, and I ascended beyond mere emotion. I became full of the spirit. I don't believe in God, but I knew Her in that moment.

Aretha took me by the throat and dragged me to the pulpit. She took it to the podium through the bridge and into the climax. She was no longer a person, she was an oracle, she was possessed, she became the wind of life, part of the chaotic maelstrom of the primal energy. I was caught in the tidal waves of emotion that washed through me. I became one with the wave, with the feeling. I became feeling itself. My face was wet with tears as my body rocked to the rhythm of the track.

I cried and Aretha sang.

The song faded out and I reveled in a minute of precious silence. Finally, I opened my eyes.

I saw Stephen sitting opposite me, his face also streaked with tears, looking at me with shock, surprise, and then delight. He had wanted to see if the music could open him up. He hadn't thought about what it would do to me. Neither had I.

He told me that now he felt connected to me in a way he never had before. We had both stood at the pearly gates and met the place's musical director. We giggled through the crying. This moment changed everything: him, me, us. His healing blew open. Whatever had kept him stuck had now set him free. I was certain of it.

But what did it do to me?

The ninety minutes were up, the therapy session ended, and Stephen left my room. Alone, my body vibrated with the experience I had just been through. Stephen didn't know the half of it, and neither did I.

The catharsis felt good, but troubling. I knew my emotion was about something more than Aretha's soul-healing performance. Hearing that song, at just this moment in my life, awoke something unfinished from many decades before, something that was still unresolved for me.

The feeling and the troubled confusion stayed in me like an after-image from staring too long at something. Incidents I hadn't thought about in years started to emerge. It was Paul Simon's song that had done this odd thing to me.

Then, weirdly, I started hearing his music wherever I went. I walked into the gas station and heard a song of his called "My Little Town." I'd worked on that track many years before, in what seemed like another life. I had known Paul. As soon as I got back in the mini-van with my two little kids strapped in the back, I turned on the radio and heard his beautiful song that captured the spirit of 1968: "America." I had actually watched

Paul copy the lyrics to that song, and I still had the scraps in a book on my shelf.

As I drove, I looked at the suburban road ahead, but saw other pictures in my mind's eye. While my kids clamored behind, I was alone in my memory world. I'd been looking out the windshield and seeing that past with a vivid intensity since the session I'd done earlier with Stephen. As a shrink, I know that if you stimulate the brain with something similar enough to an old experience, a dance of choreographed, lit-up neurons pulsating in harmonious frequencies organize themselves in your head. Pictures, feelings, body sensations, thoughts can all rise up like spring water from a well, unspoiled by time. Since the session with Stephen, I felt all lit up. But I still couldn't put a word to the feeling. I still felt more confused than anything else.

I knew one thing. I had to get up to the attic. I had to get out that tape and listen to it. Maybe that would give me a clue.

When I got home, I went right to the hallway on the second floor of my split-level house. I yanked the rope in the ceiling, pulled down the attic ladder, and climbed up the wooden stairs. The kids were a pain in the ass, as usual, getting in the way of my agenda, but this time I was willing to put up with it.

"Can I come, daddy?"

"Can I?"

"No." I felt more than the usual annoyance about trying to get something done and having to make sure the kids didn't kill themselves at the same time.

"Why not?" in chorus.

"I'll be right down."

"Not fair!"

"Who said it was going to be?"

Above the house, I pulled the old reel-to-reel tape recorder out of a pile of detritus put up there like everything else from my personal history.

I didn't know where else to keep this old stuff. I carefully wobbled down the steps with the analog relic, weighty with some big, old electric transformer in its guts.

"What's that?" my son asked.

"You'll see," I said distractedly.

I went back up the rickety staircase a second time and found the oversized translucent storage container filled with the white cardboard boxes of old reel-to-reel tapes and memorabilia from another era.

Carrying the plastic crate was another awkward trip down the ladder.

"Can I help?"

I started feeling excited now. Did I really own this tape? Did this really happen? After all, you never knew what might come out when you press "Play." Had I made it all up?

Almost forty years had passed. Forty years. Could that be true? I shouldn't have been so surprised to discover that I still felt unresolved, all these decades later. That's the way the psyche works with things like this. Despite the years of maturing, the idiotic mistakes, the advanced degrees, there was still something about those early days I couldn't reconcile.

I took the cover off the machine, revealing its knobs and meters, take-up reel, transport, and head-stack. I plugged the machine in. The machine vibrated to life. It made a weird noise and glowed. An old friend. My kids sat around me, suddenly interested, wanting to touch it, like something that had just landed from outer space. What the hell was this weird machine? It acted its age much more than I did.

I went through the boxes and played a bunch of the old tapes. Here was the basic track of "Kid Charlemagne" by Steely Dan. I had been on that session. Here was the Sinatra tune, "The Saddest Thing of All," that I'd worked on. The Stones, Bette Midler, Phoebe Snow . . .

We recording engineers had a geeky penchant for collecting scurrilous tapes of famous people saying things they oughtn't. Back in the day, before it all became universally available on YouTube, we traded these underground wonders with each other, mostly because they all provided evidence of what only we cognoscenti knew: artists were wonderful, fascinating, and, by and large, loony. We loved them and complained about them at the same time. They were a strange breed, always good for an anecdote.

"Wait till you hear this one!" I tried to engage my kids. "This is by one of the greatest actors of all time, Orson Welles!" Poor Orson. After making groundbreaking films, like *Citizen Kane, The Magnificent Ambersons,* and *Touch of Evil*, he had been relegated, in his later years, to doing advertising copy. He was a big man in every way, and his Falstaffian appetites needed to be fed. He was desperate for the dough. On this audiotape, some idiots were trying to tell him how to do a line reading about peas.

Welles's stentorian rumble rattled the tinny, built in speakers. "What do you want in the depths of your ignorance? I wouldn't direct actors in Shakespeare the way you are doing this! If you can show me how to emphasize the word in in a sentence, I'll, I'll go down on you!"

The sounds had so much meaning for me, but the joke fell flat for my little ones. They hadn't spent years at repertory movie houses in New York City studying classic films by guys like Welles, trying to discover the secrets of existence.

Within minutes the weird old machine and the strange sounds it emanated lost its cool for the kids, and they drifted off, chasing the dog. I smarted at their total incomprehension and lack of interest.

In this moment, I felt oddly distanced from them. I had lived an entire life before they were born, an entire life before I had married their mom, an entire life that no one had lived but me. Memories could be wonderful, but also estranging. I was alone within my glowing neurons.

Anyway, I soothed myself, this wasn't the one I was looking for.

Then I found the tape. The white, cardboard box had black Sharpie writing on it, in the printing style I use to this day with an "s" that looks like a lightning bolt. It said "It Was All Me." I felt this little thrill. Yes — it does exist.

Anyone could get the Orson Welles thing on line now; but only a handful of people had ever heard this one.

I pulled the clear plastic disk filled with black analog audio tape out of the box. My breath caught. I held it lightly, like a precious relic, which it was.

I deftly threaded the tape onto the take up reel, muscle memory intact. I hadn't lost my touch. I hit the play button. The motor moaned and barely turned, like a horse way past its prime that was asked to drag a heavy load. Was the machine going to die just before I'd be able to hear this thing? I stuck my finger in the hole at the center of the five-inch reel and gave it a turn. It kicked into gear and started to spin at seven and a half inches per second. I listened to the tape hiss in anticipation of what was to come.

Then I heard through the little speaker an acoustic guitar, expertly played, beautifully recorded. I closed my eyes. The neurons arranged themselves in my brain and pictures started to form. I saw the scene in my head that I'd seen hundreds of times, dark now, a little distant, but clear.

*

Paul Simon sat on a metal stool. One sleek black boot, snuggled inside a pair of impeccably cut, stone-washed '70s blue jeans, dangled down, not touching the floor. Despite being a small man, he had an unmistakable presence in this cavernous recording studio. One white spot light shone in the darkness, encircling him.

His body was compact but muscular. He was in great shape. He was young, just over 30 years old.

He held a headphone to one ear. His fingers were stubby and wide, but they had a feathery delicacy to them. His fingernails were long, pointy, and carefully manicured, perfect for finger-picking the acoustic guitar. His movements, like his music, were deliberate, almost calculated, certainly self-conscious.

His eyes fluttered in a deep, trance-like, concentration. Through the "cans," he heard the guitar, bass, and drums from a song called "American Tune," the very recording I was listening to now.

Paul's neck tipped upward, his head slightly raised as he sang this ode to battered souls and disillusionment into the cylindrical brass of the Neumann U-87 microphone. The last few notes of the refrain wavered, out of tune.

He had been struggling with this vocal overdub for hours, days, weeks. Simon did not have the most commanding voice, and his search for greatness was relentless. He had set his hopes high for this song, but he knew he hadn't found the magic yet. Maybe he never would. It wouldn't be the first time. This confluence of conditions often made for some long vocal recording sessions.

He stopped, sighed, and said, "Oh my god . . ." with a sense of disbelief in how badly things were going.

Paul had reached the end of his endurance, an extremely rare occurrence for him. The track continued to play, but Paul stopped singing. Violins entered as the song shifted from the verse to the bridge. His engineer and co-producer, Phil Ramone, sat in the control room, listening over the big Altec speakers.

Ramone heard Simon giggling, and decided to let the music continue for a while to see what would happen. Simon started to joke around.

In a fake southern accent he said, "I'd rather be an American than a human being." And then, "Won't you buy this record, please?"

Ramone, realizing there would be no more singing, signaled his assistant to stop the multi-track. The brakes of the big machine's motors kicked in and the music quickly slowed with the familiar choking sound of analog. The sound stopped.

Except for Simon's giggling.

Ramone hit the talkback and said, "Terrible," with a smile in his voice.

There was silence for a moment as Simon took a drink from a bottle of water on a nearby music stand.

"Won't you buy this record please?"

Again Simon paused. "You know, back in 1970 I had a hit with a song called 'Bridge Over Troubled Waters.' I really wish this would be as big as that one."

Now his giggle broke into a full laugh. "I used to have a partner named Art Garfunkel, and this would mean so much to me if I could just show . . . that it was, it was ALL ME!"

Though Simon broke into guffaws, I knew this was no joke.

Once, I had felt a ghoulish glee at having this rare treasure in my possession. But now, especially after what happened at the session with my client Stephen, I felt something different. I felt a strange melancholy, deflated somehow, and some fear, some fear at my confusion.

Back then, it was scandalous that Paul would be dissing Art. But now? Who cared?

As the yellowing tape reels whirled in circles, the neurons in my brain reassembled. Now, these many decades later, my mind was transported back to those days and how it was that this tape ended up here, in my attic.

Day One: Yes Sir, James Brown!

I was stuck.

The year was 1972, and I had just turned seventeen.

Should I wear my Keds or my blue platform shoes with the cork soles? I'd already put on ripped jeans, a cream-colored sports jacket with brown piping on super-giant lapels, and a polyester striped shirt with the top three buttons open. At least the rest of my outfit was done.

I had to choose soon or else I was going to be late.

I went with the sneakers. Maybe I'd have to move fast. I had no idea what would be asked of me. I looked in the mirror on the way out the door. My long red hair cascaded over my shoulders in huge banana curls. My gold-rimmed glasses with orange lenses added a distinctly John Lennon-ish vibe. Was I ready? I blew out a giant breath and left the apartment—ready or not.

In order to get to my destination by subway from my home in Sheepshead Bay, I first had to cross the trestle over the Belt Parkway, a popular place for muggers to lurk and steal the fifty cents I carried in my pocket for a couple slices of pizza. Safely over that obstacle, I plunked my

35-cent brass token with the "Y" carved in the middle into the wooden turnstile and zoomed up the stairs to the elevated train platform, with barely enough time to sneak through the closing doors of the graffiti-emblazoned Manhattan-bound D train.

Once on the train, I grabbed a seat, gripping the little piece of paper that read: *A&R Recording Studios, 799 7th Avenue, 52nd Street, 7th floor. See Tony in the main office.* I kept staring at it, holding it so tightly my hand hurt, afraid that if I loosened my grip or took my eyes off it for a second it would fly out the window and onto the tracks, causing me to forget where I was going, and permanently blowing my one and only chance for stardom and an escape from Brooklyn.

But, as much as I wanted the job, I was equally terrified to get there. With each stop, my chest vibrated more heavily, in sync with the clacking of the subway car as it descended from its elevated track and flew into the black tunnel that would take me into Manhattan.

I got off at the 47th-50th Street subway stop in Midtown. I followed the grid of New York's streets to find my way to 52nd Street and 7th Avenue, zipping between the worker bees on 6th Avenue in a race that only I knew I was running.

Standing in front of the building marked "799," I read the discreet metal plaque labeled *A&R Recording.* My blood pressure kicked up a notch. This was my big chance. Would I fuck it up? My legs started to ache, and my breathing quickened.

Because the first six floors of 799 7th Avenue were home to Manhattan Community College, there was a crush of African-American and Hispanic teenagers in the front lobby. I stood among the throng, watching the numbers light up above the elevator doors as it inched down, stopping at every floor. With every passing minute that seemed like forever, the lobby got more and more crowded. By the time the elevator had arrived, I had to hurl myself into the car packed with so many students I was sure we'd never survive the climb to the 7th floor. I plunged my arm through a passel of bodies to get to the buttons, all lit up from the 2nd to the 6th. I was the only one who pushed the number 7.

As the ride lurched to a stop at each floor to vomit out multitudes and suck up yet more people, I fantasized about a glamorous and glitzy world awaiting me, full of fabulous stars, groovy rockers making crazy sounds, and geniuses who expected me to be just like them. Despite this alluring vision, my fears overwhelmed the thrill, and I grew certain that I was doomed, convinced I had to be perfect and brilliant, when I knew nothing whatsoever about the recording business except how to hit rewind and fast-forward. A voice screamed in my head: *Just hit the lobby button, go back down, and get out of there! No one will ever know you were here, and you will have escaped!*

With the clamor in my brain growing to a screech, the doors slowly opened at the seventh floor. I stood in the car, frozen. Thank goodness the elevator was such an ancient piece of crap that the doors stayed open for a long time.

Then something in me pushed up from my center, an alternate force of determination. I told myself, *I'm gonna do this.* With all my might, against the pull of terror, I leapt out of the car. When I looked around, I felt disoriented, convinced I was on the wrong floor. The decor was shabby, cheap, and worn. I saw a dirty yellow couch with a couple of disheveled messengers asleep on it. They looked to me like homeless beggars.

Then two guys ran in front of me and down the hall, one chasing the other with a fire extinguisher held over his head, screaming, "You putz! I'll fuckin' rip your balls off!"

So much for glitz and glamor.

Strangely, that made me feel a little more comfortable. This wasn't as far from Brooklyn as I imagined it would be.

Could this really be the place? I saw an open door to the left, and walked in. A guy stooped over a drafting table with a Sherlock Holmes pipe drooping out of his mouth. He had broad '70s sideburns and a long,

Italianate shnoz.

"Yes?" he said, laconically, with a raised eyebrow. The phone rang. "Hold on," he raised a finger, signaling me to wait.

"Can't do it, pally. It's booked. Look I don't care if Donnie's having a baby. Phil's got it blocked for McCartney. All day and night." A pause. "I know he won't use it. But do you want to tell Ramone he can't have his studio?" Another pause. "All right. Good luck." The guy slammed down the phone.

He looked at me. "What do these fucking people want from me?"

I wasn't sure what to answer, but I guessed he must have been talking about *Paul* McCartney. That would mean I had arrived.

"OK. Who are you and what do you want?"

I was in it now. No time for nerves. I somehow squeaked out, "I'm the new intern and I'm here to see Tony, the studio manager."

"You got him. Perfect. Hey, assholes!" He called out to whoever was in the room. "We have a new victim!"

The other guys in the room turned to me with a look of pity. I intuited this was all a test. It was time to perform. This was something I could handle, or at least so I thought. Just look tough, I told myself.

Tony tapped out his pipe in the ashtray and leaned over so close to me that the tip of his nose almost touched mine, which, being of the Jewish variety, wasn't so short itself. I held my position and stared in his eyes.

"Rule number one. Keep your fucking mouth — SHUT. Do you understand? If I hear that you have so much as said hello to any of the artists, I will rip you a new one and your career in the music business will be over before it began. Get it?"

I nodded, not knowing if this was one of those times I wasn't supposed to speak.

"Rule number two. You do whatever I tell you to do. You never, ever say no. The only right answer is yes. Do you understand that one?"

Now I at least knew what to say. "Yes."

"Perfect."

I hadn't blown it yet, but inside I was wincing a bit. I felt like I was getting poked in the ribs. I knew I couldn't show it.

Two hip-looking young guys ambled into the office.

One of them, with a cool gait, a wispy blond moustache, scraggly beard, plastic aviator glasses and a black and white cowboy shirt, said, "Hey Remsen, Billy, come with us."

The studio manager, Tony, said, "What are you up to?"

The other guy, good looking with a black shag and beard, said, "We're just breaking down from the Foghat session so Blakin can get into A-1."

"Mathis, Devon, this is . . . what's your name?"

"Glenn Berger."

"Berger here is our new intern. Take care of him, will you? This is Dan Mathis and Greg Devon, two of our best assistant engineers. Follow them around and one day you, too, might learn how to be as big losers as they are."

The guys smiled, ignoring the provocation. Mathis said, "Come with us."

The five of us walked down the hall. My legs were still shaking a bit, but I tried to affect the same cool these guys displayed. With each step, my initial panic settled, replaced with giddiness. If anyone saw me with this crew, they'd think I was just one of the guys.

At the end of the hall was a blue door with a round window. We opened it.

I stood at the threshold and peered in. For someone who was interested in how music got made, it was like looking into the entrance of Chartres Cathedral. I stared into a huge room with a blond, wooden floor and a high, peaked ceiling. Something had just happened. Microphones hung on huge booms slanted at various angles in front of buzzing amps and empty chairs. Headphones lay tossed on the floor. A huge drum set, behind baffles, was surrounded by a web of mics. The room gave off a sweet ring like a bunch of monks chanting "om." The remnants of a pungent, skunky smell suggested rock and roll.

I didn't have much time to take in the vibe, as we hurried to a smaller room in the back. I hustled to catch up. What were we up to? Why were we cramming in this little space? Everyone huddled in a circle, silent with anticipation. I took my place. Mathis took out a folded piece of paper and carefully unwrapped it, revealing a small pile of white powder. Devon offered a tiny, metal spoon.

"Where'd you get the shit?" Billy asked.

"The guys from Foghat gave us a little gift on the way out. They told us to share it with you low-lifes."

The group of young men hovered anxiously over the offering, waiting for their toot. I watched each guy dip the spoon into the powder, hold one nostril and snort the stuff into the other one. Then they reversed the procedure, snorting up the other side.

Eventually, the spoon came to me.

"You want some?"

I had done my share of substances in my young life, but never cocaine. Being a kid from the '70s, I was all about taking any drug available. I remembered Tony's instructions.

"Yes!"

I just wanted to impress with my *savoir faire* and do it right. My shaking hand scraped up a few grains of the magic dust onto the spoon. As I brought it to my nose I tried to remember to breathe in and not out. I feared I looked the novice. Some precious crumbs fell on the artificial carpet. Looks were exchanged. My cool cover was blown. I cringed with embarrassment.

But I learned fast. We went around the circle a few more times, and I got enough in to give me a sweet, glowing buzz. It was as if someone had blown a giant wind through my head, clearing the dust and dirt away. I felt fresh. My head expanded. All the lights got brighter, my anxiety and embarrassment evaporated, and I saw the whole thing as if from above, wowed by where I was. I had to suppress a stupid grin. I had just learned my next lesson in the studio: I now knew how to snort cocaine.

If I hadn't been excited enough getting my big break to be an intern at a recording studio, I was now euphoric. I hadn't been in this place for ten minutes and I was already blasted. A cocaine-amplified thought went through my head— I was the shit! Yes, indeed!

Devon said to the crowd, pointing at me, "So what are we gonna do with this kid?"

Mathis answered, "Berger, there's a session in A-2 you might dig. Why don't you hang in there till we think of something for you to do. Come on. Follow me."

We walked back down the hall, the shabby decor glimmering a little brighter. Over the control-room door a sign lit in red announced: *Closed Session*. I hesitated. Mathis walked right in and signaled me to follow. Apparently, I'd received *carte blanche*.

I stood in a dim room lit by colored lights. The recording console glowed in the middle, a blue metal box about the size of a small car, covered with black knobs, white glowing switches and buttons, and red sliding volume controls. This was the machine I hoped to play with someday, the thing that took what came out of the artists and musicians and transformed it into that thing we called a "record."

Thick double-paned glass covered the front wall. Behind the glass was the recording room. My first session!

Mathis introduced me to the assistant, a black guy named Holley. He shook my hand and smiled. The assistants were cool. He pulled over a stool for me in the rear right-hand corner of the control room and patted it for me to sit down. He whispered. "Do you know how to run a tape machine?"

I nodded and again said, "Yes."

"When I give you the signal, you rewind this tape to the top and then hit play and record. That's your job." Holley winked, as if to say, I'll take

Never Say No to a Rock Star

care of you, kid, don't worry.

I tried to settle my ass on the stool. My first job. I silently prayed, *Please, God, don't let me hit the wrong button . . .*

Above the glass, there were speakers on the wall opposite me the size of small tanks. A relentless funk vamp pounded out of the giant woofers and tiny tweeters. Every time the kick drum popped on the first and third beat of the four-beat measure I felt my viscera lurch to the edge of my throat. Smack between that non-stop deep and hard percussion was the stanky crack of the snare on the two and four. When the stick hit the skin I checked my ears for blood. Sinewy guitar licks punctuated the off beats. Honkin' horns swirled their sexy riffs between the gravelly vocals.

In the front of the control room, underneath a spotlight, a black guy with a high, stiff coiffure held court. He looked familiar. Though I couldn't hear him over the pounding groove, I could see his lips move as he talked non-stop while his court stood around him in obeisance.

The repetitive four-bar musical pattern seemed to go on forever. Pop, stomach up, crack, ear-bleed, pop, crack, pop, crack.

Everybody seemed to be enjoying the music that just kept going, but I couldn't take it. It was too *loud*.

I had this overwhelming urge to run out of the control room. It was like someone was screwing a drill into my head. My newbie status was clear. *I'll never be able to handle this,* I thought. I held onto my stool to keep myself there.

Over the funky noise, I heard this raspy wail. "Bob, Bob! Stop that muthafucka!"

A white guy sitting at the console, the engineer, nervously pushed his long hair back, swung his chair around from his position at the board and swiped his hand across his throat, the universal signal for "stop." Holley hit the big white button on the middle of the massive multi-track tape machine. The silence was almost as deafening as the cacophony that preceded it. Holley gave me the cue, and I hit the rewind button.

"Bob, you gotta listen when I talk!"

"Yes sir, Mr. Brown."

"Five dollars."

A short, rotund man in a black suit nodded and marked something on a pad.

Mr. Brown? Wait, I know who that guy is, I thought. It's James Brown! The Godfather of Soul, Mr. Hot Pants, the Papa with a Brand New Bag! Holy shit!

I hadn't really thought of James Brown for a couple of years, probably not since his last hit, "Sex Machine," and two years was a long time back then. I assumed his best days were behind him, but he was definitely a legend. I was in the room with my first Star.

"That track is fine," Brown said. "Now this is what we're gonna do next. This young lady and I are going to work the bridge on the ballad."

Mr. Brown put his hand on the waist of a sexy looking woman wearing a tight-fitting polyester dress that clung to her ample butt. "I'll show you what to do," Mr. Brown said to her.

He turned to Holley and said, "Set up the mics."

Holley ran out into the studio and pushed some microphone stands into position in the center of the room.

James Brown started to speak with a voice that sounded like someone had shredded his vocal chords into a thousand pieces and then poured crazy glue on them to put them back together. "Here is the situation in the country today. The black man is finally beginning to assume his power. The princes of Africa, you know that most slaves were descendants of African princes, right? The princes of Africa are no longer going to play this role of bowing down to the white man. And the white man is afraid, because he knows that when the black man finally wakes up, he will be in a lot of trouble. Now here is what *every one* of you got to do."

His coterie stood rapt around him, listening to his every utterance, nodding approvingly. The tape machine I was rewinding was coming close to the top of the reel. I hit the fast-forward button to break the speed, and hit stop when it slowed to a crawl. Then I hit play and "record." I felt slick.

James Brown continued.

"You must be proud. Say it loud," he bellowed in that famous rasp, "I'm black and I'm proud! We are not the ones who are going to ruin this country. White men can do that job good enough themselves. We are the ones who are going to *save* it! It's time for payback! Get out of my way!"

I wanted to shout out, *right on, James Brown! Power to the people!* But then I remembered that I was supposed to keep my mouth shut. Also, I was a skinny white kid who was the assistant's intern. Good idea to keep quiet. But man, this guy could be funky and political all at the same time. I dug it.

Holley came back into the control room and with deference said, "We're ready, Mr. Brown."

"Get up!" Mr. Brown cackled. "Thank you, Holley." And then, "Bob, you lame-ass white mother fucker, what are you doing? Put up the ballad and go to the bridge. Let's go!" And then, with charm, "Come on, young lady, follow James into the studio and I'll show you what to do."

The engineer fiddled with some knobs to prepare for the new track.

As James Brown walked out of the control room and into the studio, a man with gold-rimmed glasses, a droopy moustache and a scraggly head of hair with a growing bald spot in the back got up from the row of movie theatre chairs that were at the front of the recording console.

He said to no one in particular, "Is this man not the funkiest cat on the planet?" still groovin' to a beat that had stopped long before.

This guy looked familiar, too. I rifled through my brain's memory drive, and up came the cover of the very first record album I bought and loved when I was five years old in 1960. It was called *Peter, Paul and Mary*. The scraggly dude, in a somewhat younger version, was on that cover. The man in front of me was Peter Yarrow from this hit-making folk trio. He was the guy who wrote "Puff, the Magic Dragon."

Now I knew I was a little high, but this was a weird combo: the godfather of soul and the pot-smoking pederast! (Yarrow had pleaded guilty for taking "immoral and improper liberties" with a 14-year-old in 1970, and "Puff" was presumably about weed.)

I barely had time to incorporate what was going on when Brown, standing in front of the mics with the young lady, commanded, "Bob, play the track through the speakers and record this!"

Bob the engineer hit the talkback and said nervously, while playing with his hair, "Mr. Brown, if we play it through the speakers that will leak into the mic, which won't be great for the sound. Could you put on your headphones?"

"Bob! Just do what I say. You make it work. Wait. Let me explain it to you. It's not about the *sound*, it's all about the *feel*. Who cares about the leakage?"

Little did any of us know at that time that in a few decades, with the advent of hip-hop and sampling, when artists could cadge a few measures from any record and use it as the basis of their own art, these nasty, low-tech James Brown recordings (probably from his album *The Payback*) would become some of the most popular "samples" in the genre.

In exasperation, Bob turned back to Holley and threw up his hands. Holley, always smiling and nodding, leaned over Bob to push some buttons and turn some knobs. He then turned to the multi-track tape machine and hit the red button. A black velvet, slow groove chugged through the speakers. James directed the girl.

"Now you just follow what I do with what you do. Just do whatever comes to your soul, girl. Just be real."

The instrumental mid-section of the song began, and James moaned, "Ooo yeah, baby, unh."

He nodded to the girl. She took it up. "Yeah, I like it like that."

Then James, "Get it on, get it on, girl, get it on."

"Sweet, sweet, James, give it to me good."

This went on for a couple of minutes. It was bad! I started to writhe in my seat, the snaky groove crawling up my spine. I couldn't help but get into it.

In a swoon, I was startled to feel someone poking my shoulder. I turned my head and there was Tony, the studio manager. With his thumb, he motioned for me to get up and get out, as if I was being sent to the principal's office. Was grinding not allowed?

When we got into the hall, he said, "OK kid, here's your first gig so don't screw up. See these mics?"

I sighed with relief. I wasn't in trouble yet.

In the hallway were two 7-foot tall Atlas mic stands. At the end of each hung a microphone the size of a liter soda bottle.

"Bring the U-47 into A-1. There's a guy in there named Blakin. Make sure he gets it."

Tony turned and walked away. I took a breath and tried to push the enormous, heavy metal unit to the big room. I could barely steer it, and the mic swung perilously close to the walls. Inching along, I made it after what felt like a half hour, sweating, relieved that nothing broke on the way and no one was there to see it.

Richard Blakin, impeccably tailored in a black vest, black pants, wireless glasses, and a "patch cord" around his neck, grabbed the mic from me. He flipped a switch on the mic and said, "Wrong one. I need the 47, not the 48. You see, let me show you. This one is figure-8. The 47 is omni."

"Oh," I said, not wanting to reveal my utter ignorance as to what "figure-eight" or "omni" meant. What I did know was that, out of the two mics in the hall, I had picked the wrong one, and now I had to go through the treacherous exercise of getting the other one down the hall without shattering it.

I guess Blakin saw the fear in my eyes, or he knew he needed the mic faster than I'd get it. "Come with me," he said, with teacherly patience.

I followed him down the hall.

"Let me show you how to do this."

He deftly grabbed the giant stand. He unlocked a big knob on the side, lowered the upper boom parallel to the floor, tightened the knob, grabbed the mic in one hand and the lower part of the stand in the other, and pushed the whole thing into the studio in about four seconds. Ah-ha.

He loosened another knob, lifted the upper stand high in the air, and deftly swung the boom into the middle of a semi-circle of five black gospel performers singing in powerful harmony, being directed by a little white guy.

Wait. The guy directing them is very short, I noticed. *It's Paul Simon. Paul Simon?* Of course the thought that got stuck in my head was, *Wow. He is really short.* For some reason, when I looked at him I didn't feel excited. I felt cold. A little scared.

But the singers! The sound of their rich, blended gospel voices in that sweet, big room was stirring. I got a little teary.

I followed Blakin into the control room where we were alone. Hiding my trembling voice, I asked, "Who are those singers?"

"The Dixie Hummingbirds. Name of the song is, 'Loves Me Like a Rock.'" (This track, which eventually charted as a number two single, would be released on Simon's forthcoming album, *There Goes Rhymin' Simon*.)

Blakin gave me my now familiar seat next to what I was to find out was called the "echo machine." The machine added a delay to the reverb, giving the effect a rich depth. I was starting to get into my gig of rewinding that tape back to the top when it got to the end and hitting the play and "record" button. Also, I felt safe and secure hidden in this corner of the room with something to do.

Blakin pointed to a fat guy with a beard who hovered close to Simon out in the studio.

"That's Ramone. Phil Ramone. The guy who owns the place. Look, steer clear of him. He's a genius, and he can be a little volatile on occasion.

Your job is to be invisible. If you can manage that, you'll survive. Don't do anything unless I tell you to."

So that was the legendary recording engineer Phil Ramone.

It was great being invisible. As I watched these musical giants at work, I wondered, what are they really like? I still had a little buzz on, and I thought this enhanced my powers of perception. I imagined I could see more deeply into things.

Ramone seemed an inexplicable combination of sensitivity, strength, confidence, and anxiety all rolled into one. He followed Simon around, hanging on his every word. I was shocked to see this studio legend treat Simon with such deference. I could see their whole relationship in a flash. It was as if Phil was simply an excellent butler to the lord of the manor. This bugged me. I felt a resistance in my working-class liberal-hippie belly. I couldn't do that, even for a superstar like Simon. Judgments came up: *Ramone is acting like such a pussy. And look how Simon expects to be treated this way.*

Blakin turned a knob on the V-shaped console, and we listened in to Simon's work through the mic he had placed in front of the singers. Simon rehearsed the choir relentlessly, singing the same few lines over and over. He must have heard something different each time they did it, but it all sounded the same to me.

Suffused with an intolerable boredom from the endless repetition of the whole thing, my mind wandered. As I looked out into the big room, I traveled back to Nov. 17, 1970. On that night, I had listened to a live radio broadcast of a concert by Elton John, recorded in this very studio, with Ramone at the helm. That had been the day my father died. I had listened to that concert in my room as I waited to put my father in the ground.

A few weeks before my dad died, I came home from school one day to find him in his wheelchair in our living room, crying. I had never seen my father cry before. I felt a tightness in my jaw that made me want to lower my eyes and turn away. Sitting opposite him, on a plastic covered chair,

I asked him what was wrong. He said that he had never achieved anything in his life except have his children.

Hearing those words, I felt a rising panic. How horrible. I told myself in that moment that I would never, ever find myself in that position. I would start doing something with my life, now.

Little did I know that two years later I would be sitting with Ramone and Paul Simon, of all people, in the very room where Elton played the night my father died.

The coke was wearing thin. I started coming down, my euphoria mixing with melancholy.

Simon started recording the background singers over the pre-record-ed rhythm section. He kept doing take after take. I rewound my echo tape over and over again. The dregs of the coke left me feeling edgy. What with the volume, the repetition, and all that had happened that day, I hit over-load. I told Blakin I had to go. He grunted, preoccupied, at the ready, his eyes on Ramone and Simon, his fingers on the buttons. I slunk, invisibly and silently, out of the control room and down the hall.

I crammed back into the front elevator, relieved that I had survived, glad to be out of there, and excited that I would be coming back again.

On the way down to the lobby, I looked at all the students, oblivious to what was going on right above them, to what had just happened to me. I felt strangely apart from them as their bodies shoved against me. Some-how, I was *different*. I had gone through the very first steps of an initiation that had already transformed me in ways I could barely understand.

As I made it into the street, back in the real world, surrounded by the chaos and grandeur of the city, revived by a blast of oxygen, the experience of that day suddenly hit me. James Brown, Peter Yarrow, and Paul Simon. Day one. I could confidently say I was doing something with my life. Remembering my first lesson, I jumped up, pumping my fist in the air, and yelled, *yes!*

The Schlepper

After three months of interning, in March of '73, I got a phone call from Tony at my girlfriend Kathy's house in Tenafly, New Jersey. *Uh-oh,* I thought, *I must've screwed something up. I'm cooked.* I was in trouble. Just not the way I thought.

"Berger. You've got a job. You're gonna be the *schlepper*. Be here Monday morning, 8 AM. And be on time, you little scumbag."

I thought I detected a small smile in his voice.

"Yes, sir!"

I slammed down the phone, screamed and whooped, and gave Kathy a hug. I was truly in the door! I felt the gentle hand of the universe aiding me. Then the hand turned cold. Could I really escape the dregs of Brooklyn where fate had indiscriminately born and bred me? The next test was upon me.

To *schlep*: to drag, to carry with shame, to slave.

Schlepper: he, or she, who is at the bottom.

A&R had studios in two buildings, one at 7th Avenue and 52nd Street and the other at 48th between 8th and 9th. Avenue. Someone had to *schlep* a hand-truck of tapes from one building to the other across midtown Manhattan.

$80 a week, $64 take-home after taxes.

Me!

Within days the glow of victory began to fade. The ignominy of my newly achieved status settled into my bones like a virus. The job was easy enough. That I could handle. But would I be able to tolerate the weary ache of my days?

Each morning I assumed the mantle of *schlepperhood* by descending to the recording Underworld. Now that I was an insider, I knew not to travel up the front elevators crammed with the *hoi polloi*. Instead, I entered the building through the freight entrance on 52nd Street. This portal was reminiscent of Dante's entrance to hell. (If you want to know what it looked like, it was immortalized on the cover of Billy Joel's album, *52nd Street).* The scene was pure New York '70s: grotty, filthy, perfect as a place for some homeless drunk to sleep it off.

I passed through the unmarked entrance and slid down the fetid, greasy steps, rank with the smell of rancid french-fry oil oozing from the Golden Griddle Coffee Shop on the corner, and headed to the basement.

There I passed the office of Doug McTeague, the Southern superintendent, with its walls covered in cheap nudie shots. I barely waved, while he said, "How-dee!"

"How fuckin' dee to you," I mumbled to myself.

I pushed open a bent metal door and entered my work home, the studio's tape library, filled with thousands of audiotapes created over the previous decade.

I'd spend my bored hours snooping through the shelves, occasionally stumbling on some amazing classic. One day I opened a box whose spine read "The Crackers" and found the original multi-track masters of the *Big Pink* album by The Band, the first album by one of the greatest groups of the rock era.

I plopped down on a ripped Naugahyde chair held together with silver duct tape, skeevy with ancient cum and coffee stains. Like the water torture victim anticipating the next drop to fall, I waited for the phone to ring. Within minutes, after I'd barely had time to take a sip of my coffee with milk and sugar, the metal clapper vibrated on the bell of the black phone that sat on my desk. Cringing, I picked up the handset to stop the clanging, and heard the dreaded voice of that hook-nosed, pipe-smoking, jive-ass Tony, whose favorite thing in the world was to make me start my day miserable.

With a derisive snarl in his voice, he said, "It's that time, pal."

This meant that I got to take the freight elevator up to heaven, to the studio floor. I walked through those halls, empty at this time of day. No self-respecting cat would be seen alive there at 8:15 a.m. Tony handed me a re-used manila envelope with the day's schedule of sessions and pointed to the hand-truck full of tapes that I was to push across midtown to what we called the "other side," meaning the studios on 48th street.

"Move it!" was the closest he got to "good morning."

I rolled the hand-truck down the hall, made a right turn to the back and pushed it into the freight elevator. The elevator operator was a guy named Reverend Blalock. He was like Vasudeva, the ferryman in the Herman Hesse novel *Siddhartha*, who teaches the young Buddha about the path to enlightenment.

As Blalock took me back down to the ground floor and the early morning midtown street, I asked, "How you doin', Brother Bob?"

"Up and down brother, up and down," he would answer.

True enough, Brother Bob, true enough.

I hit the sidewalk. New York in 1973 was a nasty, dangerous place. You had to navigate the streets with a constant vigilance, knowing how to sidestep, cross, avoid. When you were in the groove, you could feel the danger coming and it would never touch you. That's why it was always the tourists from Saginaw who got mugged on 42nd Street between Broadway and 8th, the very intestines of the neighborhood where I went to my version of college, *Screw U*. That's where I got a 4.0 in the "don't fuck wit me" class.

The city was bankrupt, dogshit was all over the streets, the sky was always a putrid grayish-green, and any minute some freak could step out of the shadows and plant an axe in your skull.

The route from 799 7th Avenue to 322 West 48th Street took me through the classic Broadway theater district, the fabled land of song and dance, immortalized in such tunes as "On Broadway" and "New York." *If I can make it here, I'll make it anywhere,* and all that jazz.

I edged the hand-truck into the gutter, and yanked it up 52nd to Broadway. I parked my load of tapes in the corner at the Playland arcade on Broadway and 52nd and, with the few dimes in my pocket, played some pinball along with the other game-freaks who hung out there 24 hours a day.

I turned south heading to 48th. One of the city's fabulous nut-jobs hung on the corner of 50th and Broadway, standing next to an overflowing trashcan. This shaggy fellow with a patchy white beard and few teeth lived for Wednesday afternoons. When some little old ladies would pass by on their way to a matinee theatre performance, he'd say, just loud enough for them to hear, "Shit."

There were a lot of great nut-jobs in New York then. One of them appeared in the Martin Scorsese film that captured this era best, *Taxi Driver.* He was a little guy named Gene Palma who looked like a bullet with tarred, shiny black hair. He was an ersatz drummer who loved the age of hard swing. He'd say in his nasal bark, "1941, 'Drum Boogie,' Gene Krupa at the Philharmonic." Then he'd twirl the sticks and play his concept of the original solo on the top of a garbage can. For years after, he kept the hope alive that his one film appearance would be the beginning of a major movie career. He'd advertise himself available for hire, his ad written with magic marker on a piece of cardboard box. He actually got in one more movie, but then disappeared.

Then there was the blind composer Moondog, who stood in front of the CBS building on 6th Avenue holding a spear and dressed in a cloak and horned Viking helmet. That was one way of getting a recording contract. He actually put out a few albums of bizarre stuff on the *grande dame* of record labels, Columbia.

Continuing on my way to the other side, I passed the Brill Building between 50th and 49th Street and said a prayer. This was the center of the musical universe, where more hit songs were written in the 60s than anywhere in the world.

Finally, I stopped in at the historic Colony Records on the corner of 49th— where aspiring stars bought their sheet music and recordings— to peruse the bins in search of some obscure King Crimson album imported from England. I'd do anything to waste a few more minutes before my daily dose of humiliations would commence.

The turn up 48th toward 8th then brought me to an even sleazier part of town. Cheap, black, junkie hookers would be leaving their corner posts, gray and pasty from a night of fucking tourists (unprotected in those pre-AIDS days). Low-life porno joints lined 8th Avenue along with down-on-your-luck Blarney Stones, where you could get a Salisbury steak for $2.99.

"322," as we called it, was halfway between 8th and 9th Avenues. The decor was much sleeker than the shabby vibe of "799"; it was '70s modern with shiny red tiles on the wall.

On my way in, I said hi to the cool, eccentric babe who sat at the receptionist's desk behind an old-fashioned switchboard with holes to plug in cords for directing the calls. A few of the receptionists through the years doubled as drug dealers, but, if not, by plugging in the right cord, they could certainly service any star or staff member with any substance required. Another couple of the hot young things behind the desk were also generally not even the least bit above giving a blowjob to just about anyone who asked nicely enough. She could be an aspiring show biz something, and if she played it right, she could get a rich studio singer to "sponsor" her up-and-coming career.

I left my hand-truck for a minute and went downstairs to take a leak. Along with the tech shop and the guy's john, it was also the home of the women's bathroom, a popular place to snort cocaine. At night, the boys of the studio would line up on the sink counter waiting with their glass bottles and tiny spoons to offer their sacrifice of Peruvian Flake to the punky girls who yanked their skin-tight Fiorucci jeans down around their ankles and splashed into the pot while absent-mindedly picking the numbing rocks out of their noses with their blood red fingernails, then sucking them into their mouths for a little extra blast.

I went back upstairs and with anticipation entered the room to the left of the receptionist area. This was the location of studio R-2, where Phil Ramone, the revered Alpha silverback of our pack, did most of his work. It was a small room, and, as I was to learn later on, it had its flaws. It had an "RF" or Radio Frequency problem as it was too close to 8th Avenue, so it was hard to plug in any electronic device without getting a nasty buzz. But that didn't stop the studio from putting out an endless string of hit records.

The studio had been "block-booked" and had been left set up from the day and night before, in order that the artist, musicians, and engineers could pick up right where they had left off. One wall, covered with the "patch bay," was crammed with a Medusa-like jumble of quarter-inch cables. On the console in the middle of the room, the big, round, black faders used for setting recording levels were turned this way and that. The sliding red faders to their left, in the "juke box," used to finesse the blend of instruments called a "mix," were each in their perfect undulated spot. Underneath it all were strips of masking tape, on which were written the names of the mics or the instruments: bass, kick drum, tom-toms, snare, high-hat, electric guitar, piano, organ, vocals. Out in the studio, all the mics in place, I could almost hear the reverberation of the tight, smoking tracks that had been cut the night before by the best studio musicians alive.

Standing in this inner sanctum of musical marvels, I felt a combination of exhaustion, thrill, and fear. We were all told way too many times by the CEO that we should be glad we got paid anything at all because anyone would be willing to give his or her right arm to have the chance to work at A&R. And he was right.

As I looked at the studio all set up and ready to burst into music at the push of a button, with its bright blue console, glowing white switches and red sliding faders, I yearned for that day when I would take the trip up the freight for good, to become a member of the squad on top, an assistant engineer. Something inside me came alive at that moment that I had never felt before: a single-minded, passionate resolve to do whatever it took to make it. I'd spend every minute I could in the studio —that is, when I wasn't pushing that infernal hand-truck across the city.

My reverie was interrupted by some internal alarm signal that hit me like a prod to the gonads. Shit! I had a job to do and I knew what would happen if I didn't get it right.

I had to make sure the rooms were well stocked: the cup had to be filled with pencils, every one with a sharpened point; there had to be ample take sheets to record the day's proceedings; track sheets were also essential to indicate what could be found on each track of the multi-track tapes.

Before I had the chance to tidy up the place, Plotnik, the guy who made the early morning tape copies, blew into the room looking for some master tape and busted me, the *schlepper*, breathing in the rarefied air of Hitsville. There I was, snooping in the control room, trying to ascertain the hidden code of the universe, intently studying the position of each knob, the placement of a microphone.

He looked at me suspiciously, and without saying a word, he slowly inspected the control room. If he would have been wearing a white glove, he would have run it along the console for dust. He looked in the pencil jar and paused, smiling with victorious satisfaction like a detective finding the essential clue. He dumped the can of pencils on the floor.

Then he exploded. "Hey shithole! Get over here! What the fuck is this?"

He got so close up to my face I could see the spittle on the sides of his mouth and smell his pickled breath. "What are you doin' just standing

22

there? Writin' a book?"

He picked up an unsharpened pencil stub from the floor and shoved it in my face.

"If the ashtray is dirty, how can you trust the pilot to fly the plane? Don't you know where you are?" He was referring to the A&R way, as passed down by Ramone. We had standards to maintain.

Then, grabbing me by the waist, he lifted me in the air, swung me up over his head, spun me around, and deposited me roughly on the floor. "And it's your job to keep the ashtrays clean. Now make this place perfect and get outta here before I give you a nootzle!"

That was the life of the *schlepper*, the sub-cretin that everyone was allowed to torment.

"Suck this!" I muttered, just loud enough for him to hear, as he turned toward the door. He turned, glared, smiled, pointed at me, and nodded, as if to say "you're dead," and walked out of the room, master tape under his arm.

As much as I resented the abuse, I felt a warmth in my belly. I longed for meaning and something to live for, and I could tell that all these people, as over-the-top as they all seemed, had *pride*. I wanted that. And, being from Brooklyn, I could handle this shit and give it back, too. If that was the game, I'd show these motherfuckers.

I left the control room "perfect," and after doing the same to studio R-1, went upstairs to where the business was done. I said hi to the sexy girls in accounting, getting a seductive smile from one (who would later initiate me into the fine art of cunnilingus), and went into Uncle Max's office to drop off the tapes and envelope.

Uncle Max, "Broadway Max", a man of a thousand monikers, officially known as Milton Brooks, was the studio Yoda, the majordomo of the place. Out of all the characters who populated this hip '70s studio, Max was the least likely resident. Dressed like a funeral director, he looked and talked like a character from a Damon Runyon story. Day in and day out, he wore the same shiny black suit covered in dandruff, a yellowing white shirt, and stained red tie. He had a white crew cut on a brick of a head, teeth even yellower than his shirt (and more crooked), a wicked smile, and a demonic laugh. He sat behind his desk with a few chewed cigar stubs in his ashtray.

"Well, well, well, if it isn't our very own Sammy Glick," Brooks said in his best Edward G. Robinson imitation and making one of his typically obscure literary references.

If for five minutes every day I could feel safe from the random acts of training violence I was subjected to, it was here in the presence of Max. His calm in the face of the studio lunacy was preternatural. It was like he was born to live in this jungle, and nothing made him happier.

Max's world was bordered by 42nd and 59th Street on the West Side of New York City. He had been born in Minneapolis, and had fled his family's haberdashery business as soon as he could get on the Minnesota-to-New York express. He loved theatre and literature, so never wanted to be far from the shows on Broadway. When he landed his job at A&R he knew that he had found home.

"How's my boy?" he rasped.

I plopped down on the chair opposite his desk. "Alright, Brooks. Who is this Sammy Glick?"

As he had many before, and would for so many after, Brooks decided to take me under his wing and give me a true education. I was hungry to learn.

"Read this," he said, pushing an old paperback in my direction.

"*What Makes Sammy Run?* by Budd Schulberg. What's it about?"

"Maybe you. We'll just have to wait and see," he said with a sly grin.

Caught in my own solipsistic, adolescent circle, I thought out loud, "Brooks, when am I going to get into the studio?"

"Patience, my boy. You will."

I leaned on his desk, and said "When?"

He retorted, "Read the book," and handing me another envelope, added, "And bring this to the *other side.*"

I grabbed both, twirled around to leave, looking at Brooks with a fake grimace, and waved the book as if to say thanks.

 I got a new load of tapes, stacked them on the hand-truck, stuck the envelope between a few of them, schlepped those back to "799" and returned to my post in the fetid netherworld of the tape library, fearing I'd be trapped there forever, and dreaming of my means of escape. I couldn't wait to get the book out of my pocket. I pulled it out and started to read, holding my breath, hoping it would teach me how to make it in this mysterious world, and help me find the path to heaven before the blare of the phone dragged me down to Purgatory again.

TRACK THREE

Phil Ramone Plucks Me from Obscurity

During that summer, before I turned eighteen, I took one small step up from my job as bottom-rung *schlepper*. I got a $10 raise and was promoted to tape librarian. I didn't have to push the hand-truck across Midtown as often, but I still had to schlep piles of audio tapes from the Valhalla of the 7th floor studios down to my personal hell, the tape library in the basement of 799 7th Avenue. It was my job to catalogue these newly-created album, film, and jingle recordings and order them in the endless stacks deep in the basement's innards so they could be easily retrieved.

I was terrible at the job. I personally knew where every tape was, but my system was chaos. I paid the price for my disorganization early one Saturday morning.

As was typical, my friends and I had spent the preceding Friday night watching a quadruple feature at a ratty old repertory cinema on Manhattan's Upper West Side called The Thalia, where the seats were higher in the front row than in the back. The first film we watched this particular night was *Even Dwarfs Started Small,* a weird, incomprehensible movie by the then up-and-coming German director, Werner Herzog. Next came the satirical sci-fi flick *Barbarella*, starring the then-super-sexy Jane Fonda, directed by her then-husband Roger Vadim. Third was *Fellini Satyricon.* By the time this rude, psychedelic favorite came on at about two in the morning, I was so high and tired that I didn't know whether what I saw was in my mind or on the screen. Finally, at around 3:30 a.m., the film we had all been waiting for came on: *Performance*, starring the Stones' lithe frontman Mick Jagger. We had seen this rocker-meets-gangster film so many times we could quote every line of dialogue, even the ones in incomprehensible cockney slang.

After the all-night show we slept on the subway back to Brooklyn, finally getting off at the Avenue U stop at about 6 a.m.. I crashed in my friend Duke's basement so I wouldn't get busted by my mom for being out all night long.

I was a bit groggy when Duke's mother shook my shoulder about three hours after I'd fallen out to tell me I had a phone call.

I put the receiver by my ear. "Huh?"

"Hey, buddy boy. We need ya." It was Broadway Max, the studio's all-purpose consigliere.

"Max, what time is it? Isn't today Saturday? What the fuck?"

"Mr. Ramone is here with Mr. Bacharach, and he needs a tape. Call a cab. How soon can you be here?"

Phil Ramone. The studio's fearsome leader. Through my time at A&R, I had learned more about him. He was brilliant and a baby, an inspiring hitmaker and a world-class psycho. Following the instruction I had received on my first day from Phil's sensei, Rich Blakin, I steered clear.

Mr. Bacharach. That would be Burt Bacharach. For those of you who don't know, he is one of the finest pop songwriters of all time, charting 73 top-forty hits. In collaboration with lyricist Hal David, he penned some of the greatest records of the '60s, including "Walk on By," "The Look of Love," "What the World Needs Now," "Do You Know the Way to San Jose," "Close to You," "I'll Never Fall in Love Again," and the one I consider to be their best, "Alfie." He was an anomaly for the times. He wasn't a rocker — his tunes had sophisticated harmonies and rhythms — but even in that time of hardness and hipness, he honed his pop chops to such perfection that he was able to knock hit after hit into the *Billboard* stratosphere.

"Brooks, can't somebody just go in the basement and get the tape?" I pleaded. Brooks pretended not to hear. "Thirty minutes? Perfect. We'll see you when you get here."

Here's what I guess had happened.

Phil probably hadn't prepared for the session and didn't request the necessary tapes in advance. On impulse, he turned to his assistant and said, "Where the hell is the multi-track?"

The assistant couldn't find the tape because he didn't know he'd need it and it wasn't there.

Normally, at that point, they'd call me in the library, and I'd scurry over with the tape. But it was Saturday.

"Get your ass over to the basement and get that tape now!" Ramone was sure to have hollered.

The assistant went but, in my mess, couldn't find the tape.

"Max!" Phil was certain to have yelled.

"Yes?"

"Get that goddamn *schlepper* down here NOW! I want that tape NOW!" Phil most definitely demanded.

Brooks was sure to have answered, "Yes, sir, right away!" and went on his detective hunt to find me.

No doubt, Milton ignored my whining because he was standing right in front of Ramone and wanted to make sure I didn't come off as an uncooperative complainer in earshot of our fearless leader who demanded unquestioning obeisance.

"I can't possibly get there in less than an hour," I said.

Again, ignoring me, "See you in thirty minutes."

"Brooks! That's impossible . . ."

"Bring the tape over to '322' the minute you get here."

That Saturday morning was my first personal encounter with The

Great Ramone and his mercurial demands.

Following the A&R ethos, I acceded. I bounced back easy in those days. I threw on some clothes and headed back to the subway I'd just barely exited. I'd get to midtown Manhattan faster that way, and I'd pocket the cab fare. Between that, and the double-golden overtime I'd be making ($5.00 an hour), this would at least make financial sense.

By the time I got on the decrepit D train, I emerged into conscious-ness and started to stew. What kind of lunacy was this? Did he really need this tape right now? Why didn't he ask for it on Friday like normal people? What the hell was Burt Bacharach doing at the studio at nine o'clock in the morning on a Saturday anyway? Pains in my ass.

After getting over my snit, the good soldier kicked in. I busted it to the basement, jogging through the streets of the city. It took me all of thirty seconds to find the tape in the library. If I'd just been a little more organized anyone could have found it. But, no, the *schlepper* had to be schlepped out of bed and made to travel halfway across creation to get it. Wow. I was *important*. I scurried over to "322" to deliver the tape as if it were the Holy Grail.

Two-inch tape in hand, I walked into the control room of studio R-2. Max was standing at attention by the door in his shiny black suit, yellowing shirt, and stained red tie uniform, always at the ready. Ramone was behind the board. He leaned back in his brown leather Knoll chair, his arms rest-ing on his leviathan belly.

Phil's newly acquired assistant, Danny, sat behind him by the tape machine, affecting coolness. Stealthily, I slid over to him and handed him the tape.

Before I could slip out, Ramone, ignoring me, whispered to Max, "Have him wait in case we need anything else."

Fuck. Now I couldn't leave.

I pulled up a stool and hung by my favorite spot near the echo ma-chine. At least I'd do something while I waited for the boss to give his next command. I faced Bacharach, who stood by the row of seats in front of the console, next to the glass that separated the control room from the recording studio.

Burt was chatting away. A minute or two into his monologue, without missing a beat, he pulled his yellow crew-neck cashmere sweater over his head, revealing a pale blue oxford shirt. Then he replaced the yellow sweater with a royal blue number. That lasted all of three minutes until he yanked that one off and changed into a red one. As I sat there, aiming to achieve my Zen stillness, bored out of my gourd, my body aching from so little sleep the night before, listening to Bacharach prattle, I must have watched him change his sweater 15 times. He sampled every color on the wheel: blue, red, pale pink, black, chartreuse, lavender, sea foam, gray, emerald, white, purple, crimson. As my blood sugar plunged and I struggled to keep my head upright, I waited in vain for the music to begin. But not a note was played.

His sartorial regimen complete, Bacharach turned to Ramone, and said, "I'm done. Let's go."

What the hell was that about? Bacharach in the studio early on a Saturday morning only to try on a stack of cashmere sweaters? Weird.

Then Max told me that I could leave. Really? They never even used the tape I brought. It was all due to some whim of Phil's. I was pissed.

Talking about whimsical, and the making of a hit record, here's a legendary story I heard years later from Phil about Burt. Bacharach had penned and produced the song "Raindrops Keep Fallin' on My Head," sung by B.J. Thomas. It was the theme song from the film *Butch Cassidy and the Sundance Kid,* a breakthrough movie starring Paul Newman and Robert Redford. The song was due to be released as a 45 rpm single, back in the days when we listened to music on vinyl. After it was recorded, mixed, mastered, pressed, and shipped to record stores, Burt decided he didn't like the mix of the intro, a three-second subtlety that would be missed by almost any living human being. But Bacharach was a perfectionist and couldn't live with it. He had all the discs recalled at who-knows-what cost to the record company. He had Phil redo the 4-beat intro and edit it to the body of the tape. They re-released the record and it went to number one, selling millions of copies, and winning an Oscar for best song. Would it have anyway? Who knows?

*

I wanted desperately to get out of the basement and into the studio. But given the tales of woe I'd heard, and the glimpse I'd gotten of his majesty that day, I didn't want to work with this Phil Ramone guy. That would be way too scary. But I was certain I didn't have to worry about that. It would never happen. Phil had just gotten a new assistant. He only worked with the most seasoned, brilliant guys anyway. Once hand-picked, this assistant worked exclusively for the King.

All the heavies at the studio had come up this way, apprenticed to the master. At that time, the staff of disciples included Elliot Scheiner, who eventually won Grammy awards for mixing Steely Dan; the Canadian funkmeister extraordinaire Don Hahn, who went on to run A&M Studios; and the eccentric, deeply musical, tuba-playing Dixon Van Winkle, who worked with McCartney. The distance between myself and these top-notch senior mixers felt infinite. I barely contemplated ever getting to that level. But I did hunger to be an assistant, one day — just not for Phil.

I knew that if I stood a chance of getting into the studios I'd need to work hard to get my shit together. I did this by arriving at the studio before anyone else. I would find out what session the assistant would be setting up for that morning, and I would do the job before the kid would arrive. The assistant wouldn't mind the help, and I'd work on my chops. I learned what microphones were used for the different instruments and where to place them to get the best sound. The bass drum had an Altec 633 mic called a "saltshaker;" the snare, a Sennheiser 421; we used Neumann U-87's on the brass; woodwinds, the Sony C-37.

But most of what I learned was what it meant to be the best. We were there to help the greatest musical artists in the world make timeless music. In order to do that our work had to be impeccable. Any mistake in our work meant that the artist would be made aware of the technology, and this distraction would interfere with their flow of creativity. The recording quality did not come from the engineers, but from the players and the incredible sounds they were able to make with their instruments and voices. The less they noticed they were being recorded, the more likely they'd be able to make beautiful music. Recording, in the A&R school, was about ensuring that there would be as little interference as possible between the sweet sound of inspiration and what landed in your ear.

The studio work went on around the clock, and if I was the first to arrive, I tried to be the last to leave. Even this wasn't enough for a kid as hungry as me. With the tacit encouragement of management, I'd sneak into the studio on weekends, stealing rolls of tape to record anyone I could. Thus began my training in going without sleep, seven days a week.

After months of this self-imposed discipline, I had managed to get myself to assist on a handful of sessions when an extra hand was needed. I fucked up badly at least once on every session and would get my pipes cleaned by anyone in the room. That, I knew, was the price of admission. I'd put up with it for as long as I had to, if it meant I was getting closer to the castle in the sky.

One day in my rank, underworld confines, I was doing one of my mind-numbing *schlepper* tasks, endlessly screwing together hubs and flanges, the center rings and the flat metal coverings that together made up the reels that held our magnetic tape. Through the monotony, I couldn't help worrying if the day would ever come when I would get through a session without making a horrific mistake and having to endure the subsequent emotionally abusive pummeling. I knew that without that, I'd never be good enough to get out of this shit-hole.

While I was enduring this physical and mental torture, the vice-president of the studio, David Sterling, who had once been a top engineer until cigarette advertisements were banned from the airwaves, wandered into my basement lair. He had taken an early dislike to me. I was all firecracker, a grasping street kid, ready to do anything to get my seat at the console, and he was on the other side of that, a bitter has-been. He was *Mad Men*-early-1960s in his neat silver haircut and finely cut narrow-lapelled suit. I was a post-hippie, '70s freak with flame-colored hair, Elton John platform shoes, and living in a cloud of pot smoke. I was more than a little obnoxious. He was a drunk.

After his daily ritual of a four-martini lunch at the China Song restaurant, he arrived in a tormenting spirit.

As I screwed together reel after reel, Sterling said, "You better get used to this, because I'm going to make sure that you're going to spend the rest of your life in this smelly hole of a basement making reels."

I could feel the heat rising up through my belly and vibrate through my body, a mixture of rage and terror. *Oh my god,* I thought. My worst fear was coming true. *I'll be trapped in the basement forever. I'll never get to the 7th floor!*

Having dropped that bomb, satisfied with the splatter, Sterling meandered over to another of the basement offices to bullshit and snicker with one of his drinking buds.

Alone and in despair, I began to think of escape routes. I was ready to quit. Maybe I'd get a job over at the Record Plant, our rock n' roll rival of a studio across town like my friend Jimmy Iovine, who had just gotten fired from A&R. (Jimmy went on to become a billionaire. Maybe I should've gotten fired, too.)

Later that afternoon, while I was sitting in my blackness and finding no exit, the phone rang. *Fuck. Just what I need,* I thought. I was sure it was Tony the studio manager with one of his annoying tasks. But it wasn't. It was Max, sounding not his usual self. He was awfully serious.

I could hear him chewing on his cigar. "Don't worry," he said in a raspy growl. "It's going to be alright, see."

Well, that would scare anyone.

"What's wrong?" I asked.

"Phil needs you to do a session tonight."

"Who's the engineer?"

"Phil."

I felt an instant cramping in my hip-sockets.

"What do you mean? I can't do that, I've never . . . Where is his assistant?"

"He's not available."

"Not *available*—to Ramone? That's not allowed, is it?"

"Let's not discuss it. And everyone else is working. So you're the guy."

"Brooks, I'm not ready, I mean . . ."

"You'll be fine. We'll all be right there to back you up. Now go over to R-1. The session starts at 7."

Ramone, like the giant in *Jack and the Beanstalk*, was known to eat assistant engineers for breakfast, lunch, or dinner if they committed so much as the tiniest fuckup on one of his sessions. If I had yet to get through one date assisting on my own without screwing up royally, and inevitably getting emotionally beaten within an inch of my psychological life by whichever of the rest of the staff engineers I was working with—and these guys were merely pale imitations of Phil, the big monster who trained them—what would happen when I screwed up on Ramone's date?

I was certain of one thing. I would never live through the night. I started making phone calls to say goodbye to my friends and relatives.

"I have to work with Ramone tonight, Mom, and I'm going to die!"

No one seemed to be as scared as I was. Well, that made sense. I was the one who was about to be eviscerated.

After saying my farewells to all, I zoomed over to R-1 at "322", the *other side*.

The session was a demo for Lucy Simon, Carly Simon's sister. It was a simple rhythm section: bass, drums, guitar and keyboards, with Lucy singing in the booth. I sped around the studio and had it set up in minutes. I checked the mics and cans over and over again. By the time Phil and the musicians walked in, I couldn't think of one thing left undone. The control room was spotless, the console was set. The take sheets, track sheets, and tape boxes were filled out in a snazzy calligraphy.

Lucy came in with her manager Ron Delsener, who was a legendary concert promoter. Carly, the bigger and more famous sister, made her grand entrance into the control room. She was gorgeous, with her deep voice, flowing hair, and impressive, if somewhat horsey, lips.

The band members, top studio cats, took their places behind their instruments. I dashed out to the studio to set the microphones in their optimal positions.

Ramone sat casually at the console. I stood directly behind him, never sitting down, crouched, like a runner on first base taking a lead toward second. I was ready to sprint if I so much as saw Ramone take a breath.

Phil seemed relaxed. He offered no critique of my set-up. That was strange. He pushed the volume controls, or faders, all up at once, and the room filled with the sound of each instrument: bass, drums, guitar, and keys. I was amazed. Whenever I touched a fader, everything sounded like dog meat. With Ramone, all he had to do was touch the knobs, and within seconds, it all blended together into magic.

The musicians played, Lucy sang. I kept eyeing the clock. With every passing minute, without anything screwing up, I told myself I was one second closer to the fuck up that would ruin my career for good.

Phil asked me to make a small adjustment on a mic, and I was out in the studio and back in the control room like a blur. I hit the "record" button on his command. When he asked for a playback, I rewound the tape flawlessly to the top. Somehow the adrenaline rush arising from the fear of immolation gave me a focus I'd never found before.

Delsener, Carly, Lucy, the cats all laughed. They appeared to be having a good time, not noticing that, instead of a class act behind the brilliant one, there stood the *schlepper*. We cut one, two, three tracks. Everyone seemed pleased.

I was confused when the musicians packed up and left. Could that be it? It was as if I had just gone through major surgery without a hitch.

Ramone told me to set up for a quick mix. Shit. Another chance to blow it. Maybe it would happen now. He asked me to patch in a few equalizers and limiters. I took a deep breath and plugged in the cables. Again, it all worked. I didn't create any horrible feedback, I hadn't erased any essential drum parts.

Ramone quickly balanced the instruments with the vocals, and we laid the mixes down to quarter-inch tape. It sounded luscious. Jesus, he was good.

I made a 7 1/2 i.p.s (inches per second — the speed at which the tape moved) tape copy for Delsener, and in three short hours, everyone left happily, including Phil. Politely, as if leaving the host of a party, they all said thank you and goodbye—to me!

I now stood alone in the silent studio. I could hear my heart pounding in my chest louder than anything we had just put down on tape. Wait, I told myself, unable to take it in, I'd made it through the entire, mercifully short three-hour session without one single, solitary mistake! The first time ever! I was alive!

I bolted into the studio and ran in circles screaming at the top of my lungs with glee. I jumped behind the drum kit and played a wild, Keith Moon-esque drum solo. Yay!

I went back into the control room and flopped in a chair behind the console, taking some long, deep breaths.

The best part was that I'd never have to work with Ramone again. I was done. I could go back to my hidey-hole in the basement, safe from harm.

I broke down the studio, coiling all the mic cables and headphones, folding the chairs, lining up the mic in neat rows. I cleaned up the control room, leaving it pristine for whoever would come in the next morning. I closed up the studio, as usual, the last to leave.

I went home to sleep a full night for the last time in seven years.

The next morning, my night of torture behind me, I returned to my humble station in the basement, the smelly sanctuary suddenly seeming tranquil and safe. Then, like a predictable bowel movement erupting, I got the dreaded call from Tony to come up to the studio's main office.

"Get up here, pal."

Reverend Blalock took me up the freight. "Hey, chicken hawk. You catchin' any chickens?" I had no idea what he was talking about.

The usual characters were hanging around the office.

Plotnik laughed sardonically, "So, your Ramone's new boy!"

"Go stick it," I responded. "I'm just glad I lived through the night."

"Oh yeah," Holley added. "Now you da man."

I was sure I was just getting my usual morning dose of razzing. I felt embarrassed.

Tony joined in. "You're fucked now, big fella. Come over here and look at the book."

As I walked over to the scheduling book, I felt a strange sense of destiny in a way I have experienced only a few times in my life. Tony pointed his pipe at page after page. Phil's assistant's name had been erased from all his sessions, and I saw my name on every one: Paul Simon all day, and an unknown artist named Phoebe Snow at night. The engineer: Ramone. On top of each session was the name "Berger." That was me.

"Your *schlepping* days are through. I don't know why Ramone would have done it," Tony had to add.

I had just turned 18 years old. I made my way out of the basement and I was saved from the evil alcoholic VP. But the escape meant entering the jaws of the T-Rex.

In a moment of inspiration, Holley said, "Now you da Berger...

Queen!"

The office liked that one, and everyone cracked up, repeating in unison, "Berger Queen, Berger Queen!"

I had passed through the initial tests and now my real initiation was about to begin.

As terrified as I was, I knew this was the big break I had barely dared to wish for. On that day, staring at my name next to Phil's and Paul Simon's, I knew that a rare, perhaps singular miracle had occurred in my life. Never again would I have to walk down the fetid steps to the basement. I had made it up to the seventh floor for good. I was on my way to becoming a *cat*. Phil Ramone had chosen me to be his assistant engineer.

I was the luckiest boy in New York City.

Paul Simon: The Superstar

When I walked into "322" that next morning in November 1973, everything was different. No more would I be relegated to the rank confines of the basement; no more would I begin my day with Tony's call to schlep. Starting that day, I would be Phil Ramone's personal assistant engineer.

Out of all the people in the world, Ramone had picked me. This was an event I had both longed for and dreaded, like a liver transplant. It could save your life, or it could kill you. There was a part of me that wondered if it had all been a mistake. I worried that there would be a call from Tony, who would say, "Oh, we meant the *other* Berger Queen! Get over here and grab that hand-truck!" On the other hand, maybe it was really happening. And if that was so, maybe it meant I had something of worth inside me. As soon as I had that thought, the anxiety in my stomach seemed to say, *you don't.* Either way, I realized, I would soon find out. My options were to either resist or embrace my fate. I made my choice: whatever hell awaited me, I would face it. After all, this was my shot.

Unencumbered by messenger gear, I said good morning to the receptionist, Lana. Automatically cooler now, I sat down on her desk for a minute, and we chatted amiably. She asked if I wanted anything for breakfast. Of course, she whispered, it would go on Paul's tab. That was new. Anything? I ordered a couple of scrambled eggs on a toasted English muffin with cheese, and a coffee with milk. This was a sure sign that I had made it up a rung on the ladder.

I walked into R-2 and picked up the booking sheet to see what was on tap for the day. *Paul Simon. 16-Track Playback.* There were no further instructions.

There were piles of two-inch tapes with names of venues from across the country, like Knickerbocker Arena, Cornell University, and Boston Music Hall. Fragments of the ultra-wide tape were hung on the walls, or draped over the massive 3M multi-track tape machine. I did not dare touch anything and was at a loss for what to do.

Habituated to the task, I made sure all the pencils were sharp. While straightening up, I worried, *What would Simon be like? Would I be able to get him to like me?* I tried to fortify myself with the notion that I had always got on best with the toughest teachers in my school. As the moments passed, with the clock approaching our start time of 10:00 a.m. and no sign of Ramone, I grew increasingly worried. How could I prepare for the date without any direction?

Minutes before the downbeat, Ramone blew into the room. With a winning smile, he said, "It's you and me now, kid. You ready? Do you want to be a world-class engineer? Because that's what you'll be when I'm done with you. We're going to make beautiful music together."

I felt a small pang of love at first sight. *Wow. Me and the big guy? Really? World-class?* This guy wasn't the typical borough-tough that I found in so much of the rest of the staff. He was charming. He instantly won me over. Maybe he wasn't the monster that he was reputed to be. After all, he'd been nice to me so far.

Standing at attention, I waited for his command. I assumed that Ramone would provide me with some kind of indoctrination, some guide to the Master's method. But he said nothing.

He took his seat by the console. With no indication of what to do, I took my spot on the assistant's stool by the multitrack and waited for what was going to happen next. It took all of my powers of self-control to appear steady.

Phil stared at a small video monitor, high on the wall, among the pre-amps and outboard gear. It showed a vague black and white image of the studio's entrance. A blurry figure approached the door on the screen. Phil started breathing heavily. "Ok," he gulped, nodding his head two or three times. "Here he comes. Here he comes."

Huh? Was the great Phil Ramone scared of Paul Simon? This possibility amplified my own fear. If the alpha-dog was nervous, how should the pup assistant feel? My body tensed, but I knew I needed to keep my cool and not let my nervousness show.

A few moments later, the door opened, and my first superstar entered the control room.

Phil stood up and, appearing to tremble, seemed to almost bow and greeted him in what appeared to me as an overly-solicitous tone of voice. "Good morning, Paul."

Phil must have warned Paul to expect someone new in the room, as he showed no surprise at my presence. "Paul, let me introduce you to our new assistant engineer, Glenn Berger." I managed to smile. Paul looked through me. He didn't reach out his hand. He didn't even say hello. His basic vibe communicated, *Don't think of existing in my presence, and we'll be fine.* I wasn't completely surprised. He was, at least, willing to let me sit in a room with him and watch him work. Creating music was a sensitive endeavor, and artists didn't let people in these rooms easily. Still, I felt bruised. I retreated to the safety of my stool.

While I appeared impassive, it didn't escape my awareness that I sat in proximity to a man who had sold a few records in his day. His catalogue was impressive enough, but it wasn't really that hard for me to be cool. The tautness coming off of him made me wary, but I wasn't particularly star-struck. I had never been a fan. As I stewed, wincing at his dismissal of me, I thought, *I never liked Simon and Garfunkel, anyway.*

My 8th grade English teacher, Ms. Kantor, in an attempt to turn us on to poetry, had once played us S and G's song version of "Richard Cory," a poem about a guy who's got it all, but ends up shooting himself in the head because he figures out he's a jerk. I automatically had to hate anything my 8th grade English teacher liked. She was a priss.

What was it about Simon and Garfunkel that I found such a turn-off? It wasn't that I was a rocker and found them too soft; I liked all kinds of pop hits. I was a big fan of Todd Rundgren, The Incredible String Band, and The Band, none of whom could be considered heavy metal. I didn't like Simon and his taller half because I thought they were, to use Holden Caulfield's favorite word, *phony.*

I was sure that I was an expert on the truth. I judged like a wrathful god, and no one escaped the piercing eyeball. The thing that determined whether someone got membership in the Rock and Roll pantheon was, were they real? That's what rock was all about. So as far as I was concerned: it was and always had been, at its purest, a reaction against bullshit. *Parsley, Sage* — give me a break with the chicken spices.

I mistrusted the duo's folksiness. I thought it was just put on because it was the trend. The name, Simon and Garfunkel, was a good marketing move. It was the "next big thing," in the development of folk/rock branding. It sounded goofy, ethnic, anti-establishment, but sincere. It stuck out, in just the right way, for that mid-'60s moment. Others would follow in this trend, descending in the end to totally constructed shams like Engelbert Humperdinck.

I was convinced that Paul was a top-notch crap-meister, and his instant attitude toward me did nothing to dispel this notion.

But once I was able to watch him create in the studio, I got a different take. The first thing that Paul said was, "I'm working on a new song for my next album, and I want to record a guitar and vocal demo of what I have so far."

That was my cue. I asked Ramone which mics he wanted me to use. He told me to choose whatever I liked. That made me feel uncertain, but I didn't have time to hesitate, because the next thing he said was, "Move it!"

I boogied out to the studio to set up. Paul came out to the recording room to tune his guitar. As I adjusted the mics I had selected, standing inches from him, I felt a little awkward. I wasn't tall myself, but I towered over the guy. His Martin acoustic guitar almost engulfed his body. I noticed he moved deliberately, as if every motion was prepared in advance. There was something both impressive and creepy about that. I wanted to say something, just to make conversation, but I couldn't think of any words.

Paul said, "Move that mic over a little bit." And that was it.

I went back into the control room. Phil turned to me, and in an exasperated voice, as if he was saying something any idiot should have known, said, "Why didn't you use the C-22 for the acoustic guitar?"

I wanted to tell him that he told me to use anything I wanted, but I thought better of it. Instead, I said, "I'll go change it," and made a move to go out in the studio.

But before I could move, with his voice getting urgent, he said, "Forget it. Let's go, time to record!" I had two legs moving in opposite directions. First he told me to use any mic, then he told me I used the wrong one, and then he told me to leave it.

Ramone hit the talkback, and the tone of his voice changed completely from the pressured splash of cold water I had received, to a deep, warm, maple syrup. "We're ready, sweetheart."

Then he turned to me again, and the insistence came back. "Hit it! Hit it!"

"Record?"

"Yes, come on! Now!"

I hit play and "record." The red lights came on and the tape started to turn.

I watched Paul finger-pick the strings on his guitar. I'd never seen anyone play the way he did. The sound was inimitable— a hard thing to do on that wooden box with six strings where you can only put your fingers in so many places.

Then he began to sing some as yet unknown lyrics to a song that would later become "Still Crazy After All These Years." No one but us had heard this song before. He finished the second refrain, and then said, "Not sure where it goes from here," and the song petered out.

But what he already had composed was a finely cut jewel. You could hear the whole thing with just him and guitar. It needed no production. Way too many songs are slight and gain their credibility through the production jizz that's floofed around them. Listen to those songs naked and they are all fashion with no body. Not Paul's. This song was bright, clear, and done from the raw bones of it. Any arrangement or additional instrumentation would just put the jewel in the proper setting. Every note was there for a reason, every word the perfect choice.

Listening to him play that song was like being woken up by blinding sunshine. It left me dazed and sweaty. *So this is what brilliant songwriting is*, I said to myself. Maybe I had been wrong about this dude.

The impact was enhanced by my first experience of hearing something being created in the studio, with just a microphone and a super-clean preamp between what was coming fresh from the mind and hands of the creator and the giant speakers on the wall. There is something about hearing music in the studio that brings you all the way into the heart of the thing. But even with the sonic enhancement, it was clear that this guy was deep. Maybe if I paid close enough attention, I could learn how to make great records from this cat.

He listened back, yet seemed unimpressed with himself. He sighed and, almost as if talking to himself, said, "I'm not sure where to take this song next." He slowly lifted his coffee cup in a perfect arc, and looking off into some melancholy distance, took a sip and put it down.

Phil said, "It's brilliant. It's going to be great."

"Let's move on" was all Paul said.

*

This demo of his new song was just a distraction from our main purpose. I began my gig in the middle of Paul working on his album *Live Rhymin'*. Paul had been a solo performer for a few years now, and had established himself as a hit maker on his own with his first two albums, the eponymously titled *Paul Simon* and *There Goes Rhymin' Simon*.

In May of 1973, he'd gone on his first solo tour with the Andean band Urubamba and the gospel group The Jessy Dixon Singers. Phil captured these American and European shows on tape, and we were now making a live album out of those recordings.

I was shocked to discover that the record was not so live that it couldn't be rejiggered twenty ways from Sunday.

Phil directed me to put up "El Condor Pasa," from the show recorded earlier that year in May at Carnegie Hall. Phil made a rough mix of the track. When the recording came to the end, Simon spoke to me for the first time with a phrase I was soon to hear incessantly from him. Without looking, he waved his hand, and said, "Back it up."

I rewound the tape. We listened again and again. After several playbacks, Paul said, "I like the second verse, but that's it. Let's hear Santa Monica."

I put up that version, and again we listened, repeatedly.

It went on like this for days, with Paul and Phil closely scrutinizing all the recorded performances from around the country. The monotony was numbing. Paul was not satisfied with the whole performance of that tune from any of the shows. So, painstakingly, Phil created a complete song by editing together fragments of multitrack from different performances across America, from California to the New Jersey Turnpike. We took a few measures from the concert in San Francisco, then a chorus from a theatre in Uniondale, finally a verse from Notre Dame in Indiana.

Next we worked the song "America," which was just guitar and vocal. Again, after endless investigations, Paul couldn't find one whole live, vocal performance that he liked, so he decided to replace much of his singing by overdubbing it in the studio. While listening to his live guitar through his headphones, he recorded a number of vocal takes on several empty tracks on the multitrack. Then, he wrote out the lyrics and "comped" together a complete performance, taking one line from one track and a word from another. He put a circle around the number eleven for one line, while adding another lyric that came from track fifteen.

As I watched Simon replace each organic musical part with their bionic replacements, I began to wonder what "live" really meant.

Throughout this endless, tedious work, Paul continued to treat me like little more than a well-trained monkey, which fit my job description. I pressed buttons: *play, record, stop, rewind, play, record.*

There was an absence of feeling that blew like a cold wind from him. He was obviously keenly intelligent. I had always thought of myself as pretty smart, but in his presence, I felt my own confidence shrivel, and I became unusually stupid and inarticulate. Outside of taking a lunch order, I kept my mouth shut. As Simon finessed some musical detail on a single measure of music, his only words to me were the automatic phrase, "Back it up. Back it up."

After air-brushing all of his presumably live musical parts on *Live Rhymin'* to make them into something between real and fantastic, it was time to mix. This is when the engineer blends together all the disparate musical elements of a track into a coherent whole. One part of the job is to set the relative volumes between the instruments. For example, how loud should the drums be in relation to the vocals? But creating the proportion and relationship between the musical elements is only one aspect of the sonic landscape that can be controlled in the mix, which is what makes, for instance, Radiohead sound different from The Beach Boys.

In the same way that Paul scrutinized every note, creating the perfect "live" performance, he also quested after the ultimate mix. We mixed each song several times, as Paul was always finding something wrong with what we had already done.

Back in the 1970s, there was no automation of mixes. Since the advent of digital technology in the following decades, every move in a mix can be remembered — you make a modification once and the computer will replicate that change eternally. But in ye olde days, we crafted mixes by hand, starting fresh each time. It was artisanal. Though this method could be nerve-wracking, it had its advantages; it allowed for the serendipitous moment. Sometimes an imperceptible nudge of a fader would allow magic to occur.

On this day, we were mixing "The Boxer" for the four-thousandth time. In order to redo it, I began by recreating all of the settings from the last time we had mixed it. Getting to the studio early, I set all of the relative volumes and the reverb; I patched in, and tweaked, all the out-board equalizers to modify the timbre; and I set the limiters and compressors to narrow a track's volume swings, called dynamic range. After whipping all that together, my breakfast having arrived from the deli, I collapsed in utter exhaustion, because I'd only slept two or three hours the night before.

I had completed the recipe just moments before the heavies arrived. We got right to work. Simon sat down next to Phil on one side, to supervise the mix, and I sat on the other, to lend my helping hand.

The mix was Ramone's chance to perform. As the song unfolded, with the instruments entering and falling out, with parts rising up to prominence and then blending back into the background, Phil continuously massaged the sliding volume controls called faders. He finessed these subtle relationships to create an emotional arc, in search of the combination that would have that spark where it all came together, sounded right, and most important, felt right.

We rehearsed all the changes in volume and proportion throughout the song, learning what Phil called the "choreography." I memorized all the moves as he perfected them. With each run through, as I learned the parts, I called out the alterations to him.

Simon's blank, sharklike stare made Ramone's hands shake. No matter how many subtle refinements Phil would make, Simon would hear something else that needed to be fine-tuned. Once every last detail had finally been considered, Phil gave me the go-ahead to start recording the mixes to quarter-inch tape. I hit "record" and pressed the talkback button to lay down an identifying slate at the top. "The Boxer, take one." I hit play on the multi. We started the mix. Right in the intro, Simon said, "Let's do it again. Let's move the *charango* a little bit to the left, and duck it a smidge at its entrance."

We started again from the beginning. "Take two."

This time we got to the first interlude. Ramone missed the entrance of the *quena*. "Shit!"

Simon, to me, "Back it up."

This went on and on. Simon never had an encouraging word. In his single-minded hunt for greatness, there was no space for human consideration. This could wear anyone down.

I could feel Ramone's frustration building. He added some midrange to the reverb. Unhappy with the sound of the acoustic guitar, he zoomed to the back of the control room to change the setting of an equalizer. Seeing where it had been set, he stamped his feet and threw his hands up in the air. "No wonder! Berger, you fucked it up again! I'd *never* set EQ like that!"

But I knew he had. He could get into such a fugue state when he was mixing that he could wail a knob and have no memory of what he had done.

The more the hours passed, the more relentlessly Simon drove Ramone. And equivalently, the harder Ramone pushed me. "Berger, let's do it, come on, faster! And don't fuck up that vocal switch in the outro."

We were always one wrong moment away from blowing the whole mix. This pressure got Phil deeper into the groove, and he worked the thing, hard. His hands became one with the band. Following the shifting feelings of the song, he "rode" the levels of the instruments like he was riding a winged stallion, building the song, hitting escape velocity, rising off the ground, pulling it back, creating tension, galloping, then another burst, building to a bigger peak, emphasizing the *antara* here, then the vocal, closing his eyes, breathing deep, putting his emotional back into it.

I called out the moves. "Track 13! Fade it out! Cross-fade to 12! Push the *charango*, now!" The musical measures went by; we were getting it all right. Ramone started tapping his foot, on the ball, and then the heel. When that happened, I knew we had something. The closer we got to the end, and the greater the excitement, the scarier it became. Ramone reached his hands over his large belly, delicately manipulating the faders. Simon barked, "Careful with the *quena*! Goose the vocal!" The end of the song came into sight. Ramone pumped it, the needles going into the red, loading all the magnetism onto the tape that he could. Finally, the horse leaped skyward into some spontaneous, unpredictable, emotionally radiant moment of brilliance, revelation, and ecstasy.

Big finish, the song ended. Silence, and then Ramone nodded to me, and I artfully pulled down the master fader. We let the tape roll for a few seconds of bias tape. It was always a scary adventure to live through those three or four minutes, but when he nailed it, it burned. I was sure this was the take.

Phil said, triumphantly, "Playback."

I rewound the quarter-inch to the top. I listened with more trepidation than satisfaction, but I couldn't clamp down on my hope all the way. The beauty still took my breath away. When it was done, Simon turned to Ramone and said, "Let's do one more."

What the hell more could he want? Whatever it was, I couldn't hear it. I just wanted to go home and get some sleep.

As the days wore on, and we couldn't get anything that made Paul happy, Ramone got increasingly frazzled. After our eight-hour days with

Simon, at night we were recording Phoebe Snow's first album. At 3 a.m., when we were done, Ramone would crawl up to his couch in his office on the second floor and sleep the few hours before it was time to begin again. One of the world's most successful recording engineers didn't even sleep in a bed. He almost never went home to his wife in Pound Ridge. He'd shuffle down to the studio in the morning, dressed like shit, his beard unkempt. Every day he seemed to get fatter. He ate pork ribs from the House of Chan for dinner every night. The lack of sleep, the bad diet, and Simon's inhumane treatment were putting him into an increasingly foul mood.

In the same way that Paul could not find a complete performance that he liked—he barely approved of any complete mix—so too was Ramone forced to edit together the mix fragments. At one point, after chopping for hours, Ramone turned to me and said, "Berger, get over here. You do this one." The surgeon held out his hand, passing me the scalpel to make the cut.

I stood at the machine, with one hand on each reel, and rocked the tape over the playback head, listening for the optimal spot at which to sever it. I tried to keep my knees steady, while Simon stood an inch from me on one side, and Ramone hovered on the other. With their eyes focused on my fingers, I stood at the chopping block, slicing the acetate with the one-sided blade. It was surgery on their baby, with the mean old daddies breathing down my actual neck. Keep the hand steady, show no fear, cut cleanly…patient lives, I told myself. I imagined, if I blew it, my own head under the blade, clean cut, right into the bucket. I had to do this to survive, and I did. The edit worked. Nobody applauded. Simon said nothing, walked back to the producer's table, and sipped his coffee.

During one of these editing marathons, just about at the end of the day, with tiny ribbons of audio tape all over the control room, Phil made a cut. Listening back, Paul said, "It just doesn't sound right, does it?"

By this point, Ramone's hands could barely handle the blade. He muttered under his breath, "Fucking shit."

Frantically, he cut out an inch of tape, to see if that would work better.

We listened again, and Paul said, "Nah, that's worse."

Now Ramone's frustration started boiling over. "Fucking, goddamn . . ."

Paul said, "I don't know. Maybe the first one wasn't so bad. Let's go back to what we had and listen to it again." Amongst the scraps of tape scattered around the machine, Phil found the one inch of audio tape, and put it back in where he had taken it out. He hit play back. However, when we listened to it this time, it sounded different, weird.

"What the fuck?" Now Ramone's voice was getting louder. He took the piece out again, and put it back in, pushing down hard on the adhesive tape that held the fragments together. Again, it sounded wrong. How could that be? He had merely taken the tiny fragment out, and put it back in again. Why did it sound so strange?

Now he lost it. Ramone kicked the tape machine. "Goddamn mother-fucking piece of goddamn shit!"

I backed off into a corner, scared.

He stomped around the control room like a giant toddler who couldn't get his way. He threw the pile of take sheets onto the floor. He knocked over a pile of empty metal reels. All the while screaming, "Shit!"

The guy had snapped. I felt bad for him, and offered to help. "Phil, do you want me to give it a shot?"

"What the fuck are you going to be able to do? What the fuck is wrong with this goddamn . . .?" And he kicked the machine again.

At least I tried to help. I looked over to the other grown-up in the room, hoping for some assistance. Simon was wholly aloof, as he glanced at a magazine. He looked at his watch. "I've got to get out of here. I'll see you tomorrow."

One word of reassurance from Simon would have been nice, something like, *Don't worry, I'm sure if we give it a break, you'll figure it out tomorrow.* Maybe that would have helped to calm Phil down. But this was not Simon's style.

After he left, Ramone stormed out of the control room, screaming. I peeled myself off the wall.

That night, as I lay in bed at around four in the morning, almost hallucinating from the lack of sleep, the answer came to me like a revelation.

The next morning, I couldn't wait to get to the control room. Sure that I was right, I thought, *Now I'll show these guys!* I removed the fragment of tape, and turned it upside down. I put it back in, and played it. It was, as we used to say, tight as a duck's booty. *Yes.*

When the masters appeared, I hit the button, and played the tape back for them. Simon looked over at Ramone. Phil raised an eyebrow, and almost grimaced. He barely mumbled, "How did you do that?"

I tried to suppress a boast, and said, "Trade secret."

Simon showed no pleasure in my trick, but he smirked, because he could tell that Ramone had been outdone by the *schlepper*.

It was obvious that Paul was not the kind of cinema verité artist who was comfortable with revealing his own flaws. Our job was to make the record — a patchwork of performances, edits, and overdubs — seamless, like one perfect, spontaneous performance. This was no easy thing to accomplish. Live albums usually took a few days to mix. We worried this thing for months.

One day, we were all sitting in our usual spots: me, on my stool by the tape machine in the back of the control room; Ramone at the console; Simon at the producer's desk next to Phil. We were eating lunch from the Gaiety Deli, a rare moment when we were not engaged in some microscopic surgery.

Breaking the silence between bites, without making eye contact, Simon said to Ramone, "My friends are saying this album is taking a long time to get done."

Phil didn't respond, but, although this remark seemed fairly innocuous on the surface, the air suddenly got thick, and there was a distinctly noticeable shift in the room. All you could hear was the crumple of wax paper and the chewing of corned beef on rye.

When the session finally ended, Ramone put his head in his hands. "My career is ruined! Paul thinks I'm too slow. You have no idea what that one statement could mean!"

I felt a moment of panic. Phil and I had just started our beautiful music thing, and his career was about to end? Could this really be true? After all, if it were up to Phil and me, we would've put this colicky baby to bed a long time ago. It was Paul's ultra-perfectionism that was making this thing take forever. *Oh,* it dawned on me, *he's not going to get fired.* A wave of derision moved through me, as I rolled my eyes behind Ramone's back. *What a drama queen.*

Then, out of nowhere, another wave of emotion, this time, anxiety, crawled up my spine like the time I got an electric shock from putting a live patch cord into my mouth. It wasn't only the *schlepper* who could feel the icy slap from Paul. I had just witnessed how Simon could maim with the precision of a medieval assassin, pulling his bodkin from out of its hiding place, placing it precisely in the space between Ramone's ribs, and having it back behind his cloak before anyone would notice. To crush the schlepper was one thing. But nailing Ramone right where it hurt? Was this why Phil panted every time Paul came into the studio?

*

Ramone thrived on chaos. He used this lunacy as part of his alchemical brew to summon up the magical muses. He had this amazing psychic capacity to cause equipment to break down just by walking into a room. Unprepared for whatever was about to happen in a recording session, he'd come in late, and just at the worst possible moment, gear would simply stop functioning. It was standard that Ramone would push the craziness to the lip of catastrophe.

We were working day and night, and when Paul wasn't in the studio, there was always something else going on. One Monday morning, with Paul out of town, Phil booked a date in A-1. I didn't know who it was for or what we would be doing.

The standard procedure was that the instrumentation for a recording date would be called in by a producer, arranger, or contractor, and Tony would write it out on a booking order. That sheet was the first thing I looked for when I arrived in the morning: that was where I got my instructions for that session's set up.

On this day, I came in to find the sheet blank. That meant I couldn't do my job of putting out the chairs, placing the microphones, giving all the players headsets, plugging everything in, and setting up the console, so the engineer could walk in, sit down, and start the session, knowing everything was set, checked, and ready to go.

Depending on how big the session was — and in A-1, 40-piece orchestras were the norm— it could take up to ninety minutes to get everything prepared. Once I got my chops together, I could move faster than anyone, but it still took time. I didn't like pushing things too close. I wanted enough time to check everything twice. Murphy's Law had proved itself too many times: if something could go wrong, it inevitably did. And the price for being even a minute late could be enormous. Going overtime with forty musicians getting paid scale was a pretty penny.

When I got there at 8:30 a.m. and saw the empty sheet, I called Tony in the booking office. By this point, with Ramone as my guide, I was earning the status to become obnoxious. "Where the hell is my goddamn set-up?"

"Beats me, Berger. Ramone booked the session and he didn't give up any info. I guess you'll just have to wait till he shows up."

"Where is he? Can't we find him and figure out what he wants?"

"No can do, pal. Relax. It is what it is."

That didn't exactly soothe me. In my own exhausted frustration, I thought, *Fine. Fuck it. It's his fucking fault if this becomes a nightmare.*

At about 9:40, with a 10:00 a.m. downbeat (the time the session was supposed to begin), Ramone walked in to find the studio empty, without a single microphone, chair, or headphone set up.

He started to panic and scream: "Why the fuck isn't the studio set up?"

Foolishly, I tried to argue by using logic. "But Phil, there's nothing on the set-up sheet — how was I supposed to know what to set up?"

I long forgot that sweet guy I saw on our first day together. That had been merely a ruse to lure me onto the hook. Once I was securely in, his legendary brutality emerged. He answered with his own impeccable logic. "Are you a complete useless idiot? It's your job to know!"

And he was right. Ramone was the kind of guy who taught you nothing but expected you to know everything and, if you got it wrong he, to put it politely, disemboweled you. That was his style and the way you had to learn, like it or not. I realized in that moment that it was my job to anticipate his fuck-ups and to cover his ass.

He had neglected to alert anyone at the studio that we were going to be recording a 60-piece orchestra for that guy with the quaint name, Engelbert Humperdinck. But that didn't stop him from blaming me.

In a panic, with minutes to go before the session was due to start, Ramone hollered like some large, extinct, carnivorous cat, inspiring shock and awe.

He picked up the phone and called Tony. "I want the entire staff in here NOW! I want every microphone in the studio, every baffle, every platform, every headphone, every piece of equipment in this studio in the next five minutes!"

Instantly, his command was fulfilled. The troops frantically ran through the halls; Holley, Tony, Plotnik, the other assistants, the maintenance guys, Blalock the janitor, wide-eyed and panting, schlepped every piece of gear into the big room. With everyone scampering around like ants running away from a descending shoe, and with me commanding the troops, we set up for the orchestra.

"Put the podium in the middle! Three chairs for the trumpets there! Three for the french horns there! Five woodwinds! Sixteen fiddles! Six chairs for the cellos!"

Just as I was checking the last microphones, the docile string players started shuffling in, chomping their cigars, with their *Wall Street Journal* under their arms. The clock struck ten, the conductor tapped the podium to bring the cats to attention, and Ramone was behind the board, ready to set levels.

No one, no matter their official job, complained. Although Ramone could induce deep chaos, he could also in turn inspire those around him to seemingly impossible heights. That was a key to his hit-making genius. He showed his leadership in his ability to enroll us as egoless participants in the creation of his masterworks. Whatever it took, we were all willing to do it, as crazy as it might be. He convinced us that we were the cream. A&R studios may not have had the slickest equipment or the fanciest furniture. But what we did have was our unsurpassable staff, all trained by the fat man himself, Ramone. Our team could not be topped.

One reason why we didn't have the best gear and our stuff was breaking all the time was that, despite its success, A&R was — much like the rest of New York in the '70s — on the verge of bankruptcy. Ramone had lost a million bucks on a record company that had flopped and, unbeknownst to us lowlifes, the studio was on a long road toward paying off that boondoggle. In the same way that New York's infrastructure was collapsing at the seams, our brutalized and overused equipment was falling apart, and there wasn't any money to pay enough maintenance guys to keep it all working.

It was also hard to find good technical guys because everyone wanted the glory of being the engineer, rather than performing the selfless task of keeping the old crap working. In reality, the maintenance guys had a brutal gig. We were working twenty-four hours a day, and the gear just couldn't keep up. Add to this, the technology was changing all the time. Phil was constantly pushing against the boundaries of the possible, using equipment in ways that no one had tried before. Without the time needed to test-drive the stuff, the gear was more likely to blow up than work.

When everything busted to pieces, Phil would yell at me and anyone else in earshot, blaming us for all that was going wrong. It took me months to learn to swing with this and still keep the boat afloat while the smoke and flames climbed around us.

*

In the midst of all this madness, we faced the greatest challenge in the making of Paul's album. Getting the right mixes of each individual song was not the final step in putting together this classic.

As this was a live album, at least in theory, we wanted it to have the feel of a concert. We would achieve this by creating the illusion that one tune flowed naturally into the next, just as if Paul was actually doing a show. This all had to be concocted, because each song came from different venues, on different nights, in a different order.

The first step in this process was to fake the applause. The real audience response didn't always sound convincing. Stealing recorded applause from anywhere we could find it, we created an applause tape with many options: pleasant clapping, cheers of recognition, respectful, heartfelt acclamation, insane stomping, standing ovations, whatever canned business we thought would fly.

Then, in order to create the flow of a show, we needed to place this applause between one song and the next. Today you could achieve this kind of effect on your Aunt Tillie's laptop, but in those analog days, it took a lot more than that.

First thing in the morning, while I gnawed on my English muffin, Ralph, the head maintenance guy, scurried into the control room, pushing and banging the busted up metal box on wheels that housed a quarter-inch tape machine. Then he ran out and did that three more times. We would need to use these four different quarter-inch machines to get the job done.

Ralph's job as our technical maven was to turn a bunch of knobs and screws to align these finicky analog monsters for optimum performance.

He pushed his comb-over back, eyes bulging out of his head, as he stared at the clock. He knew what was coming. Phil walked in, and saw that it was almost 10:00 a.m., and Ralph hadn't finished the alignment yet.

Ramone slammed his fist on the producer's desk. "I can't get any cooperation around here! Do I have to do everything myself? Ralph, could you move any slower? Don't you realize that Paul Simon will be walking in here any minute? Paul Simon does not wait for anyone!" Ramone held his breath and took a quick glance at the front door monitor. He started to pace and reached for a cigarette.

I walked toward Phil and tried to calm him down. "Phil, it's going to be ok. He'll be done in time."

This was the wrong strategy. "Don't EVER tell me to calm down! My shrink told me I need to express my feelings!"

Oh great, I thought. *I sure would like to have a conversation with that therapist.*

Ralph turned the last screw and ran out of the control room before he could get smacked down any more.

I put up the end of the master mix of "Duncan" on one playback tape machine. I set up the chosen applause on the second machine, then added the beginning of the next song, "The Boxer," on a third machine.

I hit play for the end of "Duncan." At Ramone's cue, as the music died out, after the flutes exited and Simon finished the song with a descending lick on his guitar, I hit the play button on the audience machine. Ramone faded in the warm, devoted applause at just the right moment. As the clapping diminished, and at Phil's next cue, I started the beginning of the incoming track "The Boxer," and Ramone faded up the new track, with Simon tuning his guitar before beginning the song.

We recorded this entire *crossfade* onto the fourth machine. Once we got it right, we edited in what we had just created — end of song, applause, beginning of new song — in between the two master mixes of "Duncan" and" The Boxer," connecting the end of the previous song to the beginning of the next.

We did that with each song until we had a final master of a seamless, whole concert album.

On the last day of creating these crossfades, after endless hours, days, and months of working on this thing, there was one final decision to be made.

As much as Paul treated me, and just about everyone else, as objects, he wasn't above leaving some of the most critical decisions about his records in the hands of the guy who delivered the pastrami sandwiches. If some bike messenger walked into the control room and said he liked something, there it stayed in perpetuity. But beyond that, Paul was the ultimate and final arbiter of all things. There was no detail that he would leave unmanaged — so driven was he by some mysterious demon that relentlessly demanded ever-increasing perfection.

The last thing to be done was to put the applause tracks at the end of the last song on the album. Should it be long, or short? For the first time in six months, Paul was stymied, unable to make up his mind. He turned to Phil, who couldn't decide, either.

The two lifetime-achievement Grammy winners couldn't come to this final, rather inconsequential decision about the length of the applause. After billions of choices along the way, now, just when it was about to be born, the baby got stuck in the birth canal.

It was hard to let go. I could understand. They'd put more of their soul into this project than anything I'd ever encountered. With this last decision, the project would be declared officially complete, done, finito. They were unable to proclaim, as they say in Italian, *basta*, "it suffices like that."

After a long silence, and in a panic, they both turned and looked at me. And for the first time during all those grueling hours we'd worked together, they asked me for an opinion.

"Glenn, what do you think? Which one do you like? The long one or the short one?"

Up until that moment, I had barely been a peripheral blur in Simon's universe. I wasn't sure if he even recognized me as a sentient being.

I had long given up hope of ever being considered a creature with a neo-cortex, and on the four-hundred and seventy thousandth rewind, I had finally numbed to the point of Buddhist non-existence. I was without opinion. But, suddenly roused from my stupor by Paul and Phil's query about the final applause, I figured here was my big chance to make an impression on Paul. I could give the answer that would save the project, turn it into a hit, make it as big as *Bridge*, have him ask me to go out on the road, fire Phil, become the new Artie. Simon and Bergfunkel!

But instead, everything went fuzzy. They looked at me in torment. I had to speak. I did have an opinion somewhere, but I couldn't seem to find it.

At that point in my life, everything I had been taught was to not have a point of view. And now I was being *asked* for one. Was this a trick question? Was there a right answer? I had to figure out how to respond without getting in trouble because the silence in the room was growing unbearable.

I opened my mouth and the words that came out were: "Well, the long one is really exciting, but the short one ends nice and fast."

They both looked at me with crushing disappointment. And in that moment, that perplexing riddle, which I had failed to solve, brought me to what's called *satori*. That's Japanese for a moment of enlightenment. I got it. The only way to learn the lesson is the hard way, but couldn't I have learned it in advance of fucking up my one shot at immortal record production?

The answer was: any answer would have been fine. I should've said, "The long one," because Paul would have then said, "Let's use the short one," and we would have gotten out of the stuck moment. At these times in life, the answer doesn't matter at all. What matters is just giving *any* answer. (*Honey, which dress do you like, the blue one or the green one? The blue one.*)

The reality is, they should have used the short one. With a live album,

the listener doesn't want to be in the middle of a climactic, romantic moment and have to either endure listening to endless applause or get up to
turn the goddamn thing off. Once the album is over, you want to move on
to something else. You've got to think about how these things will fly on
repeated listenings, and applause gets tedious fast. Anyway, I think I kind
of knew that then but couldn't find it in my brain to say it.

Once we put on the, long, wrong applause, we finally finished the
project.

Working on this live album of hits gave me a chance to live with many
of Paul's classics every day for months, penetrating their depths, memoriz-
ing their every nuance. Immersing myself in songs like "America," "Home-
ward Bound," and "El Condor Pasa," I grew to love his music. Strange that
these songs possessed such deep humanity, when Paul himself seemed so
devoid of this quality at the time.

Once we were finally done, the master tape was an endless puzzle of
stitched-together fragments, made up of pieces from different mixes that
were done days, weeks, or months apart; the cross-fades where we used
four different machines to create the effect of one track going into the
other; and other fixes that turned what was supposed to be a snapshot of
a moment in time into a constructed artwork. I learned that I was right
about Simon faking it. What came as a revelation was when I came to
understand just how much artifice was required to make something sound
"real."

The record sounded gorgeous. We were done—but for the final disaster.

Ramone was supposed to fly the final product out to the coast for
mastering. That was the part of the process where some genius figured out
a way to squash all that good stuff from the tape onto a petroleum product
known as a master disk. This master would be used to make metal nega-
tives and these would be pressed into hot vinyl, i.e. the records you'd buy in
the record store.

The album was due to be released in a matter of days. Phil was getting ready to leave for the airport in a few hours. While he was heading up to the 2nd floor to complain about something or other, he gave the order to me and Ralph to make a safety copy of the master tape, in case the plane crashed and the original was incinerated. Ramone might have gone down in flames, but we'd still have the record. Ramone would've agreed that that was the most important thing.

In that age of analog, every time you made a copy, you lost something in the transfer. You got more noise and distortion. With every copy of a copy, the record got a little further away from the crisp, punchy thing you started with in the studio. The track was sure to lose some of its edge through the production process, from the cutting of the original track to it coming out of your squeaky car radio. That's why a hit record better sound damn near like a jack hammer when you first recorded it.

But we made the safety copy just in case, even though it was a slight bastardization of the original. And with this album, considering all the edits, cross fades, and remixes, we'd already lost a lot of the pristine quality along the way.

I hung in the control room with Ralph, finally relaxing, while he made the transfer. He was all bouncy — he loved the recording thing, and here was a cool, fresh master tape of a yet to be released album by a monster artist, performing his biggest hits. As we listened to the completed work, he gleefully jumped around the studio. I felt pretty puffy myself. This was the first huge album I'd worked on, and the first time in my life I had the fulfillment that comes from suffering for something way bigger than myself. I leaned back, basking in the glow of the hardest job I had done in my young life, well done.

Ralph flew over to the console and hit a square switch with a white light. Then, something very scary happened. It sounded like someone had put cotton balls in my ears. The crackle and crisp all got sucked away and the tape sounded like a dull, muffled mush. I looked at him, and he looked back at me, terror in his eyes.

He stopped dancing. He flipped the glowing, singular, thumb-sized lever on the board back to its original position. As if the tape had been fished out of the toilet where it seemed to have dropped a moment before, the happy highs came rushing back, someone pulled the cotton out of my ears, and it all sounded fine. Relief.

Until Ralph re flipped the switch, and again it sounded like something coming from an apartment three floors away. But wait — it was weirder than that. The sound started to swish, like a whirlpool of sound, drifting off into the murky depths, then flipping around into a crash of treble, and swirling back into muffled darkness. Another flip of the switch, and the sound was back to normal.

In a frenzy, Ralph flipped the switch back and forth. Swish, clear, gone, clear, swish, clear, gone-clear, gone-clear! With each flip I could see his comb-over get increasingly damp as he pushed the pathetic strands back on his head, his pallor increasing, his eyes growing wider with panic.

I sat at the edge of my chair. "Ralph, what is going on?" I screamed. I knew something was terribly wrong. I could hear the roar of an approaching tsunami and there was nowhere to run. This was months and months of work, thousands and thousands of dollars, Phil Ramone and Paul Simon, for Christ's sake!

Ralph looked at me with pathetic despair in his eyes. "Da fu . . ."

"Ralph . . ."

He stopped the tape. He sat down in a chair opposite me. "OK. We've got to figure out what to do."

"Would you tell me what the hell is going on?"

"That switch. It's the mono switch. It takes your stereo mix and it combines the two tracks together and makes it mono. You've got to be able to play the thing in mono. When they master it, they're going to check the mono, because somewhere, on your radio, or something, someone will listen to it, hear it, in mono, instead of stereo."

"But why does it do that? I mean, why does it sound like someone is flushing it down the toilet when you switch it to mono? Is that what is supposed to happen?"

"No, no, no that is exactly what is NOT supposed to happen! The tape is totally fucked up!"

"What? How?"

"The *azimuth* — the azimuth must have been off, off on one or more of the quarter-inch machines." Then with a tear in his voice, "Maybe they were all fucked up! I don't know!"

"Can you talk in English? I'm freaking out!"

A complete novice, I had no idea what any of this meant.

"A stereo recording has two tracks. To make it seem like a sound is coming out of the middle of the two speakers, the same sound is recorded onto the two tracks in equal volume. The two sounds add together and you get this big sound in the middle. That's why when you listen to this stereo tape, it appears as if the sound of Paul's vocal hovers in the middle of the air between the two speakers, as if he is on stage and you can almost see him. And the different instruments seem to be in different parts of the sound picture in front of you – that funny high guitar to one side, the flute to the other, just like they were playing in front of you. That's the glory of stereo.

"But if the 'record' head on the tape machine, the thing that magne-tizes the iron filings in a certain pattern, is not exactly straight, not per-pendicular to the tape, then when you play the tape back on a head that is completely straight, the sounds that are supposed to be in the middle subtract instead of add. And it happens to the high frequencies worse. You don't notice it in stereo, but when you put the signals together in mono, it's like all the high-end is sucked out of the tape."

"I'm not sure I understand that, but how does that happen, how could it have been off?"

"With all the banging around these machines get, being pushed from room to room, it knocks the heads out of alignment. I should check the azimuth on every session, but who had the time to check four different machines? Ramone was always yelling at me to finish up, because fucking Paul Simon doesn't like to wait, and," his voice trailing off, "I just didn't always have the time to check everything."

I looked over at the four old machines in their beaten and battered metal boxes. "Is there any way to fix it?"

"Sure. I mean, normally. If the whole thing had been mixed down to one tape machine, and the whole thing was off consistently throughout, you'd just have to adjust the playback head on the mastering machine so it was at the same angle that the record head was on the original mix machine. You'd correct for the error in the mastering, and it would eliminate the problem.

"But you can't do that in this case, because this was mixed on so many different machines and different pieces were mixed from different machines all with different mistakes. That's why, instead of just the deep-in-the-toilet muffled sound, you get the swishing thing. It's kind of like that phasing sound on the hit by the Doobie Brothers, 'Listen to the Music,' except it's awful, and most definitely not what Paul wanted. And I can't think of any way to fix that."

I saw the specter of death before my eyes. Six months of work, ruined? The new Paul Simon album...destroyed? Discovered on the day that Phil is supposed to take the tape to get it mastered so it could be released in days? No. This could not be happening!

My panic started flowing over. "Whatever you do, don't tell Phil, look, I've got to get out of here. I'm, I'm leaving. I don't know where I'm going to go, but it's over. Anyway, maybe he'll never hit the mono button. If he doesn't, he'll never know. He never hit the mono button once during the whole six months . . . I mean . . ." Then the shock flooded me. "*Should he have?*"

Ralph started speaking softly, as if there was a microphone in the room, listening in. "Of course he should've checked. You've always got to check. That was his job. He should have checked the mono after every mix. If he had, he would have caught this right at the beginning."

I grew numb. *Could Ramone have fucked up that badly? No Way!*

Ralph must have been processing the same thing. Ralph couldn't accept that answer either. "It was my fault. Goddamn it! I should have insisted on taking the time, Phil and Paul be damned! How could I have been such a . . . Look we *have* to tell Phil. We have to tell him."

Ralph called upstairs and asked Phil to come down. As I waited in the control room, silently glued to my chair, I had post-traumatic flashbacks dancing before my eyes of every time Phil had been a complete and utter maniac. He would just as likely throw a chair at my head if my breathing was too loud. The sound of his screams rang in my ears, a volcanic, Jurassic vomiting that would rip your toenails off. And his favorite rant played over and over: "You've destroyed my reputation! You've ended my career!" Though I came to understand that his explosions were usually histrionic bullshit, this time there was some merit to the argument. If he bit off large chunks of people's legs for far less than this, how would he react to this, this news, comparable to the annihilation of the solar system?

Phil walked into the control room. Ralph asked him to sit down. Ralph spoke deliberately, in quiet tones, like someone telling a parent that his child had terminal cancer.

Ralph told him the worst of it. Everything in my head was telling me to run, but when I looked down and saw my own body, I didn't know what it was there for. I felt something more than fear, an anticipation of horror, a blackness so complete, like an antelope that plays dead, knowing it is on the verge of being eaten by a lion.

Phil was quiet. Then he, too, spoke in slow, measured tones. His voice was different than I'd ever heard from him. I was surprised. There was no yelling. "This couldn't be worse. I'm supposed to bring this tape to Roy Halee, the guy who did the Simon and Garfunkel records. The engineer I respect more than anyone in the world. He will definitely hit the button, he'll hear it. He'll know." He paused. "I can't let that happen. I can't do that."

I watched Ramone dig deep. This crisis was too real for him to pull some diva stunt. He could be a preening cocker spaniel with each day-to-day crisis, yapping and nipping and pissing all over the studio floor in some neurotic hissy-fit. But when things got really, truly, horribly bad, Ramone turned Olympian.

"All right," he said, nodding with a fierce, determined look in his eye. "Get me the Allen-head screwdriver."

Ralph knew what he wanted. He wanted the screwdriver that would change the azimuth.

Ramone straddled the tape machine, his mammoth belly pressed up against the metal box. He held the screwdriver over the six-sided metal post that jutted out from the top of the head-stack used to adjust the angle of the tape head. He breathed deep and hit the play button, listening to the sickening sound in mono.

As the timbre went from squeaky to mud and back again, Ramone twisted the screw, following the random changes. When the highs disappeared down the wormhole, he'd twist the screw in one direction, causing the sound to become clear; then as they thinned, he'd twist it in the other direction, and the sounds would once more become full.

He rode that Allen-head screw like he was in a car chase on the Riviera, screeching around hairpin turns, barely staying on the road. For hours, in total concentration, Ramone played the master tape endless times, learning the curves, the hills, the dips, the cliffs, the falls, bit by bit, of a 40-minute album.

I followed his every order, in total respect, and stunned shock, at the full weight of the reality that Ramone — *Ramone* — fucked up this badly, and it came back to kick him up the keister at the worst possible moment. (Then I said a prayer of gratitude that none of my fuck ups, no matter how bad, had reached this epic level. At least not yet.) But at the same time that he was a giant screw up, he was also the guy who could rally and do the impossible, saving the project from imminent destruction.

Untold hours later, his flight postponed, drenched in sweat and blind with exhaustion, he completed the fix. We made a safety with Ramone turning the screw for 40 straight minutes. He did it in one pass, so there would be no edits.

We removed the original tape from the box labeled "master" and replaced it with the doctored copy. Ramone took the new tape, put it in his bag, and got into a limo to take him to the airport. We put the original master in a box marked "Safety copy." That tape was sent to the bowels of the library.

We never spoke of that incident again.

The glory of my first project with a major artist had been irretrievably sullied. A vague echo of shame reverberated within me.

Had I passed my first test? All signs said that I was in with Ramone. I now held a huge secret, and that offered some leverage, not that I would ever think of using it. But somehow, even though it appeared that I had crossed the first threshold, I felt something less than elated.

After the loss of my father, whom I saw as a weak failure, all I wanted was to be mentored by men I could look up to and admire, respect, emulate. I longed to find men who were good, honest, and powerful, so they could teach me how to be a man. But how could I make sense out of this? Who were these people: the superstar, Simon, whose music provided succor to the masses, but was so cold; and Ramone, my teacher, so successful and heroic, and yet so out of control, and capable of such incompetence?

I started to absorb the confusing reality that great people were just as screwed up as anyone else. Maybe more so. My firm and rigid beliefs about the world started to unravel. Black and white began to bleed into each other. In my old worldview, there were good people and bad, truth-tellers and bullshitters, champions and villains. Now, I found all those qualities to exist in one person.

As my perspective of the world turned gray, my emotions also blended together. Only now, looking back from this great distance, have I been able to distinguish the multiple and subtle shades of feeling that I was suffering.

I can still feel the echoes of my disappointment that these men gave me neither the love I sought, nor the modeling I craved. I felt this as a personal wound, as if they had some obligation to be what I needed them to be, and took their limitations as a personal rejection.

I can sense the burning ambition and murderous competitiveness that lived in me, that led me to want to supplant them, and my smoldering resentment when they out-maneuvered and prevented me from doing so.

With hindsight, I can appreciate the confidence I was beginning to possess from having survived the game with the big boys.

I can admit to the awe I felt in the presence of these men who gave their all, risking so much, without guarantee of success, with a quality of caring that I could not allow myself to have. I can own my fear then, doubting my capacity for such courage.

I can mourn the numbness I forced on myself, in order to endure the humiliations I was put through and to appear strong.

And I can still get in touch with the envy I felt at being in the presence of such talent that seemed so inscrutable yet so close. I was right there, next to these titans, who appeared so ordinary, yet managed to create things of subtle beauty that seemed infinitely inaccessible to me.

All of those varied emotional colors roiled inside of me, but at that time, I was only aware of one feeling, one I had learned from all of the men I had been working with over the previous year. It was the only acceptable emotion at A&R Studios.

I was mad.

Bob Dylan's *Blood on the Tracks*: The Untold Story

In 1974, Bob Dylan was looking for renewal. His marriage to his wife Sara was broken. Over the previous few years, he had made two records for Asylum Records. He had been disappointed with sales and didn't cotton to David Geffen, Asylum's leader.

That September, Ramone excitedly came to find me after a phone call. Dylan was returning to Columbia Records, the venerable label he'd started with, and he was going to record his new album with us! This was the way it was in those days. We were hot. Amazing projects were coming in one after another.

The date that Dylan picked to begin recording was propitious: September 16th, which was Rosh Hashanah, the Jewish New Year. The recording was to take place in studio A-1. This room had once belonged to Columbia, until they sold it to Ramone in 1968. This was Columbia's earliest recording room, operational since the 1930s. The walls echoed with past sessions featuring the likes of Sinatra and Streisand. Dylan had done his early work there. Not least of the astounding hits recorded in that room was "Like a Rolling Stone," his signature.

From the street, you could see this big box with a peaked copper roof (the copper was there to keep out stray electronic interference), stuck on top of the building. It has since been torn down and replaced with the Equitable Insurance Building. (So has my city of dreams descended from music to finance.)

Dylan was doing what the Akan people of Ghana call a *sankofa*, a return to beginnings to move into the future. And I would be there to witness the sacred ritual.

It was a central part of my job to make the artists we were working with feel safe. Only then could they create freely. There were a few ways to do this. One was to be cool in their presence. Blasé was the order of the day. The other was to do all we could to protect the star's privacy. Discretion had been drilled into me.

I was used to spoiled artists and was trained to cosset them. But Dylan's reputation for self-protection was unmatched. Phil, in his nervous way, made an extra point to warn me about him.

"That call I got from Columbia? They told me he's totally paranoid about exposure, so we've got to keep the room off limits to everyone. He's coming in with a protector. It'll just be you and me in the control room—and you…stay clear."

Minutes before the date was supposed to start, Ramone told me that Dylan had asked him to put a band together. However, given the holiday, there were few cats around. Phil found Eric Weissberg, banjo and guitar player extraordinaire. Weissberg put out the call to the "Deliverance Band," a bunch of top players who were famous for having done the soundtrack for the movie of the same name.

The musicians started showing up for the gig, Weissberg the first to arrive. He was a lovely, friendly man, as most studio musicians were. Even though I was just the *schlepper* who set up the chairs and the microphones, he greeted me warmly. Once Eric told me who was coming in, I set up for the band: drums, bass, guitars, keyboard. I put Dylan's mic in the middle of the room.

During all this hubbub, Dylan skulked in with his gatekeeper, a

Columbia exec, and his main squeeze of the moment Ellen Bernstein. He grunted hello and retreated to the farthest corner of the control room, keeping his head down, ignoring us all. No one dared enter his private circle.

As I dashed around the studio and control room getting everything prepared, John Hammond arrived. This lightened up the room. Hammond, a visionary record-man who discovered and promoted artists from Billie Holiday to Bruce Springsteen, was the guy who had originally signed Dylan to Columbia. He and Bob hugged briefly but then barely interacted. Hammond was unruffled. I guess he knew the guy.

Hammond sat behind the producer's desk, massive disks for blue eyes, a spike of salt and pepper hair, and the big smile of a true fan on his face. To any Dylan aficionado, this was a classic moment: Dylan and Hammond in this studio, together again for Bob's comeback to Columbia.

The studio cats, who spent their days and nights working with the best in the biz on groundbreaking shit and who usually embodied the essence of cool, were palpably pumped. It wasn't every day that you got to work with Dylan. You could feel the buzz in the room.

I ran as fast as I could to get it all together so we could get the session going. Having checked out all the gear, I gave Ramone the go-ahead, and he got sounds on everyone in minutes. We were ready to rock.

I gingerly approached Dylan in the corner and told him we could start whenever he liked. He nodded and let me lead him out to the studio. He slung his acoustic guitar over his shoulder and placed the signature harmonica holder around his neck. Standing inches from him, I brought the mics in close. We used our venerable Neumann microphones, the kind he would've used in the early '60s. I adjusted the position of the mics precisely for optimal pick up.

Time stopped and the snapshot became clear. I'm standing next to Dylan: the little wiry body, the hipster-rabbi black vest and white shirt, the tangled up Jew-fro. He was thirty-three years old. He looked past me, to some place in another dimension. Maybe he muttered thanks. I retreated into the control room.

He called off a tune.

"Let's do, 'If You See Her, Say Hello.'"

He ran through the song twice. The players were just beginning to figure out the changes and what to play. On the third try, he played the opening chord on his guitar, but then threw everyone off by singing the lyrics and melody to a different song, "You're a Big Girl Now." The song was in the same key, but the chord changes and structure were nowhere near the same. The musicians stumbled. They hadn't been prepared for this. The chords they played, from the previous tune, clashed against what Bob was playing. The cacophony jarred. Quickly, the cats tried to pick up on the new harmonies, but the keyboard player wasn't fast enough. Dylan waved his hand, like shooing off an annoying gnat, signaling him to drop out.

The musicians were rattled. They scrambled to pick up the new tune. Barely having recovered from the shock, after a run-through or two, Dylan changed songs in midstream, again, without letting anyone know. This time, it was to "Simple Twist of Fate." Another of the cats crashed a wrong chord into what Dylan was playing, and he got swiped down, too.

The excitement in the studio began to fizzle, like air leaving a balloon, replaced with fear and tension. No one would tell him he couldn't do this. After all, he was Dylan. But this was wrong. You're at least supposed to tell the musicians what song you are doing, let them learn the chords, and come up with an arrangement. You've got to give them a chance.

One by one, the musicians were told to stop playing. Like swatted bugs, they writhed on the ground, waiting to die.

Studio musicians are a tough lot; they're hired to do whatever it takes. They might work on a basic track for twelve hours in search of an impossible perfection, but they'd never say no or show the slightest bit of attitude. Those were the rules.

This, on the other hand, hurt. You could see it in the musicians' eyes, as they sat silently behind their instruments, forced not to play by the mercurial whim of the guy painting his masterpiece with finger-paints.

The feeling went from tense to grim. We stole looks at each other, not understanding what was going on, not knowing what to do, hardly believing it. It slowly began to dawn on the musicians that the dream of playing on a Dylan record was not going to happen.

After a few disastrous takes, it ended up with just Bob and the bass player, Tony Brown. Tony sat inches from him, watching his hands, trying to follow the chord changes as Bob played them, never knowing what chord or song was to come in the next moment. This was particularly treacherous, because Dylan was using an "open tuning," which meant that he wasn't placing his fingers in the conventional positions on the guitar's fret board, which would signal what chord he was playing. Dylan was on his own wavelength: you either were on it or you didn't exist.

Listening in the control room, we heard some clacking sound, Bob's button against the guitar, or something. We'd usually stop a take to get rid of that kind of imperfection. But even Ramone was too freaked to say anything. He didn't want to be the next to go.

We cut an entire album's worth of material like that in six hours. That blew my mind. I was nineteen years old and trying to learn how to make art. The style of the time was set by guys I was working with like Paul Simon, who would take weeks to record a guitar part only to throw it away. I thought that was the way one was supposed to do it: one note at a time and a year to make an album. Dylan did the whole thing on a Monday night. I was flabbergasted. It was like the floor, barely built under my young soul, was being ripped apart, board by board.

As if I wasn't confused enough, Dylan came back in on Tuesday and recorded most of the album again. The full band, except for Tony the bass player, had been officially fired. This time he had the keyboard player Paul Griffin come in to try it out. Paul, a garrulous guy, tried to sunny up the date with his charm and smile. But he, too, didn't make the cut. His smile gone, he shrugged, and departed with his tail between his legs.

Wednesday we cut one song and did some overdubs.

On Thursday we recorded the album for a third time, this time just with the bass. The dark and painful vibe in the studio reflected the material Bob was recording. The songs of loss and heartache were riveting.

I sat on a stool with a tape box and a take sheet on my lap. My job was humble. It was to get the thing down on tape. The goal of the recording engineer, as Ramone taught me, was to capture an eternal universal truth so you could stick it in your ear and listen to it, without the artist ever knowing you'd done it. Any screw up on my part would bring Dylan's attention to the proceedings. That was why I needed to be flawless.

I was in the groove. The studio gear hummed. The instant Dylan moved in front of the mics, my hands flew to the multi-track tape machine. In a flash, I'd hit the red button.

Ramone was at the "flying V," what we called the custom-made recording console in A-1. In the 21st century, all consoles are manufactured by a handful of companies. Then, in the ancient 20th, everything was being invented. New techniques and methods came out daily, and we were always adapting: 8-track, 16, and then 24. The consoles were made by individuals, by hand. Ramone had a crazy concept for this board. There were knobs in multi-colors in the shape of hearts, diamonds, clubs, and spades.

This ship was like Han Solo's in *Star Wars* — that was the era — the 1970s. It wasn't the antiseptic space cruiser of *2001: A Space Odyssey*. Our cockpit was dirty and falling apart. Right before we were ready to go, the machine began to sputter, and sparks flew from the patch bay. I picked up the intercom and screamed for the tech crew: MAINTENANCE! The whole thing stopped working, and if we didn't get it up and running fast enough we might lose the moment of inspiration. The technical guys flew in. They stood frozen with a perplexed look.

Ramone bellowed, "Come on, you stupid fuckers! Bob Dylan is ready!"

One guy took a shot and kicked a metal box in the right place. The console shuddered, the lights came back on, and we were traveling through hyper-space again. We were on tenterhooks like that, always one transistor away from the damn thing failing.

We were ready just in time. I could feel the burn of creation from the other side of the glass. Dylan. Songs were bursting out of him like lava spewing from a volcano. He was mainlined to the source. What they call genius. I saw him write a song's lyrics on a yellow legal pad like he was taking dictation, he couldn't write fast enough. And the songs would rewrite themselves as he sang them. Take 1 would have a verse that sounded so good you could gasp with revelation, and then he'd do Take 2 and it would blow away the last one like so much ash after a fire.

We could feel it coming fast, and when that happened the pressure was on to capture it. Ramone's foot would start tapping, his hands on the big round black knobs, controlling the levels, making sure that what went down on tape was clean. One chance, no going back. He whipped around to me,

"Roll tape, roll tape!"

The red lights were already lit. I had achieved the sweet spot, I knew what Ramone wanted before he did. I was Ramone, we were one. We locked eyes, no time for appreciation, *was it going down on tape?* I checked the lights, all tracks in "record", I checked the meters, console, tape machine, the same. What was coming out of Dylan's mouth and guitar was going to the console, coming out of the mammoth Altec 604 speakers, cranked to a volume that reached the limits of human tolerance, 101 decibels, going to the tape machine, to be etched into eternity. Or if I forgot one thing, oblivion. *Can't mess up, not now, not with Dylan.* Meters moving in rhythm to the song. And Dylan, just a few feet away, behind the glass, throat tight, Tony Brown watching his fingers blast against the fret board, also trying to stay alive, Dylan, sweating, feeling it deep, the way he'd twist his vowels, rasping the lyrics.

Dylan! Holy shit! Me, nineteen years old watching rock and roll history being made right before my eyes and ears, seeing the spit flying out of his mouth against the U-87 microphone that I placed there.

The whole studio throbbed, the big box with the copper roof about to blow off with all the pain, the anger, the truth. The tape machine flew in circles, the tape whirred, it seemed faster and faster than the thirty inches per second that I knew it travelled, the red lights seemed brighter, the needles pushed into the red zone, Ramone's shoulders tensed, his total focus on what was in his hands, temperature rising, I started to hallucinate, the red lights turned to blood, the blood ran on to the tape machine, blood on the tracks . . .

The plaintive moan of his harmonica, then the final, clangorous chord.

Then silence.

The song over. No one speaks when a take is done.

We sat and waited. Just the sound of the tape machine still whirring: flap, flap, flap. Now the needles still. The blood back to lights glowing, telling us it was all down on tape. We waited.

Dylan turned to us in the control room and snarled sarcastically, "Was that since-e-e-re enough?"

Vertigo. I was spinning like the fat tape on the machine. Ramone gave me the signal and I hit the stop button. Rewind.

I looked down at my feet and watched the last floorboard give way. I fell. A lifetime of ideals washed away in one sentence.

What could this possibly mean? I had taken the oath, that's what you did when you apprenticed to the master in the house of recorded art, you'd go to any length for the sake of rock and roll music, the highest state of truth yet created by human design. And now the high priest of it all was just a guy behind a curtain yanking the world's chain? He'd murdered his musicians with the aplomb of a psychopath; he recorded his album sloppily in a day and then did it again two times more, and now this? Was it fucking *sincere* enough? I was ready to puke.

The egotistical pricks I'd indulged were all good fun compared to this. The icon of an age, the guy who punctured all pretense, who brought down the whole hypocritical building, the guy who sneered at sanctimony — totally full of shit?

I was lost. And I was to stay lost on a dark journey that was to last twenty years. Disillusionment can really mess with your head.

Dylan didn't show up for the mix. While most artists were using the studio like an instrument, he didn't care about the recording thing. He left it in Ramone's hands. At that time we were working twenty hour days. I hadn't slept more than three or four hours a night in a year. That week we were working with Mick Jagger during the day, mixing live tapes from the Stones' 1973 European tour for a King Biscuit Flower Hour radio broadcast. But that's another story for a later chapter. We had to cram in the Dylan mixes after we were done with the rest.

It was after midnight, just me and Ramone left in the studio, with one tech guy asleep down the hall.

Lighting was a big deal in the rooms. It was all about setting the mood for creativity. I turned most of the lights off. All was black except a glow over the flying-V mixing console. When you blocked out all external stimuli and listened for endless hours, the space between the beats would expand to the point where you could hear inside the sounds all the way down to their quarks.

The mixes were just Dylan and the bass mostly, so the sound of the voice and the guitar was the whole thing. Ramone spent a long time messing with the reverb. This was the signature Phil Ramone sound. He had these big boxes, called EMT's, in the basement that, when tweaked just right made this beautiful echo, rich and evocative of something you couldn't quite name. Ramone got it right, as he always did, and we were ripping through the mixes.

I wanted to know all the secrets. I was trying to grasp onto any shred of sense, any rule, that would give me something to hold onto when the bottom had fallen out. How did you make great art? Paul Simon, one brilliant guy, did it one way. Dylan, another master, couldn't have been more different. What was I to believe anymore? I still wanted to know.

I sat behind Ramone watching, listening. Exhausted from lack of sleep and too many drugs, I struggled to focus. I noticed that the meters looked strange. Usually they all lined up, bouncing up and down in parallel, but this time they were lopsided. What was Ramone up to? What was he doing to get his incredible sound? How did he get it so good that the heaviest cats in the world flocked to his door? I wanted to know the magician's spell so I could have the power, too.

With the clients breathing down our necks, we rarely had time to talk. And given how erratic Ramone could be, I hardly dared to open my mouth. Mostly, I had to learn by screwing up and getting drained and dressed. If you learned how to take it, you could become a major cat. But here was a chance, I thought, with no one around, to learn from my sensei.

Between takes, I said, "Phil, can I ask you a question? I notice the meters are uneven. What are you hearing? Why are you doing that?"

He didn't answer for one minute, then two, as we sat there in silence.

Then, without warning, he twirled around, his face purple and trembling with rage, his breath smelling like Chinese pork ribs.

"Who the fuck do you think you are asking the great Ramone a question? You are just a little piece of worthless shit. You don't question what I do! I do everything I do because I am the great Ramone! You will never be one percent of what I am! You think you're going to be a recording engineer? You don't have ears. You'll never make it! You should just be content to sit behind me and wipe my ass! You don't question, you just obey!"

I realized that Ramone must've thought I was busting him for a mistake. That wasn't my intention at all, but clearly I had stepped in it. I tried to protest, to tell him I meant no harm, I just wanted to learn . . . but every word just incensed him further.

There was no arguing. His voice got louder and louder, the screams more incoherent, the insults more vicious. "You're nothing! To you I am a god! You're the lowest piece of shit in the presence of a god! You will never be anything!"

"But, Phil, but Phil . . ."

It all started to swirl around me: the hours, the brutalization, the cocaine, "Idiot Wind," the lack of sleep, nineteen years old, *was it sin-ceeeeeeeeere enough . . ."*

I hit the stop button on the tape machine. I thought I saw blood on my fingers, I couldn't hold onto the edge of the cliff any longer. My face started to crumble, there was no way I could hide it. I was going down. I ran out of the control room and through the silent hallway to the bathroom. Under the glaring fluorescent lights, 2 a.m., I sat on the pot, putting my hands over my face, and blubbered.

My only passion had been to sit in the engineer's chair. Since I was eleven years old and first heard "Land of 1000 Dances" by Wilson Pickett, I wanted nothing else but to make those mind-blowing things called records. But at that moment, as I sat on the toilet in that grim stall, I wondered if the whole thing was worth it. Ramone was probably right. I didn't have what it takes.

Despite my new-found certainty that I was utterly worthless, I knew that Ramone needed me to get through the mix. The folks at Columbia were expecting the final product the next day. I had made the blood promise. I had to pull it up from somewhere and do my job. I dug deep, wiped my eyes with the particular brand of fancy-ass toilet paper that Ramone insisted we have in the bathrooms, and breathed.

I staggered back into the control room. The room was empty. I walked over to the flying V console. I sat down in Ramone's chair and touched the sacred knobs. I saw little scraps of paper crumpled up on the board. I unfolded one, and in a mangled scrawl was written "Ramone is God."

Suddenly feeling nervous, I recrumpled the scrap, got up, and silently took the schlepper's seat next to the tape machine. With box and take sheet in hand, I was ready to keep my mouth shut for the next century and just do my job, or at least till this long night was over.

Ramone came back in with a big smile on his face as if nothing had happened. I knew what this meant. I'd been through this routine before. He had popped a tranq and was mellowing into a good mood.

"Glenn, we're going to get out of this place. We're going to build a studio together, you and me; it'll be the most amazing place where everything will always work. Who do you want to record? Stevie Wonder? We'll get Stevie in and you'll be his personal engineer. Stick with me, kid. We'll do amazing things."

Phil wanted to do that with me? Really? Ok, Phil, I'll go all night, I'll take any abuse . . . I was back in all the way.

We finished the record that night. I stayed up 'til the bagels arrived at the crack of dawn, sequencing the thing, splicing together the master mixes with a razor blade and tape into the final order of songs. Watch out for the blade, especially late at night. You never knew when it could meet your flesh instead of the acetate.

The record was to be released after the first of the year. The studio life was insane, but I was back to believing the dream. 1975 looked like it would be a great year. At the peak was to be the release of the Dylan album. With this run, my star was ascending.

Phil and I started on our next amazing project, *Judith* by Judy Collins. While we were sitting in the control room of studio R-2 working on overdubs for that record, the phone rang. This must have been an important call to interrupt Phil during a session.

I heard Phil say, "Bob, it's amazing. Really, probably your best album ever. Don't worry. It's great."

Phil looked over at me with a perplexed look on his face. We shook our heads in disbelief. Dylan insecure? Huh?

This went on, week after week, with Bob calling Phil for reassurance again and again as we approached the New Year deadline.

When we returned from the Christmas holiday, Phil sat down with me, pale and dispirited. Bob had panicked. While visiting his family in Minnesota over the break, he had decided to re-record a bunch of the tracks in the nearby twin cities. Minneapolis was in its pre-Prince days; a recording nowhere-land. The only studio and musicians available were from the local jingle studio, where they recorded commercials for Mom's Biscuits and the Oldsmobile dealership on Nicolett Avenue.

Phil handed me the new master tapes. It was my job to cut out the tracks we had worked on, and splice in the new ones he had done in bum-fuck Minnesota. My breathing stopped as I listened to the stuff that was going to replace what we had done.

Dink, doink, dink doink, bum, bum, bum . . .

These searing, wrenching, burning, bloody songs…turned into bouncy little jingles? *What?*

I cut into the tape like an old, drunken, western surgeon with a rusty knife. I cut out pink, vibrating, living, breathing body parts and left them bleeding on the floor. It wasn't my job to choose, it was my job to plunge in the blade and kill the baby that I had helped deliver.

The album came out a few weeks later. When I got a copy, I quickly flipped it to the back. That's where the unsung heroes of recording look first. We take it all for the glory, but we also like the credit. I looked at every word of the smallest type but was to find myself suffering the final indignity. No credit. My name nowhere on the cover.

*

Blood on the Tracks went on to become a number one record and has been heralded as one of the greatest albums of all time, some saying it is Dylan's best. So what do I know? What do I know about anything, really? Have I really learned the lessons of those days? I learned what a trickster is — a mythical archetype — the shape shifter. Bob Dylan as Bugs Bunny. Hey, what's up doc? Always popping up from a hole you don't expect, outwitting us slow-witted mortals. He's meant to confuse, to upend the money-changers in the temple. The artist is not supposed to be nice. He's on a mission from beyond. He goes down, deeper into himself than any of us dare, goes through hell on the journey, steals the sacred fire, and brings it up to share with the rest of us. Who are we to judge the way he behaves when he does that much for us?

And Phil. He's left a legacy that will endure for generations. His job was to break me down so he could put me back together as a man. I carry his vision and standard with me in my fingers right to this moment as I write this. "That sucks, Berger, do it again," I hear him say. I'm fighting with Phil to this day, father and son, locked in the eternal struggle for domination of the universe. The old man still wins every time, damn him.

Ramone and Dylan taught me, but I don't know how well. I've certainly been a major jerk in my day but never made anything immortal like these guys.

*

To look at me now, in my fifties, in my trickster uniform of middle-aged shrink, you'd never know I'd ever been there. Recently, I ran into another dad, a major record exec at one of my kid's birthday parties, the only place I'm likely to meet a guy like that now. Looking for something to chat about, I told him I'd been in the biz, and he asked if I worked with anyone big. I said my usual sentence: I worked on the album the hip New York radio station, WFUV, named the greatest album of all time, *Blood on the Tracks*, by Bob Dylan. He looked at me skeptically and said nothing and the conversation ended awkwardly. I slithered away in embarrassment.

When I was driving home, I thought about the guy's expression. I imagined him Googling the credits to the album, and, not finding my name, deciding I was full of shit. I began to wonder, had I been there or was I making it all up?

Then I remembered, there was proof. My name was on those take sheets that I filled out as part of the schlepper's humble job. It was the place where I wrote down the names of the songs and the take numbers. In the top right-hand corner of that sheet's notations of the sessions' events, there would be a slot that said "Engineer: Phil/Glenn." I had written those words myself.

I knew the internet had everything and there were some major Dylan freaks out there. Maybe I could dig this up. Maybe I needed to prove it to myself. I Googled "take sheets for *Blood on the Tracks*." Amazingly, a guy named Michael Krogsgaard had found the take sheets of every Dylan recording, and posted the data on the web.

I scrolled down the page to find the information from our album. I read the words: Studio A, A&R Recording, September 16, 1974. New York City. 6PM - Midnight.

Here it was! Or, so I thought. The next line read: Engineer: Phil/ Lenn.

Ah well. Another drop of blood. Dylan's final joke.

Blood on the tracks. It is painful to be an artist. That's why so many of them break. Dylan poured his guts into these songs, and that's why they will long endure. He was plugged in in a way that I can only sweetly envy. I can see the prize, I can almost taste it, but it eludes my grasp like the fruit above the mythical tortured Tantalus. I had stood so close that the blades of brilliance ripped my flesh, but it was always on the outside, apart from me.

The bloody wounds of those days have mellowed into impressive scars, leaving me with the bittersweet satisfaction that one time, long ago, I had sacrificed and suffered for a cause greater than myself — art.

I know it's Dylan's blood that's on those tracks, and that's what makes those songs so great. But I take some small measure of solace for what my life has been by telling myself that, along with his blood, there is also a little bit of mine.

TRACK SIX

Judy Collins and Arif Mardin: A Turkishly Delightful New Years

It was New Year's Eve. We were about to enter 1975, one of the low point years in recent New York City history, but the Big Apple's woes made it possible for a kid like me and my best friend, Duke, to afford to share an apartment on 73rd Street and 1st Avenue in Manhattan. The rent was $240 a month for the two-room, 4th floor walk-up apartment, so we each paid $120. You can barely get a decent bagel for $120 in New York these days.

We were relatively new in town, and New York is a hard nut to crack. Still, all things considered, we were living a pretty glamorous life.

Duke was an actor and was about to perform with an offshoot of the Performance Group, the coolest avant-garde theatre troupe anywhere. It made its home in an off-beat neighborhood of abandoned industrial warehouses called Soho, which is so trendy now, but at that time was virtually unknown. The first time I went to see the Group do their thing at the Performance Garage on Wooster Street in 1972, tumbleweeds blew through the wind-swept streets of what was essentially a ghost town. I was blown away by the ensemble's adaptation of Sam Shepard's "The Tooth of Crime," not only because of Shepard's archetypal tale of the battle between a cowboy and a rocker, but also the acting and production, in which the audience was encouraged to move around the industrial space to be intimately close to the action. These were heady days in the New York culture scene.

While Duke was cool for hanging with these über-hipsters, I wasn't doing too bad myself, for a nineteen year-old kid. Apprenticed to the master-maniac, Phil Ramone, I had just helped finish recording an album by Judy Collins called *Judith*. It was to become one of her most popular albums, featuring the perennial hit "Send in the Clowns." Participating in the recording of that album during the autumn of 1974 was an honor and a joy.

We cut the tracks in the big room, Studio A-1. After a take, Judy would come join us in the control room for the playback and stand next to me behind the recording console. Reviewing freshly cut tracks was always a serious affair. Was this the version that had the magic? Was there something subtly off that would render it a useless outtake? The control room was hushed, and everyone listened with the deepest concentration.

When the song ended, Judy, inches from me, looked at me with her intense, blue eyes. She leaned over so close, her long, flaxen hair would brush against me and she whispered, "What do you think?" A pure thrill spread through my adolescent body.

I'm not sure why she asked. Judy had unerring taste. She had put together the premier production team in the business to create this masterwork. The legendary Arif Mardin was the album's producer. His equal, Phil Ramone, was on the engineering controls. Jonathan Tunick was the orchestral arranger. Yet she encouraged me to find my own way to evaluating the merit of the recording. She helped me learn how to listen.

Of course she had a great ear and knew how to pick the best songs. She was responsible for virtually discovering Joni Mitchell and Leonard Cohen. She herself received profound artistic mentorship from her teacher, Antonia Brico, the first female conductor, whom she spoke of with reverence.

Judy was one of my great teachers. Perhaps the deepest learning I gained in getting to work with Judy was about this artistic sensibility. I came to appreciate that this sensibility is in an attitude, a way of being in the world, and a sensitivity and responsiveness to the highest levels of quality and feeling. It is an approach to life and work that involves aspiring to the most penetrating insight into truth. It demands that we be willing to put all of ourselves into everything we do with total passion. Simply being in the presence of that ethos to living and work helped inspire and teach me how to be.

After I had assisted on two of her albums, Judy gave me the opportunity to engineer on my own, one of the first artists to do so. I had the incredible fortune to engineer her retrospective album *So Early in the Spring*, which covered her career from 1961 – 1976. I got to listen to all of her recordings and learned to appreciate the early work of this master on the deepest level. Judy was not only a role model in mentoring me, but by giving me the opportunity to work as her engineer, she advanced my career and artistic development.

This depth of being has held Judy in good stead. Her recent work on her own label, *Wildflower*, continues a career of beauty, depth, and meaning. Her voice is more radiant, powerful, and gorgeous than ever.

We finished *Judith* at deadline, the last day of the year. My job was to make a tape copy of the whole thing and deliver it to the producer, Arif, at his apartment on the Upper West Side of Manhattan. Duke and I didn't have any major plans for that night, so since we had nothing else to do, I asked him if he wanted to come along with me to make the delivery.

I had gotten to hang deep with Arif during the months of the recording. He was the rare exception to the rule that the most talented and accomplished among us were assholes. Arif proved you didn't have to pull people down to make yourself look more brilliant. Arif was cultured, well-mannered, and real.

Mr. Mardin was truly musical. There's a scene in the film *Amadeus*, about Mozart, in which the court composer, Salieri, plays a ditty he has composed for the young, up-and-coming genius. The composition is pedestrian, and you can hear the obviousness of its harmonic structure. Mozart sits down and riffs on the theme, and in a few moments, turns the exercise into *music*. That's the magic that a guy like Arif embodied. He exemplified tastefulness at its ultimate.

The Mardins lived in a big, old pre-war building on the Upper West Side, one of those Manhattan real estate palaces consisting of huge multi-room apartments called "classic sixes" and "classic sevens."

Duke and I were somewhat intimidated by the building's stately dimensions and class, but we would never show it, knowing how to be cool. We sauntered in, telling the doorman where we were headed, me with my tape in an envelope, delivery boys with a difference.

We rang Arif's doorbell. I assumed he would grab the tape, say thanks, and we'd run off into the night, gleeful at getting that close. An elegant, impeccably coiffed woman with caramel colored skin, coffee colored eyes and black hair came to the door. She had a welcoming smile. I told her my business.

She said, "Oh, we are getting ready for a party, but Arif will be here in a minute. Please come in. I'm Latife, his wife."

Come in? Arif was one of those legendary cats Duke and I both idolized. Here was an opportunity not to be missed. We looked at each other quickly and stepped over the threshold. Latife rushed away, and we stood in the apartment's foyer, breathing in the wooly aroma of antique rugs, absorbing the muted glow of golden light reflected off old wood.

Arif came dashing out. He looked like a falcon with a round head and a sharp beak of a nose. He wore a white shirt with an ascot and some well-tailored trousers. His black hair was slicked back over his mostly bald head, and his thin moustache added the final touch of panache.

He reached out his hand to shake mine, as if we were old buddies, and I introduced Duke, whom he greeted warmly. His deeply intelligent eyes and confident handshake eased our embarrassment.

"Boys, good to see you!" he said in his aristocratic Turkish accent. "Sorry it has taken a minute, I'm preparing for a party."

Before I could make excuses and turn to leave, he said, "Come in! Come in! Do you have a minute? Please!"

I stammered, "Are you sure? I mean, we don't want to get in the way, with your party and all that."

"No, no," he giggled. "Please come in."

Again, shocked, we agreed. Our feet started to rise from the ground. We were being invited inside to hang out with Arif Mardin on New Year's Eve? This was fun.

He brought us into his study and invited us to sit down. We sat on a couch facing floor-to-ceiling shelves filled with boxes of audio tape.

Both Duke and I knew a few things about Arif. He was one of the key people responsible for the "Atlantic Sound."

Looking at the tapes, I said, "Wow, knowing the stuff you've worked on, you must have some amazing tapes here."

This was all the encouragement Arif needed. Like a kid who has been asked to show off his toy trains, Arif jumped at the invitation to play.

"You want to hear some?" he said, clearly hoping we'd say yes.

We both nodded enthusiastically. "Yeah! Of course!" we said in unison.

He rushed over to the shelves and pulled out an outtake by the Young Rascals, saying, "You've got to hear this."

The Rascals were a great '60s New York, blue-eyed soul band that had a string of hits including, "Groovin'," "People Got to be Free," "Beautiful Morning," "How Can I Be Sure?" and Arif's first production hit, "Good Lovin'." It was thrilling to hear an unreleased track featuring Felix Cavaliere's deep-feelin' voice and organ, the Brigati brothers' background vocals, Gene Cornish's guitar, and the propulsive pop of Dino Danelli's drumming.

Arif was dancing. With the enthusiasm of a twelve year-old, Arif said, "Do you hear that? These guys cooked. Wait. If you think that's something. . ."

He impatiently rifled through the shelves, intent on finding some-thing he really wanted to play for us. His wife, Latife, came in. She carried a silver tray with an array of tan-colored morsels.

"I made these for the party and thought you might enjoy some."

Arif, distractedly, said, "You must try my wife's Turkish delight."

Duke and I said thanks, and each grabbed one of the round, soft balls.

While that was going on, Arif had found the tape he was looking for. He threaded it onto his reel-to-reel tape machine and hit the play button. I put the sticky Turkish Delight into my mouth just as the track found its groove. Everything hit all at once. Now I knew what my jazz cat friends were talking about with heroin. The sweetness exploded in my mouth and the funk exploded in my ears. The Greeks talked about the food of the gods, ambrosia, the ideal taste, the perfect combination of ingredients, and here it was on my tongue. Through the speakers, down my ears and straight into my belly, the queen of soul, Aretha Franklin, was singing her petunias out, playing her gospel piano with backing by the Muscle Shoals rhythm section that played on so many Atlantic Records hits, on a track no one had heard, played by the guy who was there and made it happen.

Arif was in a transcendent state. He beamed, swaying his hips from side to side. He looked at us with tears in his eyes, nodding, as if to say, "you get it, you get it!" In that one moment we shared the secret of the universe and the word was one sweet, funky, turkish yes.

Latife had left the tray, and I couldn't help but reach out and put another one of those magically addictive confections in my mouth. I feared the second could not match the first — it rarely does — but this was the time it did.

I don't know how much longer I swirled in this psychedelic euphoria, or what else Arif played for us. From then on, it all became a blur.

But the moment stays with me forever. What this lovely man did for two boys from the depths of Brooklyn on that night transformed me fundamentally. He taught us what it meant to be really cool. When you are that good, you don't have to lord it over others. You can be not only magnanimous, but a genuine human being as well. The thing I saw in Arif that night— no matter what he had achieved, what family he came from, or what his talents were —was that he was at heart a fan. He was a fan of the Rascals and Aretha, just like me and Duke. I'm sure that what made him such a great producer and arranger over his half-century career was that he was a fan of all the acts he worked with. I'm sure he was a fan of the Bee Gees whom he pushed to stellar heights, and a fan of Norah Jones, his last great triumph, not long before he died in 2006. In fact, I'm sure that Arif was a fan of life.

What he taught me that night is that that's what I wanted to be. I wanted to be classy by sharing all I had with anyone open to receiving it. I wanted to take in the whole damn thing, everything that was going into my mouth, ears, eyes, and hands, and find the beauty, the sweetness, the funk in it, and sway my hips from side to side, saying to whoever is with me, an unequivocal, euphoric, turkishly delightful, *yes*.

Too Much Too Soon: The New York Dolls

I was hanging at the front desk at "322" with Lana, the receptionist, between sessions. In walks a guy about seven feet tall. He's got hair in that poof-spikey seventies rock post-Keith Richards mullet-esque style, but it's blondish and longer and more outrageous than anyone ever. He's a giant because the soles of his boots must be nine inches high. He's got a minor gut, but this doesn't stop him from wearing a skin-tight shirt with the occasional loose sequin and skin-tight shiny satin gray pants. His scruffy, black platform boots go up to right below the knee.

Like a freaky Frankenstein's Monster, he lumbers up to the reception desk, and says, thickly, "Hey."

Lana says, "Hey, Killer, what's up?"

In unmistakable New Yawkese, he says, "Yeah. I'm here for the session."

In a history of legendary chicks at the front desk, Lana was one of A&R's best. Some people, they just had the natural cool for the gig. Unflummoxed, with a perpetual wry smile, she tossed her straight-black hippie hair back and snuck a raised-eyebrow glance at me.

"Arthur Killer Kane, bass player for the New York Dolls, meet Glenn Berger. Glenn's going to be covering tonight's session."

I looked at the clock. It was four in the afternoon, and the session was booked for seven. That meant they probably wouldn't start till ten.

I reach out a hand. He shakes it limply and mumbles, "Yeah man, hey."

Back on my seventeenth birthday, October 12, 1972, I went to see the Dolls at the Mercer Arts Center, in the old University Hotel on Broadway between West Third and Bleecker in the Village before the whole building collapsed a few years later. The Dolls were *the* band to see in NYC at that time. They were a bridge between glitter, glam, and punk. They were trailblazers, one-of-a-kind, harbingers of the scene to come. They dressed in trashy drag, played ridiculously loud, and blasted onto the scene with the first track on their first record, "Personality Crisis." This was a free show on a Thursday night, their last at the Mercer Arts before going on their tour of England.

After the show, my girlfriend, Betty, who had hair as crazy as mine, gave me the ultimate birthday present. It was a good night.

So I'm looking at Killer Kane, putting it all together with the first time I got laid.

Lana, with a perfect combo of sardonic wit and compassion in her voice, said, "Killer. The session won't be starting for hours."

He stared at us blankly with his mouth open, looking like he was about to drool. A paramecium had to have a better functioning brain than this dude. He scrunched up his nose and kept silent for a minute. Then said, "Ya gotta TV?"

Suppressing a laugh and knowing the A&R rule of never saying no, Lana, as if she were consoling a toddler, said, "Wayyyll, let me see what I can do."

With her usual flair, she got on the horn and called upstairs to see if we could secure a TV and a place to watch it. For those of you reading this in the mid-teens of the twenty-first century, I suppose it is fair to remind you that there were no smart phones, computers, or even cable TV at this time, so a real TV screen hooked up to some antenna was the only thing possible to entertain this empty-headed lunk for the next five hours, and we didn't just have one lying around.

The thought popped in my head, *Hey Killer, if you want I can lend you a coupla bucks and you can check out the peep shows on Eighth Avenue . . .* But as usual, I kept my mouth shut.

The band were cutting their second and, little did we know, final album (with the original lineup), to be titled *Too Much, Too Soon.* The eponymously titled first album was produced by Todd Rundgren, my teen idol. The album became a cult classic but didn't sell too well.

This album was being produced by girl-group legend Shadow Morton. Shadow had written and produced some of my most beloved hit singles, including "Remember (Walking in the Sand)" by The Shangri-Las and "Leader of the Pack," a tragic song, which featured sound effects of a motorcycle crash.

The engineer was one of my favorites, Dixon Van Winkle. Dixon sported a walrus moustache and round gold glasses at that time. He was a tuba player who had been spotted by Ramone at the Rochester School of Music and was invited to come down and enter the playpen of A&R. He was deeply musical. He was tight with the rest of the Rochester crowd who were the most elite studio players of the time, including drummer Steve Gadd and bass player Tony Levin. My favorite accomplishment of Dixon's was the track he cut with these guys of the Bacharach/Carpenters tune, "Close to You," done in the style of Spike Jones, with lots of kazoos, squeals, breaking glass, goofy percussion, and sneezes.

As early as Killer was, that's how late the rest of the band arrived. With nothing to do but wait, Shadow and Dixon, who got along like engineers and producers tend to do, sitting side by side at the console in the same soup of trying to herd these street cats, started drinking hard long before anyone showed up.

One by one, the band straggled in with an extended coterie. To the last of 'em — lead singer David Johansen, guitarists Johnny Thunders and Sylvain Sylvain, and drummer Jerry Nolan — these guys were no joke. Like

Killer, the band dressed in their satin drag 24/7. They and their entourage immediately started trashing the place. As the band coagulated into some kind of congealed mess, they plugged their instruments in and futzed around, warming up, while I ran around, moving a mic, replacing a broken set of cans. Killer had twin Marshall stacks, six feet high, for his bass set-up. When he banged a note on his bass, my legs shook like plucked rubber bands, and they gave out from under me.

As I saw Johnny Thunders about to windmill his guitar, I swiftly swooped a pair of unused headphones off the floor, shoved them on my head, and stuck the plug in my pocket. I didn't want my head to be singing a 1K tone for the rest of the week. It was still awesomely loud, and I'm sure I suffered some permanent damage.

The control room was barely better, with the monitors cranked to eleven. But loud was what these speakers were for. Out of the noisy mess something started to happen and we chaotically cut that old doo-wop novelty tune, "Stranded in the Jungle." I loved that song.

Meanwhile, back in the jungle . . . the lyrics went, and *these* monkeys were throwing their banana peels all over the place. Lana stayed late at the front desk but gave up trying to be an agent of control and joined the debauchery. (She had a debauched streak anyway. At a party at my loft in Tribeca, she and my girlfriend of the time, another A&R staff member named Helen, invited me for a threesome during the revels. Unused to such invitations, I foolishly demurred.) Broadway Max would be chagrined when he came in the next day to see the mess and destruction, but what were any of us to do? This was rock and roll apotheosis, The Who squared, you're not nobody unless you're playing it to die, and most of the Dolls ended up doing just that, too much, too soon. (Billy Murcia, the original drummer, died in 1972; Johnny Thunders died in 1991; Jerry Nolan in 1992; Arthur Killer Kane, in 2004.)

At about 3:45 a.m., unable to create any order out of this mess, Shadow and Dixon drunk as shit, after flying in jungle sound effects of chimpanzees and screeching birds, decided to bail. They turned to me and slurred, "You take over. We're leaving," and weaved their way out of the control room, out the studio, and onto Eighth Avenue into the New York spring circus, circa 1974.

I didn't really have much of an idea of what I was doing at that time, but no one seemed to give one flying crap, and I had no choice anyway, so I took the big seat at the console and manned a few guitar overdubs and a background vocal or two. I was feeling puffy anyway, having done a few toots in the downstairs bathroom. I needed it for sustenance.

It's all a bit of a blur, as sessions at four a.m. could prove to be. This, though, did contribute to the development of my chops, and the cachet (to say nothing of access to cheap studio time as an up-and-coming post-*schlepper*) that led me to record a few seminal pre-punkers of my own. Some sleazy chap named Stan with a few dollars that I wouldn't want to know where they came from worked me into cutting tracks for a band called The Harlots of 42nd Street who sometimes opened for The Dolls.

Stan invited me for a production meeting at the Continental Baths. I thought, cool, I'd never been, and had always wanted to check it out. The Continental Baths was a gay bathhouse in the basement of the Ansonia Hotel, an ornate gem of a building on 73rd and Broadway. The place put on shows, and Bette Midler and Barry Manilow, among many others, built their fan base there. At that time the Upper West Side was fairly raunchy. You just wouldn't walk between Columbus and Amsterdam at all if you wanted to live. The Ansonia, long since renovated, now costs a pretty penny. Then, you could live there for nothing.

I descended the stairs, entered the post-Roman decadence with everyone hanging in their towels, and searched for the Harlots' manager. I saw a guy with hair in a ponytail down to the middle of his back. He was fully dressed in this den of near and total nudity. As we had a drink, I checked out the scene and scrutinized this guy. He seemed like an inno-cent-enough lower-tier music biz producer. Whatever his scam was, when he was done, he convinced me to talk Max into giving us a "weekend rate," so we could record the band.

Stan put out a single, with "Cool Dude and Foxy Lady" on the A side, and "Spray Paint Bandit" on the B side. I did a decent job, considering that The Harlots sucked in just the right way and so did I. Nothing happened with the track and the band faded into oblivion until being resurrected on the internet, where anything can find 50,000 fans, even people who like to have sex with furry stuffed animals.

We didn't do a lot of punk stuff at A&R — our studio was too expensive. One exception was Television, who cut their great first album, *Marquee Moon* in studio R-2 with Andy Johns at the helm. My total punk career consisted of mixing a single for a band called Harry Toledo, and then I cut a single for Harry's girlfriend's band, Janis and the Bumble Bees, with a cool tune called "B Movie."

Meanwhile, back in the jungle of the Dolls session, everything fizzled as the sun began to glow over the East River. Some groupie shook Killer, who had crashed out on the couch in front of the console, and he and everyone else stumbled out, leaving me with the killer mess. That was my job: cleaning up the crazy artists' shitshow.

There was no point in going home. Once I broke down, maybe I could crash for an hour or two on that couch where Killer had passed out earlier, before I'd have to start setting up for the next morning's session. Another twenty-hour day. No REM sleep, slightly more psychotic. The coke had left me grinding my teeth, unable to remember what sleep even was. As I lay on the couch, staring at the big monitors on the wall, everything getting dark, I thought, *we're all on that M-60 to nowhere, exploding like glitter in the night sky, too much, too soon, big bang, quick fizzle, star at twenty-one, washed up at twenty-two. Nothing a little more blow wouldn't get me through.*

TRACK EIGHT

Oddballs and Angels: Phoebe Snow

In April of 2011, I learned that, at the age of 60, singer/songwriter Phoebe Snow had died. When I heard the news, I walked into my hallway and stared at the gold record of her album *Second Childhood* hanging on my wall.

I remembered the time I first saw her name. It was on the day I became Ramone's apprentice. As an eighteen year-old, I fantasized about what a woman named Phoebe Snow would look — and be — like. I visualized an evanescent sprite, a fairy like Tinkerbell, with translucent skin and white hair. She and I would connect in some cosmic-love way. I was a teenage boy — what would you expect?

The night we started her album, my fantasy plummeted back to Earth when the real Phoebe Snow walked into the studio. She shuffled into the room, clutching her black acoustic-guitar case. Her chin jutted out over an ill-defined body. She had a dour look on her face. Her first words, in a nasal, Teaneck, New Jersey accent were "Where's the food?" Her real name was Phoebe Laub.

In contrast to my fantasy, Phoebe was my particular adolescent nightmare. Five years older than me, she was the annoying older sister I never wanted. Nothing was right for Phoebe, and as the assistant, it was my job to try to fix it.

At 22, Phoebe was attempting to make her first record. The project had, up until then, been a disaster. Her producer was a pleasant, bearish guy named Dino Airali. He was clearly in over his head with this difficult young woman. He had followed her around the country for more than a year, blowing the recording budget on Phoebe's whims, none of which ever panned out.

Dino handed me two multi-track tapes with just a few bare recordings of Phoebe's guitar and vocals. This was not much to show for the six-figure budget he had already blown.

In a wise move born of desperation, Dino had hooked up with my mentor Phil. It was a timely fit. By that time, Ramone had been a world-class recording engineer for more than a decade and had ambitions of breaking into producing. Engineering was technical. The job was to get someone else's ideas down on tape. With producing, you get to participate in the creation of those ideas. And you get to earn royalties. With a hit record, you could potentially make big bucks.

Phil had agreed to engineer the project if he could co-produce. Dino needed help bad. His record company, Shelter Records, was on the verge of bankruptcy. If he couldn't come up with a finished product in a few weeks, cheap, there would be no record and no company. Dino saw Ramone as his last big chance. Ramone, who had uncanny ears for a hit, must have heard something in Phoebe that he thought he could shape into success.

Before we started recording, Phil and I went down to a gig of Phoebe's at The Bitter End, the most revered of the early folk clubs in the heart of Greenwich Village. There were three people in the house that night: Phil, Phoebe, and myself. This was not an auspicious beginning.

Phoebe had a one-of-a-kind voice. Instead of gliding seamlessly between notes, each change in pitch was accentuated with a sharp edge. Her singing was geometric, angular, precise. Her vibrato, too, was unique; more a staccato warble than a gentle undulation of sound.

She had major chops — that is, she had great technical ability —

and while she may have been out of control as a person, she was musically tight. She had an infinite range, from an earthy baritone growl to dog-whistle high notes.

Her songs were as quirky as her singing style, personal, with a flowing, off-kilter structure. As a female vocalist, she didn't play the sexual card or act out conventional feminine personas. She neither played the soft innocence of a Karen Carpenter nor the over-the top raunch of a Madonna. She was insightful about human nature, and there was a depth of feeling and pain in her music that went beyond her years.

At first, I didn't get Phoebe's music. I'd come home from her sessions and make fun of her songs. "I wish I was a willow –ow –ow- ow –ow," I'd mock, imitating her vibrato, and my roommate would crack up. I thought that this was a loser headed right for the $1.99 bin, the place where flop records would be relegated to in that obsolete place called a "record store." My guess did not require any particular prescience. She was an unknown, unsexy artist on a failing label.

It wouldn't be the last time that my musical prediction would be totally misguided. The record was a smash. How did that happen?

In any life activity, we can operate in a trance and do things half-assedly, or we can act with awareness, intention, and integrity. This is true for the production and arrangements of recordings that could be done either in a thoughtless, derivative way or in an aware, deliberate process in which the artist is mindful of every choice. The result, in art, as in all things, depends on which of these approaches you choose. In order for art to succeed such clarity of vision is crucial.

Many of the great artists with whom I worked in the '70s made albums that were more than just a collection of songs. The recordings were works of art in themselves. The path for this was laid out by the Beatles. Before Lennon and McCartney, records were more or less representations of live performances. Acts went into the studio and took a day to cut an album. Bands or orchestras would play, and singers sing, all at once, and the producer was there to render as faithful a reproduction of the performance as possible.

But with the advent of multi-track recording, where different musical parts could be painted one at a time onto the canvas of tape, the studio itself became an instrument. For the Beatles, and many artists whom they inspired, every instrument selection, every note, every electronic effect, every sound, every piece of an interweaving production and arrangement were vital and intrinsic parts of the artwork that lifted a song beyond its harmony and melody to its ultimate creative manifestation. To grasp this revolution, listen to the difference between "I Want to Hold Your Hand," one of the Beatles' earliest singles, recorded in the live style, and "Strawberry Fields Forever," from their middle, psychedelic period that was recorded and overdubbed in a studio over many takes.

Now, any artist will also tell you that having limitations sometimes contributes to great art, or to quote an old phrase, necessity is the mother of invention. We certainly had enough of those on Phoebe's album. We started with a few basic tracks, a tight budget, and a couple of weeks to make an entire album. With the style of recording popular at that time, an artist could easily take months, if not a year, to finish a project.

This time-and-money stricture, along with the '70s pop art sensibility, forced Phoebe and Phil to choose each part with the care and precision that makes for the most impressionable art.

Now all that theory is well and good, but art is, in the end, one of the great mysteries, which is one reason I love it. I'm a big fan of the ultimate unanswerables. That's why I'm a psychotherapist now. Music, like human nature, can never be fully comprehended. I've studied music all my life, and with increasing age, I get a little closer to understanding what makes a song great. There is melodic variety, a cool hook, a moment of surprise, the contrast between symmetry and imbalance, a beat you can move to, an individual sound, and most important, undeniable emotion in the performance. I get it, but I can't write one. There is something indefinable that occurs when all of these elements come together in a unique way. Though a song that works has all its predictably simple elements, it emerges from the background noise with blinding clarity. It can bust through the tiniest speaker, reach out, and grab you by the belly. It can shake you to your soul, make your eyes spring with tears, wake you out of a life-long slumber, put the hope back in pop. And Phoebe had written at least one song in her life that entered the heart of this world. That's a lot for anyone's lifetime.

Phil's production approach was to put Phoebe's magical songs and exquisite vocals at the center of the record, and then surround it with just the right, and only the right, musical colors. He did this by asking Phoebe: *if you could have anyone in the world play on this song, who would it be?* Phoebe had a fertile imagination, and she came up with tasty answers.

If Phoebe could dream it, Phil made it happen. The smart and cool saxophone-player Zoot Sims, blew his axe and wrapped the songs in ever-changing wisps of gray smoke. Margaret Ross, a session harp player who was usually relegated to playing cliché glissandos, turned out to be a jazz cat at heart and played deep and hard, layering on a shiny gold filigree to the tracks. The great pianist Teddy Wilson added his sophisticated blue voicings, bringing a touch of class to the proceedings.

Then came the silver ribbon on the box. Ramone booked Ralph Mac-Donald to add percussion.

Ralph was a cosmic musician. He had a shiny skull and big, brown, laughing eyes. The ultimate in cool, he was from Harlem with a West Indian heritage. He had been taught the congas by his father. He once told me that his dad taught him not to hit the drum but to caress it like a lover. He'd learned his father's lesson well. His hands were soft. His touch was incomparable. The sound of his skin against the skin of the drum was deep and sensual.

Like most studio cats, he was humble and generous of spirit. Though I was a kid barely out of high school, he treated me as both friend and worthy student. I went out into the studio to plug in and place the microphones. As he prepared his instruments for the overdub, which meant that he would add his parts to the music already recorded, he listened to the songs for inspiration.

He put together a small wooden table, about two feet across, with a wooden bar hanging across the top. Next he laid a few small percussion instruments on the table: two woodblocks, a string of bells, and two film cans with beads in them. On the bar he hung some chimes and a finger cymbal. That was all. He told me to place two microphones, one aiming at each end, to get a stereo effect.

While listening, Ralph rolled a fat joint. Now let's be honest. There were a lot of drugs at the studio at that time. A&R was a play-pen for grown-ups, and in the '70s, drugs were part of the fun. I usually didn't get high during sessions, especially in those early days with Ramone because I didn't want to screw up. Besides, Ramone wasn't a big pot head. I worried that he might not approve of my smoking, and I certainly wouldn't want to do anything to piss him off if I could help it, even though I inevitably did.

But Phil was in a good mood that day. As producer, he was getting to do his thing his way. He was excited about what Ralph was about to bring to the tracks. Ralph brought the doobie into the control room and offered a hit to Ramone. He took the joint and inhaled. Then he turned, and offered the "j" to me. I looked at him as if to say, really? He nodded and said it was ok, but instructed me to only take one hit. Ralph said that would be all I'd need anyway. I drew deep from the fat joint, mixing in air with the smoke to cut the harshness. It was sweet, premium weed. I came not to expect less from Ralph. Before I had finished toking, my ears started to crackle.

I sat behind Phil by the tape machine, and we watched Ralph through the studio glass. He put out the joint, put on his headphones, and signaled me to roll tape. We started with a song called "Poetry Man."

Phoebe's guitar picked the intro. Ralph hit the chimes: sparkle. Then, the finger cymbal: ting. Then, he tapped the bells: chik, chik. In the second verse, he added the woodblocks: tick, tock.

Ralph finished his first take and asked to put on another layer. This time he shook the film can with beads. He interweaved this rhythmically with his first track. Shak. Shak. Then, on the chorus, he added a third layer: shaka, shaka, shaka, shaka. By the second chorus, all of these accents played off one another, in a shimmering play of colorful sound. His playing was spare, tasteful, brilliant. I knew I had just witnessed a simple moment of sublime creation.

Ralph's sparkling rhythms created a juxtaposition that intensified the emotional depth of Phoebe's vocal. In the contrasting and intermingling of the green, gold, and silver silk of the guitar, harp, sax, and percussion, with the crimson and caramel hopsack of Phoebe's voice, a hit single was born.

Each element of the album was created in this way. One part at a time was scrupulously thought through and played by these masters, instilling each musical shade with significance, meaning, depth. These choices were guided by Phoebe's vision and manifested through Ramone's sure hand. This was what made this album so singular and astonishing in the end.

On the last night of mixing, we'd worked late and managed to finish the album on time and on budget. I stayed up all night, putting together the final sequence. I threaded the master onto the tape machine at dawn. I called in Phil, Dino, and Phoebe for a playback of the completed album. This was the first record for both Phoebe and me. She asked for bagels and cream cheese, and we ate.

Despite its quality, I was still convinced the record didn't stand a chance. It was a modest album for that time of overproduced decadence. No matter what was in their grooves, most records required lots of payola to make it on hit radio in those days. After blowing her budget, and with Shelter Records going under, there wasn't much cash left for that.

But then, the magic hit. The cream really did rise to the top. Spontaneously, with little promotion, Phoebe had a number-five hit record with that song called "Poetry Man."

We all changed a great deal after that. Phil went on to become a world-class producer, I was promoted to senior mixer, and Phoebe got on the cover of *Rolling Stone,* and was signed to the world's most prestigious record label, Columbia Records. We made another album: the gold one hanging on my wall.

Sometime during 1975, Phoebe came in to visit us at the studio. I was shocked when she told me she was pregnant. She had none of the glow that pregnant women usually have. I had a bad feeling. This time, it turned out that my intuition was right. Phoebe's daughter was born with profound developmental disabilities.

After the birth, Phoebe walked away from fame and fortune. Maybe she didn't realize all that she had attained with her stardom, money, and big record contract. It had all come so easily; perhaps that it is what made it possible for her to have taken it for granted. Or maybe she didn't like the way she was treated in the rough and tumble recording world that was New York, circa mid-seventies. More likely, she sacrificed her path to superstardom for a higher calling. Phoebe turned her full attention to caring for her helpless daughter, Valerie Rose.

The awkward, self-involved girl from Teaneck matured. After living through the flimflam of the music biz, she knew what was real, and that was what was going on with her child. Phoebe was, at heart, not only a true artist but, more important, a caring human being.

Before too long, Phoebe was dropped by Columbia. She was never abandoned by her band of faithful followers, but to many she was just another one-hit wonder.

*

I didn't recognize what I had either, with my front-row seat to the making of the greatest albums of the era. Also disillusioned with the scene, a few years later, I left A&R and New York, and went to live in the country.

Years passed, but unable to evade the siren's call, I eventually moved back to the city. That was when I saw Phoebe for the last time. It was a dark period of my life. One night, at about two in the morning, I was walking alone through the streets of my beloved West Village, not far from The Bitter End where I saw Phoebe perform all those years ago. Those old streets were narrow and silent.

I noticed a Volkswagen, double parked, with the lights on inside. Something seemed odd about the car. I walked over to look inside, and there was Phoebe was sitting alone in the driver's seat. We started to talk as if we were in the middle of a conversation that had started decades before. She didn't seem surprised to see me at all. There was a warmth and familiarity between us. We had been kids together in something big, all too long ago.

Earlier that night, on impulse, I had bought a key chain with a miniature motorcycle jacket on the end from a guy on the street. Phoebe was wearing a motorcycle jacket. So, as we finished up our talk, I handed her the keychain as a gift. She took it, as if she understood exactly what it meant.

Phoebe had some odd beliefs. When we'd hung out together in those early days, she would bring in cassette tapes that she had recorded in silent rooms. She was convinced that if you listened carefully enough, you could hear voices from the spirit world.

I didn't go in for such mumbo jumbo, but there was something strange about us stumbling into each other here, the only two people alive on this street, she alone in a car, me wandering around in the middle of the night.

After chatting, I walked away into the lonely dark. She sat in the car. We never asked each other what we were doing there. I never saw her again.

*

As I stood in front of Phoebe's gold record on my wall, her music played in my head. I heard the cool electric guitar riffs of her friend, Steve Burgh, who played on those early albums. A talented guy, he, too, died young and unexpectedly.

I began to wonder. What was it in Phoebe that engendered such fierce loyalty among her adoring fans? Of course she was a natural singer. She had a voice like no other, and when she opened her mouth, a sound came out that was joy burnished with pain. She was all contradiction: a jazzy, folky, bluesy, rockin', funky Jewish chick from Jersey. But it was more than that. Phoebe was an oddball.

I understand this misfit thing. I've always been drawn to these types. I guess I'm one myself. That's why I was into music, and that's why I'm now a psychotherapist.

There's something about the ugly ones, the weirdos, the freaks, the queers, the geeks, the musicians, the addicts, the losers, the left-handers, the nuts, the lonely and unlucky ones.

I think those among us who are different have a little less of a psychic immune system than everyone else. They are a little closer to the source. They don't quite make it in this world, and they feel the pain a little more acutely than the rest. But they bring us a gift we all need to know and feel.

I can imagine chubby Phoebe Laub, with her kinky hair and moles, sitting in her bedroom in Teaneck, playing her guitar and singing to the ceiling, while the cute girls were flirting with the jocks. She was sitting alone in that car the last time I saw her because, I bet, she was alone much of the time.

Phoebe touched this sensitive, longing part of us. There are plenty of misfits in the world. Maybe there is a misfit residing in each of our secret hearts. I can picture all the lonely freaks out there, sitting alone in their bedrooms in 1974, listening to "Poetry Man," and feeling some solace because they knew that she knew.

When we listen to Phoebe sing now, we can hear through and beyond that obnoxious girl I met the first time she came into the studio. We hear the contours of the essence. We hear the cry in the darkness of the West Village, that late night sound of vinyl, the echo of Zoot and Teddy Wilson, that distant reverberation receding into the dark, that voice, strong, loving, and speaking for us.

That's what the artist does — sees for us — suffers for us, because we'd rather not go there ourselves.

I call the Phoebes of the world angels. They have been given wings — an incredible voice, or some other gift — in exchange for some deep vulnerability. That's why so many artists die young. Phoebe was so powerful in her unique voice and profound love. However, all this was in contrast to her body, which was all too often a source of suffering for her.

As an eighteen year-old, I couldn't see past her appearance. Today, with nothing left of Phoebe but her music, I realize she was that radiant creature I imagined before I met her. Despite how she looked or acted on the outside, inside she was made of the rarest alloy. She was the essence of beauty.

Phoebe cared for her daughter every day of her life, until Valerie Rose died at the age of 31 in 2007.

In honor of the dearly departed Phoebe Snow, I invite you to look for the strange ones out there, or the oddball in you, and be a little kinder and a little more understanding, because you never know — you might be in the presence of an angel. And the next time you are in a quiet room, turn on that digital recorder in your smartphone, and wait. When you play it back, and listen real close, you might hear Phoebe singing in her supernatural voice.

> *I strut and fret my hour upon the stage*
> *The hour is up, I have to run and hide my rage*
> *I'm lost again, I think I'm really scared*
> *I won't be back at all this time*
> *And have my deepest secrets shared*
> *I'd like to be a willow, a lover*
> *A mountain, or a soft refrain*
> *But I'd hate to be a grown-up*
> *And have to try and bear my life in pain.*
> — "Harpo's Blues"

The Freaks, the Pricks, and the Gems

S oon after completing *Live Rhymin'*, Paul Simon returned to A&R to begin recording his new studio album.

The first song we tracked was "Still Crazy After All These Years," the one we cut a demo for on my first day working with Paul, and what turned out to be the title number.

To cut the basic track, Paul collaborated with Barry Beckett, a large, gentle man with a blond moustache, a bulbous nose, and an ample gut. Barry was the keyboard player from the famed Muscle Shoals rhythm section that hailed from Sheffield, Alabama.

Beckett sat for hours behind a Fender Rhodes electric piano with Paul standing at his side, as they meticulously worked out every note of the keyboard part that formed the backbone of the arrangement. Barry was a consummate cat. Despite the painstaking work, he never flagged, never got frustrated, never allowed his ego to get in the way. He smiled throughout the process, as he accompanied Paul on his meandering journey in search of the lost chord.

Paul was experiencing a time of growth and learning. He was studying music with the jazz composer and bassist Chuck Israels and was taking singing lessons, too. In his restless pursuit of innovation, his compositional style moved toward ever greater harmonic and melodic sophistication. His goal was to use all twelve notes of the scale in a song; in rock and roll, the usual maximum was seven.

In his recent biography of Paul, author Marc Eliot asserted that it was Ramone who created the musical arrangements for the *Still Crazy* album and, taking an influence from his work with Billy Joel, was responsible for its mellower, keyboard-inflected sound. Eliot got this dead wrong. Ramone had nothing to do with any of the music on Simon's album. Ramone never arranged anything in his life. That wasn't his bag. Simon was in control of the content, as evidenced by this day with Beckett. This meant that he determined every single note played by anyone.

Eliot was also wrong in suggesting it was Ramone's work with Billy that influenced this album's sound. Phil didn't start working with Joel until long after *Still Crazy* had won its Grammy awards. And besides, Paul didn't necessarily like his record label rival. Joel eventually crushed Simon as the top seller on the Columbia Records roster.

Ramone's real contribution was in introducing Simon to the most prominent New York studio musicians of that time, cats like Eric Gale, Richard Tee, Steve Gadd, and Tony Levin, who came from a jazz/funk/gospel/R&B background, and had the tight, hard-hitting sound that New York was renowned for. Simon used these guys for years, some even now.

Ramone, who moved gracefully toward a greater production role with Paul, was patient in bringing his influence to bear on his strong-willed client. On this first track, Simon had yet to meet Phil's New York cats, so he worked with Beckett, the guy who had helped make his number-two record "Kodachrome" a hit.

Beckett did a spectacular job on "Still Crazy." His keyboard part on that track is iconic.

Though Simon was influenced by the people Ramone knew and suggested, his arrangements grew organically out of the songs themselves. Never satisfied with the conventional or tried-and-true, he was always chasing down the unique setting for each composition.

I got to witness Simon's process in the creation of the singular interpretation of a song through his tracking of the next tune we worked on, "Gone at Last." He went through several iterations of this arrangement before he found the one he liked.

His first attempt at creating a musical foundation for this song resembled what he had done on his Simon and Garfunkel hit, "Cecilia." The secret sauce for this recipe was the participation of cosmic percussionist Ralph MacDonald, who had not only turned Phoebe Snow's, "Poetry Man," into a hit, but had also written huge hits himself like "Where Is the Love?"

Along with Ralph, Simon also invited a group of friends into the studio. Ralph and Paul created a basic rhythmic pattern, and everyone else played a supporting rhythm on some found object, whether it was a Styrofoam cup, a cardboard box, or any other thing that could be tapped, hit, or banged with a pencil, stick, or hand.

During this time, Bette Midler had arrived on the A&R scene. Bette was hot, in more ways than one. Having found her audience in the nascent days of gay liberation at that place called The Continental Baths, her debut album, titled *The Divine Miss M,* had sold over a million copies and landed her the best new artist Grammy award in 1973. She was more chanteuse and comedienne than rocker, and in the looks department more Fanny Brice than Angelina Jolie, but she had a personality, a set of pipes, and a pair of boobs that cut through all categories in those ambisexual days of the mid-'70s. This made her a rising superstar.

She had worked with producer/arranger Arif Mardin on her hit second album. Having produced *Judith* with us, Arif was now a part of the A&R family. Bette was starting to work on her third record, and Arif brought her into our studio to cut some lead vocals.

I engineered a few of the tracks that Bette was fooling around with. She was all over the place. No two vocal performances were even close, and Arif couldn't move her in a certain, progressive musical direction. The work went nowhere, and all the work we did was eventually thrown out.

Hanging out in the halls of A&R, Bette met Paul, who was romantically flailing after his break up with his wife Peggy, and Bette was free. The two cute, Jewish New York stars began a fling.

This romance blossomed right before Paul began working on "Gone at Last." He had envisioned this song as a duet with a woman. Maybe he even wrote it with Bette in mind. She agreed to sing the female part. When we cut that basic rhythm track, Bette was in the studio, too, singing a rough guide of her vocal.

Paul fussed with this version for quite some time, as it never sat quite right with him. He tried adding a bass part played by David Hood, another mellow dude from the Muscle Shoals band. That didn't quite do it. Next he tried adding the gospel group, The Jessy Dixon Singers, with whom he had toured recently, and who had appeared on *Live Rhymin'*. The ladies in that group were the sweetest. They were really, really big. They'd enter the studio and give me a hug that felt like I was falling into the ultimate queen-sized mattress of love.

I got to see Paul fall into a swoon of inspiration during our recording with them. His eyes fluttered as he had me play one verse of the tune over and over again. On the spot, he invented a tasty vocal counterpoint part. With Paul being flush, and the music scene being what it was at the time, he could afford to write in the studio, no matter how much time that ate up on the clock. This was impressive, considering he was paying $200 an hour for studio time alone, and that was in 1975. Even though I liked the part he created, this also didn't satisfy him, and he abandoned this too in the end.

Paul and Bette soon fell out with each other. I can't be sure what really happened, but I bet that as a rising diva she didn't have an extra minute for his egotude. She was too sassy for that. I think she dumped him, and in his fashion, not really cottoning to rejection, he closed the iron door on her. The story was they couldn't work things out contractually, which I think is a nice way of saying she wouldn't screw him anymore.

Paul ultimately threw out this entire version of the song, but not because of Bette; he was far more cunning than that. If he thought this arrangement was a hit he would have figured out any way to use it, Bette be damned. He would have recut the whole thing if he had to in order to eliminate her vocal. When, in the end, he couldn't make it work musically to his standards, he chucked it. That was a stunning lesson in the pursuit of the superb.

Paul's self-scrutiny was relentless. He didn't always feel good about these decisions down the line. Later, there were times when he'd listen to early demos and realize that he'd lost something in the long, arduous production process that he grinded all his songs through. In this case though, listening to the original, he made the right call. (You can hear a rough mix that I had done of the Paul/Bette version as a bonus track on the re-released *Still Crazy* album.)

Towards the very end of making the album, he re-recorded the song as a gospel rave-up. It was during this session that he got turned on to the piano playing of the big-handed gospel master Richard Tee. Paul loved this guy, and worked with him till Tee's untimely death in the '90s. Instead of Midler, Paul had Phoebe Snow sing on the track. She was the far better choice. Midler couldn't really blast this kind of gospel tune, and Snow sang her ass off on what turned out to be a top-25 single.

During the recording of this album, I had the incredibly good fortune to sit in a room with a man who had accomplished about as much as anyone could in a short lifetime. He was a poet, a tunesmith, a unique guitarist, a visionary, a producer, an artist, a famous celebrity. He was one of the creators of the culture of the 1960s, and he was the writer of some of the most successful and important songs in the history of the entire pop music era. He captured the mood and feeling of his generation. There wasn't a person in the world who didn't know "Bridge Over Troubled Waters," or the guy who wrote it, Paul Simon.

Everyone wants to know what the famous are really like. Hell, that's one of the reasons I'm writing this book. The problem is that with a guy like Simon, no one really wants to know the answer. We want to see our heroes in a golden glow. You see, the truth of the matter is, back in the day, there were people who thought Simon was — well there's no other way to say it —a prick. Now don't get mad at me. I'm not the one who said it. Steve Berlin, of the band Los Lobos, called him "the world's biggest prick." Walter Yetnikoff, the head of Columbia Records, Paul's label for many years, hated his guts and had him banned from the company's corporate headquarters. Heavens, Paul even said it himself in his unfortunate movie *One Trick Pony*. (Character in film, saying to girlfriend, about the character that Paul Simon played, "He's a real little prick, isn't he?") Biggest or smallest, the synecdoche appeared to fit.

What do I mean? Paul just didn't seem to care much about other human beings. It didn't matter to him if his words or actions hurt. I've got lots of stories about Paul being a little shit, and some so bad I can't even tell them here. But here's one example.

By the late '70s, a few years after we'd recorded *Still Crazy*, I had graduated to senior mixer, and Ramone was a full-fledged producer. He hired me to engineer some sessions for Karen Carpenter's one and only solo record. I was curious about why she and her brother were not recording together. When I asked her, she said to me that he was at home, in the garage, working on his cars. It turns out he was nursing a Quaalude habit.

Karen, at this point, was extremely anorexic. She must have weighed about 90 pounds. One of the young women on our staff would pick Karen up from her hotel and try to get a banana or apple down her before getting her to the studio.

It wasn't only her eating disorder that made Karen a bit of a freak. She was obsessed with Disney, not unlike another oddball singer who within a few years would become the King of Pop, and would also die an untimely death. Her Mickey Mouse tee-shirt hung limply on her skeletal frame. Her

Goofy watch banged against the bones of her forearm.

She may have been so frail as to be on the verge of falling to bits, but when she went out to the studio to sing, her voice had the clarion ring of pure crystal. Her vocal quality was supernatural, uncanny, numinous.

She spoke obsessively about finding a husband. Already the nascent therapist, I asked her, "So, Karen, what are you looking for in a husband?" Did I ask because I wondered if I might be a suitable candidate? I don't think so. She was awfully straight and clearly in a lot of trouble. Well, maybe a little.

She answered, "I want someone rich."

I said, "But Karen, you have all the money you could want. What about love?"

She didn't answer that, only to say, "He needs to have at least five cars." That eliminated me.

Ramone had decided to take Karen, musically, in a late-disco direction. To arrange the songs he brought in the Quincy Jones team that would eventually go on to make Michael Jackson a mega-star, including the guy who wrote "Thriller," Rod Temperton. We cut a bunch of tracks. Karen seemed increasingly emotionally and physically fragile with every passing day. Her vocal chops were amazing, but her body was becoming ethereal. She was literally disappearing.

One day, Simon was passing through the studio and popped in for a visit. I'm not sure how well he knew Karen. I'm guessing they didn't have the closest of relationships. He asked to listen to some of the tracks we were cutting. I played him some songs.

Ramone stood anxiously behind Karen, who sat at the producer's desk, while Paul listened. I sat next to them at the recording console, fiddling with the knobs, and scrutinizing Paul's face for a reaction.

When they were done, Simon turned to Karen. He paused. Then, in a voice that combined derision, snobbishness, concern, and alarm, he said, "Karen. What are you doing? This stuff is *awful!*"

Ramone blanched. Karen stopped breathing. Remember, this was her first foray into recording solo, alone, without her brother, working with a whole new production team, in a city far from home, and clearly in profound psychological and physical distress, suffering as she was with acute anorexia.

The air was sucked out of the room. Simon didn't pick up on the vibe however. He just plowed on. "Karen, this isn't what your fans want from you! They want Karen to be Karen Carpenter. They want what they have always gotten from you. This is all wrong."

With every word Ramone was shrinking smaller and smaller, until one could barely see him behind the producer's desk, having been reduced to the size of a hedgehog. I sat behind the controls, trying to keep my jaw attached to my head, astounded at what I was hearing.

Paul may have been technically, musically, and from a marketing perspective, right. But from a human perspective, he was all wrong. His insensitivity was stunning. He seemed to have a complete lack of care or understanding of the emotional toll that such a declaration could take. Couldn't he see Karen's condition? He was a smart guy — wasn't he capable of coming up with a more tactful, humane way of protecting her, if that was, in fact, his intention? The truth was, from my perspective, that this was just one graphic example of how Paul was completely insensitive to other people's feelings.

Karen never released that album during her lifetime. Within a few short years, she was dead.

The fact that a great artist like Paul was a prick wasn't so unusual. One of the things that everybody who spent time in the studio knows is that the artists we worked with were often crazy, or jerks, or both. We enjoyed that—unless it caused us too much personal indignity—because it provided us with great stories and stuff to complain about.

Now I don't have any problem with musicians trying to make a buck or get laid. It ain't easy being an artist. So I get it now that these guys had to do whatever it took to survive.

But it got under my skin that a guy like Paul would go on in his songs about "laying himself down," and that kind of bull, when he usually treated people like garbage. For some reason, the thing that pissed me off more than anything was when someone pretended to be a savior but was really an ass. I call that sanctimony.

Simon was far from the only star I encountered in the biz with this character trait. Another Paul I worked with, who was sanctimony personified, was a soprano sax guru named Paul Winter. This Paul won many humanitarian awards for his recordings with endangered species like whales and wolves. To his chagrin, his records ended up in the New Age bin. He hated thinking of himself in that way, certain that his music would be of universal appeal. But the pigeon-hole wasn't so bad, because he rode that Kumbaya wave to the peak when it was happening in the 1980s.

It wasn't that this Paul was without talent. He was a great musician and conceptualist. But he was also just a bit of a *gonif*. Was this a necessary combination for success?

Winter got his career start by winning a contest for amateur musicians, the prize for which was a record contract on Columbia Records. The story that I heard was that the first year that Winter competed he lost, so the second year he broke the rules by hiring professional ringers, and he dominated the field. If true, that early act of breaking a few eggs to make an omelet set the tone for what was to come.

In 1972, Winter had something of a hit with a revelatory record called *Icarus*. This album was this super-cool fusion thing with top-flight musicians playing all kinds of unlikely instruments for a hit record, including cello, sarrusophone, and mridangam. Despite his name being on the cover, most of the songs were written by someone else, a genius named Ralph Towner, who soon thereafter dumped Winter and went on to fame in a group called Oregon.

I call Winter the Max Bialystock of the New Age. Remember

Bialystock? He was the guy in the Mel Brooks film and smash Broadway hit *The Producers*, played in the film by Zero Mostel and on Broadway, most famously, by Nathan Lane. Bialystock was a desperate Broadway producer who seduced little old ladies to give him money to put on his money-losing productions.

Winter did the same. Except in his case, he would seduce little old ladies by telling them that he was making music to save the whales. Then he would use the dough to take trips to Lake Baikal in Russia, or some such, because it was absolutely necessary to go to these exotic locales for "inspiration."

When I worked with Winter, we made our records at the Cathedral of St. John the Divine, the largest gothic cathedral in the world, on 112th Street and Amsterdam Avenue in New York City, where his axe was bathed in reverb twelve seconds long. He had a rich, smooth, lyrical sound that no one but him has ever gotten out of the often reedy and narrow-sounding soprano sax.

We would record at the Cathedral from dusk till dawn. It was very undyed hemp. We took a lot of cantaloupe breaks, and there was much deep breathing at 3:45 a.m. A twelve-hour night would usually result in a few acceptable notes recorded on tape.

But it wasn't all melons. After a night of musical meandering, there was something magnificent about the sun rising in the rose window of the cathedral to the golden sound of Winter's horn. Paul had great ears and he and his fellow Consort members, brilliant musicians all, worked diligently to create beautiful sounds. Whatever corners he's had to cut to get there, he does have an impressive catalogue of quality music.

One night, looking at me with his puppy-dog, gray eyes and speaking in his yoga-instructor voice, Paul asked me to take a walk with him. We wandered to a staircase in the back of the cathedral.

Paul said, "You have made such an amazing contribution to this record. Really, you are like one of the musicians. I value what you have done so much. I want to reward you in a special way. I'm going to give away some of my royalties on this record to you. I'm going to give you a *point*."

This meant that, after recouping expenses, I would share in profits, receiving a percentage of future sales. Winter owned his own record company, and he could pass on the royalties anyway he liked.

I was blown away by this gift. Recording engineers were never given royalties. We were paid by the hour. To share in the profits meant that yours truly had special status. It was reserved for producers and artists. I felt a tremendous sense of gratitude and pride in the gift. It was hard to take in such generosity. It meant that Paul would sacrifice some of the money he would be making off the album to give to a *schlepper* like me. I was ready to go all night as many nights as Paul wanted to, and do everything I could to help create a musical masterpiece.

The fine print in this offer was that little thing about "recouping expenses." What I did not know at that time, but Paul did, was that there would be no royalties from this record.

Winter had expensive tastes. His breakthrough disc, *Icarus*, was produced by The Beatles' producer George Martin, who gave Paul permission to spend whatever he wanted on this record. Martin was used to working this way from his days with the Fab Four. The Beatles could run up a tab while recording, because they made their record company a bit of cake.

Winter took to the privileges of a rock-star budget, but his sales were more on the order of bands like Harry Shields and The Bones of Contention. Since he planned on selling those billions at some point, he figured he wasn't doing his job unless he was going over budget, and he continued to spend profligately on his projects.

While he was gallivanting around the globe harmonizing with sea otters, back home, because he spent much and earned little, his debts mounted to the millions of dollars from cost overruns on his several previous recordings. His crackpot schemes to sell beaucoup disks never came to fruition. Even the best New Age noodler rarely sold over 50,000 copies.

Hence the need for the old ladies.

When he bequeathed me his one percent, no album of his had ever recouped costs and turned a profit. Not only would this album have to be his first multi-million-seller to earn a single royalty dollar, but he would have to pay off all his previous debts before he could disburse a dime.

What Paul knew when he "gave" me a point on his record was that he was giving me 1% of, as they say in show biz, *bupkes*. But hey, who cares, as long as the music turns out great. And really, he did it all for the sake of his art.

Winter wasn't really such a bad guy. His hijinks didn't stop me from working with him. In fact, I worked for his record company for a bit, even knowing the facts. He was generous enough to let me produce a record on his label by a wonderful singer named Susan Osborn. When we'd be working on a record and someone would make a musical suggestion, he'd say, "Let's let the music tell us." That really meant "no fucking way." I guess to this Brooklynite, I would've appreciated it if he had just been direct. At a certain point I wouldn't drink the Kool-Ade anymore, and he fired my ass. I hope that isn't the reason I'm telling this tale. That would make me the prick.

Stories like this are legion in the music biz.

Art Blakey was a jazz drummer who was renowned for discovering monster talent. Years ago, I was hanging out at the old New York Jazz club, Sweet Basil, chatting with a waitress who worked there while studying art. She was saying how wonderful Blakey was because he gave first shots to innumerable jazz greats.

I said to her, "You know what that means, right?"

She didn't know what I was talking about.

I said, "It means he doesn't pay."

"What?"

"Mark my words."

A short time later, a sax-playing friend told me this story. Like many young cats before him, he came to New York, hoping to make it. He was excited beyond all measure when he found himself with an opportunity to audition for Art Blakey! Here was this fresh cat's big chance. He could follow in the footsteps of reed-players Lou Donaldson, Branford Marsalis, and Wayne Shorter among dozens of others, who had also made their way into the biz by playing with Blakey's band, The Jazz Messengers. When my buddy got to Art's house, Blakey was rubbing his ass and grimacing in pain.

"Man," Blakey asked, "could you go out and get me some Ben-Gay? My butt is killin' me!"

Wanting to please, the young musician ran to the corner drug store and got Blakey the unguent to soothe the pain where he had stuck one too many heroin needles.

Blakey thanked him for the stuff. They played together, and Art invited my buddy to do a gig.

Telling me the story, my friend said, "Not only did I never get paid for the gig, but the mother never paid me back for the Ben-Gay!"

Hey man, musicians are poor and so they have to hustle.

So artists can be cheap bastards. So what. No artist is that bad, right? I mean, it's not like they are starting unnecessary wars or anything. We live in venal times where very, very fat cats rip off the unsuspecting poor with exotic mortgages and then crash the economy so no one can get a job. So no matter how opportunistic an artist might be, in general the worst they are doing is sneaking a third portion at the buffet.

Except for the few who are really bad.

The worst guy I ever worked with? That would be Joe Brooks. He was truly a psychopathic music dude. You think you've never heard of him, but if you were born before 1970 he owns a piece of your inner iPod. He's the creep who wrote the song "You Light up My Life," one of the biggest hit singles of all time. At least as big as Paul's "Bridge."

The hit record was sung by the virginal Debbie Boone, Pat Boone's daughter. Pat was probably another low-life. His comments comparing gay-rights activists to terrorists tells you something about him.

In the 1950s, Pat Boone's scam was selling records off the backs of black cats. The original rock n' rollers like Fats Domino and Little Richard had a hard time selling records, so an attractive white feller like Pat Boone could sing their songs like "Ain't That a Shame" and "Tutti Frutti" and sell millions.

Pat's daughter Debbie said she sang "You Light up My Life" to God. This song being about God is the ultimate bullshit. And I'm going to tell you why.

Joe Brooks was a no-talent bastard. "Light" was one of the lamest songs ever written, and it won every Grammy. So much for the taste of the elite. It's not just that I hate treacly sap. I can listen to Celine Dion sing the theme to *Titanic* and the money note gets me every time. It's that "You Light up My Life" genuinely sucks.

Brooks recorded a lot of his shit at A&R. He would come to the studio with nothing written: no charts, no parts, not one note. Then he'd scream and yell at everyone. Because they were getting paid, everyone would pretend the emperor had talent.

The guy who sat in the first chair in the string section, the savvy and political David Nadien, who had been first chair at the New York Philharmonic under Leonard Bernstein, would whisper behind his hand, telling the violinists, violists, cellists, and basses what to play.

Nadien, who was a gorgeous musician, put up with this crap because that's how much better the money was in the studio than at the concert hall at that time. The story goes that Bernstein once told him that he had to make a choice between the studio gigs and the orchestra.

Nadien said, "My dear fellow, there is no choice."

All the musicians would make up their own parts.

Not everyone worked like Simon, or groups like Steely Dan, who would take sixteen hours to cut a basic track, but it was conventional to at least take enough time to get something of acceptable quality. The quality thing was our ethic. That was our pride.

Joe's regular engineer, an old English legend named Malcolm Addey, wasn't available one day, so I was asked to sit in the chair. Before I had a chance to set levels, or the band had time to figure out what notes to play, Joe screamed at me, telling me to hit "record." I did as he demanded. The thing sounded like a musical rat nest. Before the take was even finished, he ran into the control room ranting, demanding a playback.

When he heard that it was all a putrid mess, he started screaming at anyone in proximity, including me, "What the f-f-f-f-f-f-f-uck is going on here? What the f-f-f-f-f-f-f-f-uck is wrong with you? Are you a f-f-f-f-f-f-f-f-ucking idiot?" (Brooks did have a bad stutter, among his many other issues.)

I suggested it might be a good idea to do another take, and stop saying fuck. "No!" he continued, "Fix it! You fucked it up, now you make it work!"

There was a limit to the crap I would put up with. The combination of Brooks not having his shit together and being abusive to everyone was beyond my limit. He wasn't paying me enough and his music sucked. But I could sense something worse than that. I didn't like being in the presence of evil, especially without skill. So I, for once, refused to work with the guy and ended up not working on his hit record, something I can say I'm proud of. I wasn't above doing just about anything for a dollar like anyone else in the studio, but this freak skeeved me. (Confession: I recorded the music for the 1992 Republican National Convention even though I'm a member of the Radical Passé Party. I charged top dollar, and knew they'd lose anyway.)

Brooks screwed over the dearly departed session singer Kasey Cisyk, who performed the original vocal on "You Light Up My Life." Because she didn't have a nice American name, or connections like Debbie Boone, she got dumped for the single. That kind of thing happens all the time, too.

Brooks made it on pure shamelessness, which is the root of sociopathy. What would normally hold a person back —a little class, healthy reticence, not wanting to look the fool, or an actual conscience — simply didn't exist for Brooks. We have a tradition of this in our country. Clever sociopaths, who lack healthy shame and are willing to do anything to get what they want, are often able to bamboozle large swaths of the public and become exceedingly successful.

People like this have what is kindly referred to in my current profession as a "personality disorder." You see, there are basically two kinds of nuts in the world. The average neurotic, and if you're lucky you fit in this category, generally feels bad about him or herself and ok about everyone else. If you feel depressed, or anxious, you want to get rid of the bad feeling. But people with real personality disorders, or what we call "Axis II," are in a different category entirely. They believe the problem is "out there," not "in here." Everything would be fine, if everyone just realized what a genius they were.

All this exists on a continuum. You could have some narcissistic traits, where it is hard for you to say you're sorry, or you could be a full-blown psychopath where you can kill people without remorse. When you are like this in the extreme, you believe you can do nothing wrong. You can do anything without any sense of guilt, because you have no human limits. If anyone should point out that what you have done is in any way other than perfect, it is that person who has the problem, not you. These people, it would makes sense to say, are much harder to treat than what we in the biz call the "worried-well," who belong in category one (hopefully, you). These Axis II types are often attracted to celebrity and politics (think Sarah Palin or Donald Trump).

Everybody in the studio knew what kind of low-life garbage Brooks was. But we all kept our mouths shut, because a gig is a gig, and what's the difference between one kind of prick and another? Our job was to get out the product.

Brooks's ego was so boundless that, after his big hit, and the movie that went along with it, he parlayed his success into making a second film, called *If Ever I See You Again*. This time, this lunatic produced, directed, wrote, and starred in (!) the movie. This sorry excuse goes down in my book as the worst film of all time. The direction makes Ed Wood of *Glen or Glenda* fame look like a Lubitsch.

In the movie, Brooks gets to live out his pathetic fantasy. After having been rejected for being a dweeby freak in childhood, he is finally able to nail the *shiksa*-goddess, played by the perfectly mediocre — and appropriately named — actress Shelley Hack. She falls in love with Joe after seeing him conduct an orchestra, or that is, wave his arms awkwardly in front of about 120 musicians crammed willy-nilly into studio A-1. Talk about a Portnoy's Complaint!

By the way, Shelley Hack was famous for being in Woody Allen's *Annie Hall,* in which she played the beautiful woman on the street who says she is happy because she doesn't have a thought in her head. She was also renowned for getting thrown off the TV series "Charlie's Angels" after one season. But this doesn't make her a bad person. She has actually gone on to do some very noble stuff in her life, including helping the Bosnians. I credit her as a human being far above the more famous and talented sanctimonious schmucks I hung with in the biz. In the end, she'll be remembered for the "Charlie's Angels" debacle instead of her good works, but that's because we live in a very sick society, which, if you haven't noticed yet, is one of the points of this little section.

My favorite line in Joe's film? "I've got to go to Carnegie Hall (where he will, of course, be performing) to check the acoustics!" You gotta love it.

I would get in trouble, back then, for saying that "You Light Up My Life" was an awful song written by an evil man made in the worst way possible; that Joe Brooks not only didn't deserve success, money, fame, and awards but he really deserved to burn in Hell. Who cared and who listened? Hits talk.

After his second movie bombed, though, the *dreck* did sink to the bottom of the bowl, and Brooks was no longer invited to the A-list parties. Years passed, and I wondered what had happened to the creep.

He turned up again in 2005 with another grandiose project about himself, a musical named *In My Life*. This one was considered a total joke and people only went to see it on Broadway for the sheer horror spectacle of it all.

The next I heard of Joe, things had taken a decided turn toward the dark side. He was indicted in 2009 on 91 counts for an endless string of casting-couch rapes. Assisted by someone named Shawni Lucier, he would place ads in Craigslist for women to audition for a movie. The gullible wannabes would be flown to New York. Brooks would get them drunk, have them read some dirty script, and then rape them. It turns out that, by the report of at least one victim, he had been raping women, using this ruse since the '70s, during the time he was in our orbit.

It all ended as it should have. On May 22, 2011, Joe wrapped his neck in a towel, put a plastic bag over his head and breathed from a hose attached to a helium tank. Unfortunately, this is a quick and painless suicide method that is now highly recommended in the euthanasia community.

But let's assume that Joe had his share of pain in life, if not death. He was a stutterer and probably suffered from many mental disabilities beyond being a psychopath. The characters in his ill-conceived Broadway ditty to himself *In My Life,* had Tourette's syndrome and Obsessive Compulsive Disorder, so who knows what the hell was going on with Joe.

It was obvious he was consumed with self-hatred, the source for all narcissistic maniacs. But that's no excuse. The guy was a total reprobate. And he fucked up his son, too, who was convicted of murdering his girlfriend and will be sitting in a cell at Rikers for the next twenty-five years.

Most of us weren't anywhere near as bad as all that. But in New York in the '70s, people paid extra for the abuse. If you went to the Carnegie Deli for a pastrami on rye with Russian dressing, part of the fun was getting insulted by the wait staff. We learned at the studio that being obnoxious increased your cachet — it made you more of a *star*. Add in not sleeping for years, and anyone can get pretty psychotic. We'd work all day to make the money to buy the cocaine to keep us up in order to work all night, and then it would start all over again. Things got pretty flippy, and Ramone, the most volatile of us all, was the ringleader we were all trying to emulate.

"I want a full staff meeting NOW!" the fat man would command, and Uncle Max would set out the call and everyone would come running. Phil would scream some kind of incoherent gibberish, and we'd all nod obediently. Then Plotnik would call Friedman a putz, and they'd chase each other down the hall spraying fire extinguishers. One time there was no cheese on my tuna melt, so I threw it at my ex-girlfriend Kelly, for whom I got a gig as studio manager. We were all nuts.

If it wasn't violence and drugs, it was sex. One time I went down to the basement and found three or four staff members in various stages of undress, blasted out of their minds, in the middle of a game of strip poker. In those pre-AIDS days, everyone was doing everyone, and talking about it, too. You could barely walk through a vocal booth without tripping over people fucking.

During my quick rise from *schlepper* to senior mixer, these perfect atmospheric conditions made my nascent arrogance blossom into full flower. My jerkiness could compete with the best of them.

Before I started at A&R, I had interned at the top jingle house in New York, Herman Edel Productions. That was my way into the biz. My mom was close friends with Willie Edel, the brother of the owner. Willie called Herman, and soon I was walking the dog from this impressive town house on East 53rd Street in the Turtle Bay neighborhood of New York. Herman was rarely on site. The company was being run by what we called the musical "Mod Squad," the name taken from a hip TV show from the era: a woman, a black guy with an afro, and a long-haired white guy. This was not your father's advertising supplier. The woman in the trio at Herman Edel was the leader, and one of the most impressive people I've ever met in the biz. Her name was Susan Hamilton, and it was her dog, Mendl, that I used to walk.

Susan was a child-prodigy pianist. In an era when music production was completely dominated by men, she ran the biggest and most successful jingle house of the day. They created music for countless TV and radio commercials for the biggest accounts of the time like Chevrolet, Dr. Pepper, and Eastern Airlines.

Susan was one of those musicians who possessed an ear far beyond those of mere mortals. She'd listen to an orchestra run through a piece and say, "In measure 35 on the second beat, the oboe should be a b natural instead of a b flat." Not even the conductor heard that nuance.

Susan was a powerhouse — she had to be in order to survive in that male world, but she was also terrifically sensitive and supportive in ways that were often overlooked, because she did this in unassuming ways.

I remember one incident from those early interning days that revealed who she was. All of the top Chevrolet clients were assembled in the office for a presentation meeting. She asked me to put up and play the reel-to-reel tape of the music for the new campaign.

Now, I'd never run a professional tape deck before. I threaded the tape on the machine just fine. Like all master tapes, it was wound "tails out." This meant that you had to rewind the whole thing to get to the beginning. I pressed the rewind button and the tape zoomed on the turbo-charged machine. So far, so good. I felt pretty slick. What I did not know was that before hitting stop, you needed to slow the tape down first by hitting fast-forward. Instead, I just hit the stop button, which applied the brakes immediately. The tape machine screeched to a full stop. The momentum forced the tape to spill off the reel and get sucked down into the guts of the machine! Dots danced before my eyes, the slickness draining out of me as I was consumed with embarrassment and panic. She could have — and had the right to — scream at me, and fire me on the spot, ending my nascent career on a dime, as there was a chance that I had ruined an extremely important presentation with a major client. But instead, having comprehended what happened, she stayed cool, and quickly launched into some funny anecdotes to entertain the clients while I pulled myself together and gingerly pulled the tape out from under the capstans of the machine and smoothed out all the tangles. She kept one eye on me, and when I finally accomplished the task, she simply nodded, signaling me to hit the play button. Catastrophe averted. That's the way she always was. She understood what was important and supported the growth of others for the greatest good.

Most people in the business, and perhaps in life, are followers. They do not have the inner security to lead, to take a stand, to know their own mind, and to risk the courage of their convictions. But not Susan. She knew what — and who — was good, and she gave many of us our first opportunities, because she was great at recognizing, supporting, and promoting talent and hard work.

She had a deeply generous spirit. She brought me, and many others, into her world, sharing her homes, her wonderfully eccentric parents, her talent, and her wisdom with all of us.

With Susan saying the word, the door was opened for me to intern at A&R Recording, and the rest was history. She was also the very first person to give me the chance to sit behind the recording console as an engineer.

From her, I learned how to be cool under pressure. We could take on the toughest challenges, and through top-quality work, we'd succeed. One time, we worked with Ray Charles on a campaign for the United Negro College Fund. While many of the stars we worked with could be extremely demanding, Ray had a reputation as the toughest. Any mistake could bring the session to an ignominious end. Susan ran the session, and I was the engineer. We rocked the house. Ray left a happy man, and we felt like we had won the NBA championship.

Susan embodied many qualities that appear to be in short supply today: brilliance, excellence, generosity of spirit, and a deep loyalty. She was a gem.

I was lucky enough to have another wonderful mentor when I hung out at Susan's jingle house: Willie and Herman's other brother, Buddy. The Edels were an impressively talented family. But they had something else unique about them. Three out of the four siblings had a rare disease called retinitis pigmentosa, a progressive illness that left them blind. Herman was the only one of the four that didn't have it. But Buddy did. He would hang out on the top floor of the townhouse, and I'm not sure what his job was exactly. Maybe Herman was just giving him a place to hang his hat. But Buddy was invaluable to me. When I, a seventeen year-old, would get overwhelmed at being in the presence of these Don Draper-like creative advertising superstars and feel as small as a bug, I'd run up to Buddy for some perspective on the whole thing. He was always cool enough to bring my anxiety level down and encourage me to go back down the stairs and bravely face the next daunting task. He was compassionate, funny, and wise. We hung out, and I even went to his apartment a few times, where I helped him out with a few things.

After Susan helped me land the job at A&R, I got caught up in my own bullshit and lost touch with Buddy. A few years later, after I'd graduated to senior mixer, Buddy and Herman came in to do a session, and they booked me as the engineer. I felt so proud that I could show Buddy and Herman, who had known me from the beginning, that I'd made it!

After the session I got a call from Buddy. He said it was great to see me after so long a time and suggested we get together for dinner to catch up. I admired him and was excited to get together. I met him near his apartment on Irving Place and he took me to a tony restaurant on that special block near Gramercy Park.

After a few pleasantries, Buddy said he wanted to talk to me. He got serious.

"Glenn, Herman and I were quite upset after our session with you."

I became alarmed. "Why?"

"We're disappointed. You've become rather arrogant. I don't know what happened to that sweet kid I knew a few years ago. You've lost your way, young man."

I had gone in a very short time from being a kid from Brooklyn who used to run to him in a panic to being the wunderkind, the youngest senior mixer ever, the 21-year-old former *schlepper* who was working with the stars. I had forgotten who I was and become an ass.

Buddy fit the cliché: he was blind, but he could see right through me.

"You're hot now, but if you continue down this path, soon enough, no one will want to work with you. Herman certainly never wants to work with you again."

At first, I felt defensive. Arrogant prickishness seemed to work for a lot of my cohorts. But I didn't say anything. I burned with shame.

I could feel his indignation rising. "You better get your shit together, and show some humility."

I hung my head, averting his gaze. Then he paid the bill, and we left.

I reeled away from that meeting dizzy and disoriented. I was shocked, embarrassed, and depressed. Then I felt strangely thrilled. This guy really cared about me. He took me out to bust my ass, but I could tell he did it in a loving way.

It took some time to absorb what he said, but I knew he was right. It wasn't the first, or the last, time that I would get knocked off center, lose my core, become less than I could be. Things at times got far worse. I could be just as big a jerk as many of the people I worked with and complain about.

Along with the players, my favorite people in the studio were the arrangers. The cats who occupied each role in the studio scene seemed to have their own personality traits. Arrangers were usually kind and generous.

I am reminded of this when I think of the brilliant composer/arranger Pat Williams, who wrote the orchestral interlude for the song, "Still Crazy." Pat, like most arrangers, was a lovely man.

Since the time that Paul had done his demo of the song for us, he hadn't found the solution to the middle section of the song. He hired Pat to compose something that would connect this new part back to the third refrain. But Paul was still unclear about what was going to happen in the bridge leading up to Pat's section and had not written any lyrics. While a small orchestra waited in the studio at thousands of dollars a minute, Paul sat in another room, summoning the Muses.

Though Paul was a very slow writer and would work on stuff endlessly to get it right, he managed to write the bridge to this song in just an hour or two.

Then, when Pat started overdubbing the orchestra, Paul hated just about every note. He ripped Pat's work apart. It wasn't as if Williams was incapable of doing this stuff. He has won countless awards and worked with every artist. He's a major cat.

Paul had Pat rewrite the entire section on the spot. Writers were used to working hard to get something right, but it was the way Paul did it that left Pat feeling brutalized. By the time we'd finished, he looked shell-shocked and said that he'd never been put through anything like that by any artist ever. It was in moments like this that Paul burnished his reputation as a real prick.

In the end it came out brilliantly. It is reminiscent of an earlier orchestral part from the Simon and Garfunkel song "Old Friends," but artists are permitted to steal from themselves. This interlude, with its dissonances and cross rhythms, stands in poignant contrast to the familiar, old-timey melodic repetition of the title. It has the elegiac emotion of longing and sadness, of loss and acceptance, that the song, and Paul's sensibility, best represents. I'm fucked up, I've lost out, but whaddya gonna do?

The conflicted feeling resolves into a soaring, uplifting tenor sax solo crafted by the great departed studio musician Michael Brecker. The mournful solitude resolves into something hopeful. It's as if Paul is saying, yeah, it's all meaningless, but you might as well try to have a hit record anyway. Like Jews throughout history, Simon turns his pain into a wry song, a knowing nod and smile that says, "Could be worse."

Paul's emptiness, his deadness, his limited capacity for feeling emotion, can be a real asset in making art. The damn thing is going to have to cut pretty deep to get a rise out of a guy like Simon. If the thing he's making moves him, for the rest of us it's gonna kick motherfuckin' ass.

TRACK TEN

The Night I Didn't Have Sex with Bette Midler

Bette and Arif continued struggling with the Divine One's vocals. One Friday afternoon, at the end of a long week of recording, I was given the assignment to make and deliver a cassette copy of some rough mixes to her.

I called Bette up to see when she would be around so I could bring her the tape. When I heard her voice on the other end of the line, I became inspired. I knew things had just ended between her and Paul. Bubbling up from some source of late-adolescent supreme cockiness, total unconsciousness, and massively denied insecurity, I said, "Hey Bette, since I'm coming down to deliver these tapes, would you like to go out for some dinner?" I heard my own voice asking Bette Midler out on a *date*.

With a sparkly and wicked smile in her voice, she said, "Sure."

I had not only asked Bette Midler out on a date, but she had said *yes!*

With the cassette tape in my pocket, I rode the Seventh Avenue subway down from the studio in Midtown to Sheridan Square in Greenwich Village. What seemed like centuries before, when I was thirteen, I had taken the subway in the other direction, north from Brooklyn, and had visited the Village for the first time. The moment I ascended those stairs as a newbie teen, I knew that this was where I wanted to live. Now here I was, the coolest assistant engineer in the world on my way to the house of the hottest babe on the planet.

Yes, it was all too hip, but I was so far out of my depth, I would be lucky if I didn't get the bends. I was wearing the worst pair of shoes.

As you travel south on the granite island of Manhattan toward its narrowing point, you move back through time, to where the city had its birth. Once you get below 14th Street on the West Side, the city loses its easily-traversable grid street pattern, and becomes a tangle of irrationally laid out pathways. I somehow found my way through the confusion to Barrow Street, a charming, narrow lane of early 19th century townhouses. I followed the numbers until I stood in front of her building, number 36. I walked up the stoop stairs and rang the bell.

Bette lived then in a smartly furnished one-bedroom floor-through on the parlor floor of the building. Petite, with a mess of red hair, knowing eyes, a funky nose, and an ample, sensuous body, she opened the door and invited me in.

She asked if I wanted a glass of Chablis. I remembered the first lesson the studio manager Tony had taught me when I began my internship at A&R: whatever the artists ask, your only answer is *yes*. I also figured that agreeing to whatever she said was the best way to conceal that I was a total dork. Once she brought me the glass, I figured out that Chablis was white wine. I was a quick study.

Bette was bright, savvy, funny, and a great conversationalist. Whereas I had always felt so awkward and tongue-tied around Paul Simon, with Bette, at least I could speak. Sitting in her kitchen, sipping the wine, she told me she had just met David Bowie, and we talked about what he was like. She said he was smart and that I'd like him. We were getting along, having fun.

She asked if I wanted to grab some dinner at Alfredo's. I gave the right answer.

As we walked west toward the river, down Barrow to Hudson Street, I tried to look like I knew where I was going, while following her footsteps.

When we arrived at the restaurant, it was packed. This was the trendiest spot in New York at that time. Everyone was eating Fettuccine Alfredo. Now, I was sure to find out what that was all about.

I approached the maître d' to request a table. Looking beyond me, he swatted me away like a mildly annoying gnat. I tried in vain to push through the crowd, vying for a coveted seat at this popular bistro, my raised arm and boy's voice lost in the din amplified by the tin ceilings. Then the host recognized Miss M., and his attitude immediately changed.

"Oh, Miss Midler, how nice to see you!" he said in his most sycophantic tone. "Of course we have a table for you, come right this way!"

As the diva pushed out her bosom, beamed, and sauntered past the adoring crowd to her appointed throne, I struggled to keep up, signaling to no one in particular that I was with *her*.

We sat opposite each other, with the artichoke she had ordered between us. I had never seen such a strange fruit. How was one meant to approach such a cactus? I watched her pull out a leaf, dip it in some sauce and suck the veggie meat off the end. OK. Pull, dip, and suck. Artichoke. Got it.

After slurping through the cheesy fettuccine Alfredo — a cholesterol-laden white sauce of cheese, butter, and more cheese— drinking some blush wine, and indulging in some rum-soaked tiramisu, I was feeling loose. I had survived dinner. When I wasn't looking like a spaz, we made a charming couple. I picked up the check.

We walked back to her pad, arm in arm, in the warm spring night. My feet were off the ground, something else was in the air.

Back at her pad, she poured us some more wine, and we danced to some slow, funky Marvin Gaye. Her curvy body against mine left me dizzy.

She asked, "Do you want to watch some TV?"

Of course, I said, "Yes."

The small black-and-white was in her bedroom. This being a New York apartment, the room was just big enough for a queen-size bed. She plopped on the mattress, and I laid down next to her. She turned on the set to Channel 13. I knew I had a buzz on, but I wasn't on acid or anything; yet what I saw appeared like a hallucination. The show started with some freaky animation, and a twisted martial tune. A bunch of wacky English guys were doing the strangest bits. A *blancmange*, a large, white pudding, was playing tennis. In a high voice, someone screamed, "No one expects the Spanish Inquisition!" It was "Monty Python's Flying Circus," a breakthrough British TV comedy that captured the psychedelic, erudite, Beatles-influenced zeitgeist in the funniest way. Bette and I laughed together.

Chablis, artichokes, Alfredo, tiramisu, Gaye, Python, it all started to inflate my head like a helium balloon. Then, I looked down, and saw those fabulous, famous, large breasts. I looked into Bette's eyes, and saw that mischievous smile of hers. What had I been thinking when I asked her for dinner? Did I really think I'd end up inches away from her supine body? *What,* I wondered, *do I do now?* A vague confusion started to cloud my consciousness, but I pushed it away.

Well, if I had practiced anything during my wasted youth, it was kissing. I got the vibe that she just might let me do that. I lowered my face and my lips touched hers. She didn't stop me. She yielded, and even made some approving little sounds. Our tongues touched. *Hm. Really?* I tried it again, and again. She seemed to be ok with it. It felt good. She'd apparently had some practice with this herself.

After a spate of kisses, the obvious next thought came into my head: *I could touch, fondle, grope, caress, maybe even lick, suckle, the breasts of the Divine Miss M, the queen of booblemania.* I reached down. There they were, now in my hands! Now, under my lips!

Wait. That confusion had now solidified into conflict. My excitement was met head-on with trepidation. *What was the right thing to do?* Oh, how foolish we can be at nineteen! We allow morality to enter at all the wrong moments. *Was this a first date? If so,* I wondered, *what would the gentlemanly thing be to do? Do you screw on the first date, or don't you? Could I ruin a potentially great relationship by going too far?* I could fake knowing how to eat an artichoke, but I couldn't let on that I had no idea what I was doing *here*, at *this* moment. And what of Tony's lessons? I was always supposed to say yes, but I was never, ever supposed to mess with the artists. And then there was Phil. *Shit, oh yeah, him.* Phil Ramone. My boss's ugly puss flashed through my mind. He might not take too kindly to this…I had to make a decision.

That luscious, famous body pulled me in one direction, and some inhibiting force pulled me in another. *I, I — would be gallant,* I thought. *That couldn't be wrong!*

Before I knew what I was doing, I got up, started putting on my bad shoes, and said that I'd be going. Bette looked at me with shocked incredulity, but her unlikely reaction didn't register in my still-maturing neo-cortex. As I watched myself from outside my body, as I reached the door, with me mumbling goodnight, it suddenly dawned on me. *That look on her face — she was angry!* Her willing smile had turned into a curl of wrath. Hell hath no fury.

The door closed. I saw a cab in front of her building, hailed it, and got inside. The minute I sat down, I felt the yanking pain of my post-pubescent tumescence. I saw, like an after-image, Bette's face with her wide eyes, flared nostrils, and narrowed, scornful lips as she closed the door. Then, just five minutes too late, it hit me. I had just made one of the worst mistakes of my young life. I could have, no, I should have, done it with Bette Midler, and I blew it! Then, like fragments coming together into a recognizable whole, I could perceive the next layer of truth: this had probably been my one and only chance to ever do anything like that in my entire life. As the cab went up Sixth Avenue, every few blocks I leaned toward the cab driver to tell him to turn around, and each time I told myself I couldn't, kicking myself.

The truth was, I wasn't gallant. I was scared. I chickened out. I hadn't thought when I made the ballsy move of asking her out to dinner that anything like what happened was in my future.

If that wasn't bad enough, now I had to deal with the next consequence of that ill-fated non-act. The next Monday, I was back in the control room with Ramone. It was just the two of us, working on some mix, without an artist or producer present. Since Bette was sure to come in again to record, I knew there was a chance that Ramone would find out about this date, and I couldn't let him hear the story from anyone but me.

"Phil," I started gingerly, "there's something I gotta tell ya."

"What," he said impatiently. "Come on, 30 IPS," which was his code for *get on with it.*

"Nothing happened (*unfortunately*, I thought to myself), I was just delivering the cassette to Bette and we decided to go out for dinner, and we just ate some pasta and hung out for a while and that was all that happened. I just wanted you to know."

Ramone said nothing. That made me nervous. *Well, maybe it shouldn't,* I thought. *Maybe he'll just let it pass. Maybe we got through that moment.* I started to breathe again. We went on with our work, for a half hour, or so. Few words passed between us. Was there tension in the air, or was I making it up?

I was over by the half-inch machine, rewinding a mix, when Ramone suddenly twisted around in his brown, leather chair. Reflexively, I turned, and saw his massive belly pulling him forward with a mass of momentum, making him look like a sumo wrestler on the attack, his eyes twirling with crazed rage. I jerked back, banging into the tape machine, and held on.

"You talk to me about integrity," he growled disdainfully. "You don't have any integrity. When Bette drives up here in her limo you're going to crawl out to her on your belly!"

I tried to reason with him. "But Phil, I'm telling you . . ."

Now the volume was getting to an ear-damaging decibel level. "And let me tell you something else, Berger, when you produce her next album, I won't be engineering it!"

If only I had that kind of moxie and narcissistic confidence! I just thought, in the moment, when the opening presented itself, that maybe I'd be lucky enough to get a kiss, cop a feel — I hadn't strategized quite so far as to see this as some brilliant career move.

"But Phil, I was just her roadie of the night. I'm ten years younger than her, she'll never have anything to do with me again!" I wished that wasn't true, but deep down I knew. I knew.

"Now I know who you really are! You'll fuck anybody to get ahead. You don't care about me, or the work! You gigolo! So what, now you're Bette Midler's little boy? Is she driving up here right now to pick you up? And if she comes, will you go?"

He was out of control. Now I made my next big mistake. "Phil, you're just jealous."

"GET OUT! GET OUT! I'VE TAKEN ABOUT AS MUCH SHIT AS I'M GONNA TAKE FROM YOU, YOU . . ."

Before I heard anymore, I ran out of the control room, and zoomed up to the second floor, heading straight for Broadway Max's office for refuge. Max was on the phone, trying to collect money. He gripped a pencil stub, scribbling something down, and chewed an unlit cigar. His shiny black suit was covered in dandruff, as always. He rolled his pale, blue eyes, while pointing at the black phone with the coiled cable, and motioned for me to take a seat.

He hung up the phone, and said in his Edward G. Robinson voice, "What's up buddy boy?"

I told him the story. He laughed demonically, exposing his big, yellow teeth. He relished this tale, as he loved everything about the biz.

"So you are Midler's boy-toy of the night, you don't even follow through, and Ramone thinks you are going to steal his gig! That is hilarious!"

"I'm glad you think it's funny. If I wasn't idiot enough last night, now I go and tell Ramone he's jealous. I'm in deep shit."

Now Max looked mock-serious. "You said that? Uh-oh." He scratched his white crew-cut. "That is bad. I better go down there and see if I can patch things up."

"Thanks, Max."

It was good to have an ally I could depend on.

Max called me back down to the control room after a suitable interval during which he had poured Phil a stiff cognac. When I came back in, Phil looked at me out of the corner of his narrowed eyes. I promised not to go out with any more stars. We went back to work as if nothing had happened. But he never looked at this *schlepper* the same way again. Along with a degree of suspiciousness, he had to admit a begrudging admiration.

Still, I couldn't let go of this nagging sense of guilt and shame about the Midler debacle. I thought I'd send her some flowers, just to say thanks — and I'm sorry— and maybe there'd be an opening . . . We did a few more sessions, but she acknowledged nothing. I sat quiet and cowed, back in my assistant's chair. Though I slowly grew to accept that my romance was over, I couldn't forgive myself.

*

Even now, I still cringe with regret over my missed dalliance. Was there any way to reconcile this blunder? You'd think the lesson here would be the old *carpe diem* bullshit. To a fault, for years, I rarely turned down such opportunities again, which got me into all kinds of other trouble. So maybe that wasn't the moral.

Here's another possible message. With opportunity, you've got to recognize it when it is there. You've got to take advantage of it when it makes itself apparent. But you've also got to be ready for it. Timing is a matter of luck.

You see, what would have happened if I *had* shtupped Bette Midler? I would have done a poor job of it, for sure. I still would have been just a boy-toy for the night, and my less-than-studly, nineteen-year-old perfor-mance would have sealed that deal. Having made love, I would have fallen in love, and if the bad sex wouldn't have been bad enough, my uncontrol-lable pursuit afterwards would have led to even grosser humiliations. Phil would have had something to really be angry about, and who knows how that would have ended. Certainly, if we had consummated, that would have been the extent of the story. But *not* having done it makes a much better tale. Perhaps it was the best mistake I ever made.

That leaves me with one last regret. It's just too bad we couldn't have been friends. She was cool. Now, that makes me sad.

*

There was a coda to this concerto. At that time, I was also assisting on Steely Dan's *The Royal Scam* album. Walter Becker and Donald Fagen, the two guys who made up the band, were an unusual combination for the studio. They were brilliant oddballs *and* regular guys; that is, unlike the typical superstars, they were not over-the-top narcissists. Most other artists weren't as eccentric, but were far less friendly.

Steely Dan epitomized the New York studio scene of that time. They had made some great hits in California, but deep-down they were New Yorkers in their souls, and they wanted the funk influence that only the top players in the City could bring. They came to A&R to cut the tracks for their new record and had hired engineer Elliot Scheiner to man the controls. Gary Katz was their producer, who translated the cryptic Martian commands of the bizarre duo to the musicians. The team went on to make the Dan's greatest record, *Aja*, as well as *The Royal Scam* and *Gaucho*. After that, they really had very little left to say.

The greatness of those records came from the combination of Steely Dan's arch, white college-boy wit, angular rhythmic changes, sophisticated jazz harmonies, and post-modern melodic references, with the groove and funk sensibility of the studio cats who played the music.

Donald and Walter were the most exacting artists I'd ever encountered, relentless in their pursuit for attaining the perfect realization of the sound in their heads. We would regularly take all night and about twelve reels of two-inch tape just to cut a basic track. They might have the drummer tune the snare drum for hours, or recut a track because a single cymbal crash was in the wrong place. Along with Scheiner's great ears for sounds, there was good reason why their records won Grammy awards, including for best engineering.

One afternoon, we were listening back to those freshly recorded basic tracks. They were so hot, it felt like sparks flew out of the speakers, and we were all lifted to a higher realm. While Becker and Fagen were goofing around in the control room, taking a break from our work, Midler came in to hang with the guys.

She saw me and brightened. With just a soupçon of irony in her voice, she said, "Buns! How are you?" She sashayed over and gave me a tantalizing, but kitschy, hug.

Well, Becker, Fagan, Katz, and Scheiner loved this. "Buns?" they said in virtual unison, when Bette left.

"Yes," I said, with a mixture of pride, showing off my tight Fiorucci jeans, and excruciating embarrassment. "That's what she calls me."

That became my name for the rest of the Dan project. In case you might be skeptical about all this, take a look at the credits on *The Royal Scam* album. The last credit, under "Techno" is, yeah, that's right: Buns.

Fifty Ways to Leave Your Mentor

Unfortunately, I didn't get to work on all of *Still Crazy*.

At some point while trying to make something of the first arrangement for the song "Gone at Last," Paul wanted to overdub horns and extend the ending so we'd have a longer fadeout. This meant making exact copies of the multi-track tape and editing on repeated replicates of the final chorus.

The technicians made the copy in preparation for the overdub session with a whole bunch of players, which was slated to happen first thing Monday morning.

I'd asked Phil if he'd wanted me to do the cut, but now we were talking about the big two-inch multi-track master. He looked at me with condescension as if to say, let a man do a man's work. He'd handle it. He told me that he'd come into the studio over the weekend and do the edit.

When I got to the studio first thing Monday to set up, I assumed it had all been done. The players were wandering in, I had all the mics and headphones checked, and I was looking for the edited tapes to put up. Then I realized Ramone had never done the cuts. I had the original masters, and the copies that were made, but they hadn't been spliced together, and there was no Ramone.

He finally blew in at the last minute, and in his usual dramatic panic was going to do the edit in the few seconds before we were to hit the downbeat. We were quite familiar with "Murphy's Law" in the studio, because it was always proving true. If anything could go wrong, it would, at the worst possible time. As usual, the techies hadn't checked their work. They'd made a crappy copy that didn't match the original, so when Ramone tried to chop them together, it sounded like shit. So what did Ramone do? He screamed at the top of his lungs.

"As usual, if anything is going to get done right around here, I'll have to do it myself!"

I couldn't hold back. "Well Phil, you were supposed to do this, and you didn't."

"Are you some kind of incompetent, lousy ... and you just stood around here and let this go down? Now what am I supposed to do? Where were you, loser? I can't depend on anyone! I don't know why I put up with your sorry ass! How could you do this to me?"

He was right. It didn't matter that everyone else had fucked up. I knew better by now, and I should've left nothing to chance. I should've assumed that Ramone would screw the pooch, and I should've covered his behind in advance.

Now things were really in the shitter. We had a dozen horn players, an arranger, and a big artist waiting to record this thing, and all Ramone could think of doing was scream at the top of his lungs, telling me I was a total fuck up. Then he turned to Simon and kissed his tuchus so he wouldn't notice what was happening two inches away to this little *schlepper*.

I had become as irascible and as much of a fuck as Phil, and we were fighting way too much. The rain-barrel spilled over. I was done.

I turned to Ramone and said, "If I suck that bad, find yourself someone else to save your fucking ass every day!" and I walked out of the studio.

Once on 48th St., I stormed down 8th Avenue, thinking, "Let Ramone see how he survives without me, then let's see if he treats me that way . . ."

As I angrily bobbed up and down, walking farther away from the studio, I remembered a time in my earliest days when I had been the actual *schlepper*.

One morning in bad weather I was pushing a hand-truck up the block with a double load of tapes wrapped in sheets of plastic to keep the masters dry from the pouring rain. Along the way I had to make a stop at the copyist's office to drop off some lead sheets. I couldn't leave the golden masters on the street, so I tried to pull the heavy hand truck of tapes up the stairs into a narrow vestibule that bordered the sidewalk. The hand truck pitched to the left and didn't hold, and the tapes fell all over 49th Street.

Take sheets started blowing through the street with names on them like Paul McCartney, Burt Bacharach, and James Brown. I started to chase the papers into traffic with taxis blaring, getting soaked, and for a second I thought, *what the fuck. I'll just walk away.*

But then something clicked. I realized I was in the first five seconds of my career. Somehow I dug deep into my seventeeen year-old soul and gathered it all back. I calmly got every piece of paper, closed the tape boxes, stacked them all back up, secured them, and got the hand truck up the stairs, dropped off the music, and brought the tapes to their final destination.

Remembering this incident, which by then seemed so long ago, I stopped. It had been only two years before. Now I was all of nineteen, and wasn't pushing the hand truck anymore. I was on the verge of becoming a major cat (In retrospect, when I hang with teenagers now, I can barely fathom how I had anything resembling the inner strength or maturity to handle the kind of situations I found myself in at that young age).

Recognizing what was at stake, and unable to resist my indoctrination, I pulled my shit together. I knew I had to go back. I turned around and returned to the studio.

When I walked in, everyone was really concerned. Phil had alerted the entire staff that I had bailed, and they all knew this meant trouble. They couldn't do it without the *schlepper*. It didn't really give me any sense of pride or value. I just had to pull the dick-head through.

Now Phil struck low. "I don't know what I was doing hiring someone as young as you."

I kept my mouth shut, but thought, *really? I'll show you, you out-of-date, lame motherfucker.* I took over the task of making the new copies. I yanked the second elephant-sized multi-track tape recorder in the room and linked the two machines up umbilically. I made sure the techies did their job, and we recorded a nice, neat copy. I didn't let Ramone near the machine, and I insisted on putting the pieces together myself. When I was done with the edit, I got levels on the band. All Ramone needed to do was sit down and say, "Hit it." I was now good enough so that if Ramone fell over and died of a massive coronary from eating too many pork ribs, I could take over the cockpit and bring the sucker in for a landing.

The next day, Brooks called me into his office. "You're graduating, my friend. Phil is moving on."

That was the end for me and Phil. We broke up. We were both ready. For good or ill, I was always pushing to move on to the next step, to be more independent. I didn't want to be Phil's lobby-boy anymore; I wanted to do my own thing. Besides, I couldn't keep my big mouth shut. I wasn't cut out for taking that kind of shit. I was insolent, oppositional, and defiant, and the last thing he needed was a cheeky assistant.

I was also *good* at what I did. I had become Ramone. When I started with him I could barely rewind a tape machine without jamming a tape. When I was done, I was a senior recording engineer, another product of the apprenticeship to the master. I was ready to fly out from under his wing.

One guy that followed soon after me was far more patient and lasted for years, in the hopes that Billy Joel would one day have him produce. Today, that guy is working at Staples or something. And I'm a shrink, writing this.

Phil and I had an amicable divorce. It really was like a marriage. I certainly spent far more time with him during those two years than he spent with his actual wife. After we got out of each other's hair, we became better friends. He rarely said a good word about me to my face, but showed his respect by throwing me some really nice gigs. And I would do anything for the guy. My loyalty to him was absolute. If he asked me to assist all weekend recording the horrible singing of members of the fascist religious cult he became involved with for a short time after his actual divorce, I would do it. (Which I actually did.)

I didn't get to assist on the rest of the *Still Crazy* album, but I followed its progress. Since we were in the studio together 24 hours a day, Ramone and I would occasionally hang out and he'd keep me up to date on what was going on with the record.

After the usual gruelling endless process they finished recording, and the disc was finally released. There was nothing as satisfying and relieving as finishing a project with Paul Simon. Phil was in a relaxed mood. He sat in his Knoll chair in R-2 at his usual spot behind the board, his hands behind his head, his legs stretched out and crossed before him. I faced him from the front of the control room, my chin in my hands, my arms resting on the console.

Paul had done a few shows to promote the new album, and Phil had gone along to see the reaction to the new material.

With an ironic, disbelieving smile on his face, he said, "Guess which song is going to be the hit single?"

Among the many attributes of the record guy, the ability to pick hits was seen as the pinnacle. If you could tell which song was going to succeed with the public, you were worth gold to the record company. This was one of the great skills that Phil and Paul were famous for. They had been responsible for, or participated in, more hits than anyone could possibly count.

Given the acumen of these two giants, guessing the answer wouldn't be too hard. Anyone could tell which songs were selected as singles by the way the songs were sequenced on the album. In the days of vinyl, when you had 5 or 6 songs on a side, the hits were put first, maybe second, and rarely, last on side one. If there was another single it could be first on side two.

Thinking this was a trick question, I started with the first cut on side two. I guessed "Gone at Last." That fun tune that Paul sang with Phoebe Snow was certainly a kick. Ramone shook his head. Then I tried, "My Little Town," the track Paul had done with his ex-partner Art Garfunkel. Surely a comeback single would get people to plunk down the $1.49. Nope. Then I went with track one, side one. "Still Crazy?" Uh-uh.

I couldn't figure.

Then he told me it was "50 Ways to Leave Your Lover." People were going wild for this song at the shows. I was shocked, as Ramone had intended.

Because I'd been tracking the progress of the record, I had heard how this song came to be. Simon, who struggled so hard for worthy product, could barely come up with enough material to fill a vinyl disk, which could hold about 40 minutes of music and still have good quality. "50 Ways" was a throw-away track, something slight created to fill up a few grooves.

Paul had written it using a cheap, rudimentary drum machine. He'd programmed a nice little beat on this box. He brought it in for the hired guns to get inspiration.

Steve Gadd, the heaviest of the drum cats, heard the pattern and came up with a riff that turned out to be so memorable you could sing it to just about anyone who was listening to music then, and they could instantly identify it as "50 Ways." *Um-bam doo-dam ba-dum b-r-r-r-r-r um-bam doo-dam ba-dum boooomb.*

This scored Gadd a permanent home in Simon's world where he still resides today. The success of that goofy chorus indicated to Paul that maybe his growing musical sophistication was not the way to make the shekels, but he would not really abandon this path until *Graceland*, where he had the proof of a few flops to get him to give up the 12-note thing and groove deep into musical simplicity.

So Paul and Phil were completely off when it came to predicting which song from the *Still Crazy* record was going to be a smash. The biggest ears in the business can't always hear a hit. If you don't believe me on this one, just look at where the song lives on the album. Geniuses like these guys never bury one of their top selling records of all time fourth on side one.

It didn't matter. No one was the wiser. Paul and Phil's efforts paid off. *Still Crazy After All These Years* won the Grammy for Album of the Year.

TRACK TWELVE

The Saddest Thing of All: My Thirty Minutes with Frank Sinatra

During the broiling New York August of 1975, between sessions, I walked into A&R's main office at 799 7th Avenue to check the scheduling "book." I did this every chance I could get. It was better than going to the mailbox. You never knew what cool surprise awaited. Anyone could be coming in to record.

The "book" rested on a drafting table that stood about chest high. It covered the entire angled platform with card-stock heavy white sheets held together at the top by three metal rings. Each page was one day's schedule of recording sessions in our five studios. A-1, A-2, and A-3 were at "799." Studios R-1 and R-2 were at "322".

The studio manager, Tony, was in charge of booking the dates. He sat on a high stool sporting his pipe, with his only other prop, the black Bell Telephone, next to him. That day, he was in his usual position, hovering over the book, the phone at his ear. Using the pink eraser, he was feverishly rubbing out the details of one session and swiping the rubber shavings onto the floor.

He replaced the old session data with the new information that was coming in. He did this with pencil because, as in this instance, he often had to move things around to accommodate all the clients, producers, and mixers who were certain that their session was the most important in history.

"OK. So that's Eastern Airlines in R-1, two to five with a possible hour. Ed Rice is the engineer. Right?"

I stood next to him and waited as he completed the task. When he hung up the phone, I sidled up to see what the next days had in store for us.

"Berger! What do you want?" Tony said in his typically derisive tone.

"I want to be famous, like you. Whaddya think?" I answered, in my best Brooklyn tough-guy voice.

I placed my hands on the top page as I perused the schedule for the next day. The feel of those thick sheets covered in pencil provided a tactile pleasure. I lifted up sheet after sheet. As I looked over the days to come I felt a sense of pride in our roster of clients like Columbia Records, 20th Century Fox, or the world's #1 jingle house, HEA Productions. I saw the names of artists from Bo Diddley to Barry Manilow, movies like *The Godfather* and *Carrie,* and million-dollar products like Chevrolet.

Along the left hand column of each session Tony would draw a line to indicate the hours for the date, but the allotted time usually wasn't nearly enough. Sessions were notorious for going over. I can't count the number of times I disappointed friends and lovers by saying I'd meet them for dinner and a movie at eight and then wouldn't show up till the wee small hours of the morning. It was the rule more than the exception and if my girlfriend couldn't swing with it, the relationship was doomed.

The name of the senior mixer would be in a circle in the middle. Finally, at the top, he'd put in the name of the assistant engineer. That's where I would find my name.

I'd get a warm buzz looking at the names of the people coming in to work, and it was especially fun to see "Berger" on as many sessions as possible.

This reminds me of a story I once heard about the great departed comedian George Burns, who performed 'til he was 99. When someone asked how we was doing, he'd say, "I'm booked!" Seeing my name on those pages meant everything was all right.

As I turned to the page for August 18th, 1975, I saw that in our premier room, A-1, the client was Reprise Records. The time booked was 4 PM to 6 PM with an extra hour in case we went over. A feeling of awe came over me as I saw the artist's name: *Frank Sinatra.*

When I checked to see who would be engineering, I was a little surprised that Phil Ramone, my mad mentor, wasn't on the date. Rich Blakin, one of Phil's former disciples before I had become his #1 boy, was slated to sit behind the board. Phil was generously giving Rich a shot at the big time. He was like that, especially if he had something better to do.

Underneath Rich's name it said "Vocal O/D." This meant Frank would be coming in to add a vocal to a previously recorded instrumental track.

I looked to see who would be assisting. My name was at the top. Sinatra was coming in to sing and I was on the date. The feeling I had was akin to Moses approaching the burning bush: a mixture of gratitude, humility, and awe at the imminent presence of the deity.

I had to find Blakin. I tracked him down in what we called the "back forty," a hidden labyrinth of storage space behind the studios where we'd hang between dates.

"Hey, man, did you see we're doing Sinatra?" I said, in hushed astonishment.

Rich was more reserved. "Yeah. Actually, it's a little scary."

I knew what he was talking about. We'd all heard about Sinatra. This stuff was common knowledge among the cognoscenti. It wasn't that Frank was capricious. It was just that those who were superb demanded the same from everyone around them. He represented the extreme-sport end of recording: if you lost your grip, you could be maimed for the duration.

Everything we had trained for, all the torture we suffered at Ramone's hands, was on the line.

"This is the big test, Berger."

My stomach tensed at the words. If we could do Sinatra, we were the shit. We could pull off anything. But if not . . .

When the special day came, I put on a shirt and tie instead of my usual outfit of ripped jeans, tee-shirt, and sneakers. The *schlepper* didn't get paid much, but I did what I could to show the guy respect.

As usual, I got to the studio early. I made sure to be out of my previous session in plenty of time. I was the first one there. Rich, a fine engineer with impeccable integrity, showed up soon after me, way before the downbeat. There was no question but that we had to get it right for the Chairman of the Board.

We chose a lusciously warm tube U-47 for the microphone, a favorite of Frank's. By this time I knew how to move those behemoths on their Atlas booms with ease and grace, as Rich had taught me to do. I situated the mic in a spot where we would be able to see the singer from the control room but away from the reflective glass. I placed a simple stool in front of the mic and a music stand between the two, under the microphone. I set up some burlap-covered fiberglass baffles behind which Frank would be sitting so the sound wouldn't be too 'live' in that big room. I sat on the stool and adjusted the height of the mic and stand so there would be minimum fuss when the star arrived. I figured he was about as tall as me.

Rich thoughtfully suggested something a bit unusual. Considering Sinatra's reputation for not suffering fools and our desire to impress the king with our standard of excellence, we wanted to give him every option for happiness. In the old days, Sinatra would sing together with the orchestra. Everything would be recorded at once. Back then, you actually had to be able to be great on cue to be a recording star. But with the advent of multitrack recording, you could record instruments one at a time, and add the vocal later. Singers would listen to all the previously recorded instrumentation, and could sing over and over again, if they wanted, until they got the performance they found acceptable. In order to do this, they would listen to the prerecorded tracks while they sang along. Some singers liked to listen through headphones that covered both ears. Some liked to only cover one ear; it was easier to hear yourself that way, which could make it more likely that you'd stay on pitch. We wrapped both a two-sided headset and a single-sided one around the music stand, so Frank could have either option. In front of him, just behind the mic and a little to the side, we also placed a small cube-shaped speaker called an Auratone, in case he didn't want to use headphones at all. Having Frank listen through a speaker would not have been optimal because some of the pre-recorded music would "leak" into the vocal mic, but if that was what Ol' Blue Eyes wanted, we'd oblige.

I straightened out the cables from the mic and headphone box that plugged into the wall so they were neat and out of the way. I adjusted the lights to suffuse the area around the mic with a blend of warm colors that deepened the rich darkness of the large room around it, filled with the shadows and music vibrations from time past. For this guy, we would go classic.

Blakin, a fastidious man and one of my great teachers, stroked his beard, looked at my set-up, nodded, and said, "God is in the details."

Preceding Frank's arrival, a record company functionary delivered the multi-track tape. I opened the box to find the "track split," the sheet that indicated what instruments appeared on each track of the multi. It also listed the name of the song. It was "The Saddest Thing of All." The arranger of the tune was Gordon Jenkins, a Sinatra mainstay on many of his poignant ballads.

With a Sharpie on a masking tape strip beneath the faders of the "juke box," I notated which instrument would come up on which volume control.

Professional audiotapes were always stored end-first. To get to the take we'd be using, I rewound the 10-pound, 2" tape on the mammoth

Ampex MM-1000 16-track tape machine until I passed 2 strips of white "leader-tape." The first white strip, a few feet long, marked the end, and then, after several hundred feet of black magnetic tape, the second strip delineated the beginning, of the master recording we would be using for our vocal overdub. I stopped the machine at the top of the tune.

I pressed play and Rich turned one knob at a time to create a rough mix of the lush, orchestral arrangement of strings, woodwinds, and horns. He balanced the instruments, placed them across the stereo plane, and added reverb from our sweet echo chambers that lived seven stories below in the basement, next to the library where I once worked and suffered. Later, as Sinatra sang, if he chose to use headphones, Blakin would feed the live vocal, slathered in luscious echo, back into the cans, on top of the pre-recorded track, to inspire the greatest standard vocalist of all time to do his thing.

We followed our usual approach of having the minimal amount of electronic gear between his baritone and the tape. Microphone, pre-amp, that's it. Why screw around with this guy's voice unless you had to? Better to have the pure signal on tape. Once you committed to processing you couldn't remove it but if you had recorded the real deal you could always treat the sound anyway you wanted later. At the same time, just to be safe, we kept a Fairchild limiter, LA-4A compressor, and Neve Equalizer a patch cord away. Most singers needed a little help with their sound and we were there to provide whatever was necessary.

We checked all the gear three times. Everything was cool. We sat down to wait. That was the way we liked it. When the artist entered, we'd be nonchalant. We wanted to exude the professionalism that made it all look easy, just like Frank sounded when he sang. But underneath, we were on code red, the highest alert.

A roly poly Neapolitan-looking guy barreled into the control room. He quickly shook our hands and introduced himself as Don Costa, one of Sinatra's favorite musical arrangers and producers from that time, who was there to facilitate the process.

"Frank just left Jilly's and he'll be here in a few minutes," he said, as he hurriedly prepared the pages of the musical score that Sinatra would be using to reference the lyrics and melody.

Jilly's, a saloon just up the block on 52nd between Broadway and 8th, run by his friend Jilly Rizzo, was one of Frank's favorite hangs.

My adrenaline spiked when a massive gentleman with slick black hair and a threatening demeanor ambled into the control room to size up the joint. This was clearly Sinatra's bodyguard.

The large man was intimidating as intended and I would be sure to show him the appropriate deference. Hopefully, he wouldn't be brought into service if Frank was displeased with our choice of microphone.

In his raspy, Little Italy voice, he said, "Mr. Sinatra is about to arrive."

A few moments later, Frank strode jauntily into the A-1 control room. He was dressed in a well-tailored charcoal suit, his face broadened by waning middle-age, his graying toupee perfectly plausible. At sixty, he was the epitome of fluidity and confidence.

In the world's most recognizable voice, he said, "Good evening men!"

He was in fine fettle and appeared to be in a good mood. I saw Blakin take a deep breath. Maybe we'd be OK. Still, it was early. We couldn't let ourselves get overconfident. There was a long road ahead before we got the final take.

Then Frank said, "Let's go."

With a footman's hand motion and small bow, I opened the door that led out of the control room and into the studio. The bodyguard walked through first, then Costa and Blakin, and finally, Sinatra.

I led them into the air lock that separated the control room from the studio for sound-proofing purposes and pushed open the heavy door that took us into the grand recording room.

As Sinatra passed, he turned to me and said with derision, "I see you got rid of Mitch Miller's stink."

I had no idea what he was referring to, so I chuckled, guessing this was a joke. I knew enough to know that one always laughed at the emperor's asides. He raised an approving eyebrow and flashed the smile that had made a billion bobby-soxers swoon.

Later, I found out the story. Miller had been the head of "A and R" at Columbia Records in the 1950's when Sinatra was on that label. A and R stood for Artist and Repertoire. This was the cat who signed the artists and decided what material they would record. The gig was the most coveted spot in the record company hierarchy.

Though the studio I worked for was called A&R, it had nothing to do with this aspect of the business. It was simply the initials of the names of the two men who started the company, a business man named Jack Arnold, and of course, the inimitable Phil Ramone.

(One day, a young man who seemed quite befuddled came up to our studio and asked if he could play us a tape. I agreed, telling him there was nothing I could do with it but I'd be happy to listen. The tape was garbled and I soon realized that this guy was probably mentally ill. I asked why he had come up to our studio to play this tape and he said that he was told he should find the "A and R man." He assumed he would find him at A&R Studios. An honest mistake.)

Mitch Miller, who was the real "A and R man" in those days, had the job because he made enormously successful records even though his taste ran somewhere between the conventional and crap. He was a sucker for novelty tunes, songs with some kind of gimmick that made them stick in the mind of the lowest common denominator.

Among the many cringe-worthy tunes he tried to foist on Sinatra, Miller browbeat him into making a record of a song that featured barking dogs called "Mama Will Bark," sung as a duet with a large-breasted TV celebrity named Dagmar, who couldn't sing. This song is considered by many to be the nadir in Sinatra's canon, and marked a low-point in his popularity. Though by the time I was listening to him in the mid-'70s, when Sinatra could sometimes verge on making a parody of himself, he was generally a man of unerring, impeccable taste who made the most artistic recordings of his era. He found that barking record to be a great embarrassment. Thus cemented a lifetime of enmity between Sinatra and that A and R man named Mitch.

This very room we stood in, having once been Columbia's studio, was the place where Sinatra recorded during Miller's reign. It was here that he had sung with the starlet and the dogs. Hence the "Miller's stink" remark.

I only found out all that later as part of my ongoing musical education. For now, the leader of the Rat Pack sat on the stool and, being the ultimate professional, graciously allowed me to adjust the mic.

Rich asked which headphone or speaker he wanted to use. He said it didn't matter to him. He picked up the single-sided headset. I unplugged and removed the other headphone and pulled the small speaker out of the way.

Costa draped the chart over the music stand.

I followed Costa and Blakin out of the studio and almost bumped into the hefty bodyguard, my slight frame coming up about level to his protruding belly. If my heart had not already been beating at 160 bpm, it jumped another 30 or 40 in that second. I managed to roll around his gargantuan stomach and not touch him. I smiled obsequiously as I looked up at the towering figure and produced a small wave. He glowered. I scampered back into the control room.

Sinatra said, "I'll run it down for you one time so you can set levels."

Rich hit the talk back and said, "Great."

I hit play and "record." I had learned by now that you record everything, from the first run-through to the last take of the session. You never know when the magic will hit and, even though he said this was just for levels, if he asked afterwards if we'd recorded it, we'd want our answer to be yes.

Watching the meters and Blakin's hand, we were both astonished. Sinatra was able to increase his volume and intensity while the needle hardly moved. How could he do that?

With most singers, we needed to be deft with the "pot" or potentiometer, the knob with which we controlled the recording volume. If the singer got loud, we would turn the knob down so the tape wouldn't be saturated and cause distortion. If the singer got too soft, we would turn the knob up so the signal would not be too scant and buried in the floor-level of noise that was on all analog recording tape. If we did not trust our hands to do the job well enough, we would patch in that technical device called a limiter, or a compressor, which electrically narrowed a signal's dynamic range. This device would lower the highest volumes, and in the case of the compressor, increase the lowest ones. It turned out that, with Sinatra, the job for Blakin was easy. He barely needed to nudge the dial at all.

We watched Sinatra to figure out how he did it. Listening to his own vocals through the headphones, he carefully and subtly moved toward the mic during the softer passages and moved away from it during the louder parts. He "rode" his own levels according to how close to, or far from, the microphone he stood. In this way, while his intensity would increase, the recording volume stayed within the narrow range that the equipment liked best. This is called good mic technique, and I've never seen anyone use it as effectively as Frank.

Watching Sinatra sing, I thought about his importance in the history of music. While there were many factors, I mused, that made him such a phenomenon, it wasn't until now that I realized that one of them was the way in which he used recordings and the microphone.

Just a few years before Sinatra, there had been no mics, amplifiers, sound systems, or recordings. As a result, most singers learned, as central to their technique, projection. That was a big part of what determined their vocal quality. You can hear what I mean by listening to opera. While that kind of singing limits emotional subtlety and can even sound false today, at the time it was necessary in order to reach the cheap seats of the great concert halls so everyone could hear the words over the pounding orchestra.

Remnants of that style can be heard even in early recordings by belter Al Jolson or crooner Rudy Vallee, who were the big popular singing stars before Sinatra. You can hear the style changing and becoming more real with America's next huge vocalist, Bing Crosby. Recording made it possible for people to sing in a more natural style because they didn't have to project in the same way. The vocal was amplified electronically on stage and the balance between vocalist and orchestra could be manipulated in the studio. At home, people listened with their ears by the speakers and turned up the music as loud as they wanted.

By using impeccable mic technique and taking full advantage of the recording medium, Sinatra created an intimate effect where it sounded like he was singing only to you, whispering directly into your ear. It is incredibly sexy. Sinatra was the ultimate modern vocalist. He changed our sense of what vocals were meant to sound like. His emotional directness made everything that came before it seem overwrought. He was an everyman, a kid from the street, the son of immigrants, a hot, skinny Italian guy lying next to you in bed, seducing you. That is, he embodied the American male of the World War II generation, the guy you hoped would come home alive from the war and make a baby with you.

And there I was, the son of a man from that era, looking through the glass, at *the man*.

My reverie was broken when the song ended.

Sinatra said, "Did you get what you need?"

Blakin said, "It's perfect, Mr. Sinatra."

"Well, let's do it then."

I rewound the tape to the top while Sinatra waited patiently. When I got there, Blakin gave me the nod and I hit "record" and play again, saving the first vocal on one track and recording the second on another.

Sinatra finished the song a second time. When he was done, Costa hit the talkback and said, "Sounds great, Frank."

The Voice took off his headphone and walked into the control room. He said, "Let's do a playback."

We listened together silently with the reverence that always befits such moments.

Sinatra's rendering was stellar. In 1975 he was certainly past his prime. His voice shook at moments but this only added poignancy to the lyrics of loss and time gone by. This touching song, written by Michel Le Grand and interpreted by the consummate master, resonated with what the Spanish called *duende*, a magical quality that comes from aging and pain and is suffused with an awareness of death.

As the melancholic French horns announced the arrival of the chorus, Frank sang Carl Sigman's poetic lyrics of the sadness of our lives when we are haunted by our hurts, our losses, and when our dreams no longer have any chance of coming true.

As I listened, I thought of my dad who had died at age 49 a few years before, a guy who looked a bit like a Jewish version of Frank. He would have loved to know that I got to sit in a room with Frank Sinatra, got to hit the "record" button for this guy, got to adjust his microphone. We were an audience of four: Costa, Frank's bodyguard, Blakin, and me. My dad would have loved that. But my old man was gone, and he would never know. The *duende* hit me, and my eyes brimmed with tears.

The track came to its end. I hit stop. Frank nodded and smiled. Most singers would worry a track like this for many hours, days, or weeks. But not Frank. He nailed it in one take. The whole thing was over in half an hour.

He walked over to Blakin and me. He shook our hands and said thank you. He turned and walked toward the control room door, followed by Costa and the big fella, and was gone.

Rich and I had hung with a lot of stars. On the average day, we no longer had to fake the cool. Whoever was behind the glass, it was usually just another day's work. But this was *Sinatra*. We looked at each other, both shook our heads, and said, "Wow!"

And then we busted into grins. "We did it!" We'd survived. Like the master Japanese calligraphers who after decades of practice would produce their masterwork in an instant, our years of hard work paid off. We had achieved the pinnacle. Frank Sinatra, the toughest, most demanding, magnificent son-of-a-bitch in the business, had walked out a satisfied client.

Now what? We had nothing left to do. We expected the session to go over by at least a few hours. So we rolled a fat one and breathed in deep. Blakin committed a 1/4" rough mix to tape for posterity and we listened back dozens of times to our day's work, each time amazed at the nuances we found that we hadn't noticed before, happy to be alive.

Frank had taken our game to a whole new level. This was the reason we were all there. We put up with all the lunacy for moments like this. In the end, for us, it wasn't about the size of the celebrity. It was about the beauty and the greatness of the artist.

Now I sit here, a guy almost as old as Sinatra was when he sang that song, remembering that moment and the dreams of mine that have been lost in the time that has passed since then. I can hear my father's voice, and Frank's, but they live now only in my memory, and that's the saddest thing of all.

TRACK THIRTEEN

All That Bob Fosse

ACT ONE: THE MEETING

SCENE ONE:

The Studio

The lofty room was silent and dim, except for one pale light illuminating the cluster of Atlas microphone stands. The tall booms, with cylindrical microphones hanging off the top connector, made them look like a weird, metallic family of giraffes, snoozing on the veldt. The smaller mic stands, with their triangular bases, were arranged symmetrically, the children of the larger creatures. Thick, dusty, black microphone cables, neatly coiled, hung on the mic stands' boom knobs. Green metal chairs were obediently folded and stacked against the wall. Black music stands were lined up next to them, as if waiting for their chance at the big time.

The squeak and bang of the manual elevator's metal accordion door broke the silence. A tall black man with close cropped salt and pepper hair in an olive-green uniform walked down the back hallway. This was Reverend Blalock, the janitor and elevator operator, about to enter Recording Studio A-1, the crown jewel of A&R Studios, one of the best recording studios in the world.

He opened the heavy, sound-proofed doors and flicked the row of light switches on the wall, one at a time. With each, the fluorescents illuminated sections of the room. First to be lit was the rhythm section area to the right, with its raised platforms and amps for the bass and electric guitars and a square for the drums, walled in by baffles. Furthest to the rear-right was the percussion corner. At the back of the room was the large vocal booth and a smaller booth. These rooms within the larger room were used to isolate musicians and singers with sounds too delicate to record amid the blare of the band. Above the booth was a large movie screen. Then off to the rear left, the violin area and, next to that, opposite the drum platform, was the place where the celli, violas, and orchestral basses did their thing. Following the circle to the door where Blalock stood was the area for the harp and French horns. Next to that, in the part closest to the glass of the control room, was the Hammond B-3 organ and the room's ebony jewel, the seven-foot Steinway grand. The clock on the far wall read 8 a.m.

The Reverend wheeled his bucket of soapy water into the room and began to mop the light pine floor. The swish of the mop and the occasional splash of water provided the first rhythm of the day.

A short man in a rumpled suit entered the studio, carrying a black leather bag. He had a large head shaped like Charlie Brown's with a single tuft of scraggly, mousy hair. His lips were frozen in a permanent grimace, and he mumbled as he shuffled anxiously into the room, dwarfed by the huge space with its thirty-foot peaked ceiling.

This was Willie Lanin, the old piano tuner.

Willie was one of ten boys. His brother, Lester, was a famous society bandleader. Willie was musical, too, but without the luck of looks or charm, he was relegated to this humbler task behind the scenes.

He walked over to the piano, pushed up the lid, and placed a stick under the cover to keep it open. Sitting down on the piano bench, he placed his bag at his side, and unpacked it. He set a black cube on the corner of the piano, plugged a power cord from the box into an outlet on the floor, flipped the "on" switch, and an orange half-circle glowed in the center of the gizmo. He pulled out a piano lever and a set of rubber mutes from the bag, and placed them on top of the piano. He put the mutes into some strings, placed the lever over a pin, put his foot on the piano's pedal, and struck a piano key. The first note of the day had been sounded, adding melody to the rhythm of the Reverend's swishing mop. The orange circle sprang to life with a pattern of black bars bouncing back and forth, going in and out of focus. He twisted the pin and hit the note again. This time, it sounded a little flatter. Again, and this time sharper. When the rotating bars became clear and still, he moved on to the next string.

As Willie moved up the scale, his banal melody was suddenly interrupted.

"Blalock, I'm gonna get you!" Plotnik, a large Jew with curly, dark hair on his head and a wild hair up his ass, stood at the studio door with a demonic grin on his face. He would be running the film for today's date. Blalock picked up his mop and, in mock rage, charged at Plotnik. For a minute, in a game they played every morning, they chased each other around the studio—Blalock in his green cleaning-man's outfit, and Plotnik, with his heavy bones and fat ass jiggling. Out of breath, they collapsed in laughter, hugged, and then feigned fury, before separating to return to their respective mundane tasks.

Plotnik repaired to the duplication room behind the studio and climbed the short flight of wooden stairs to the small projection booth, where he found the pile of metal canisters filled with the rough-cut cues we would be scoring that day.

At 8:30, Chuck arrived. He was my assistant, the set-up man. He was a chubby twenty-year-old black guy with long sideburns. He pushed the conductor's podium on its raised platform out into the middle of the room and placed the booking sheet, with the info for the day's set-up, on top of it.

He wheeled seven mic stands over to the drums and set up three chairs and three music stands for the trumpets in a semi-circle right in front of the podium. He then placed five chairs and stands in a row in front of the vocal booth for the flute, clarinet, alto, tenor, and baritone saxes. Completing the section, he set up three chairs for the trombones on the other side of the podium, facing the winds.

Chuck listened to Willie mumble to himself as he tuned the piano. He knew that the black box with the spinning orange wheel was the electronic device Willie used to keep the pitch accurate. Willie's ears weren't what they once were, and he depended on this clunky device to keep his tuning honest. Chuck decided to have some fun. He snuck close to the piano and started to hum the note Willie was working on, but slightly off-key. The wheels spun crazily, and Willie couldn't get the bars to line up, which signaled that he could not find the center of the note. Willie couldn't figure out why his electronic tuner was going haywire. His mumbling got louder. When he realized Chuck had been messing with his head, he started to yell.

"What the hell you doin' that for? Ah yah . . ."

Chuck laughed and put his hand on Willie's shoulder. "I'm just goofin' on ya, old man."

Willie grumbled and went back to work.

A new layer of the orchestration was added with the arrival of Kenny, the delivery man from Carroll Music, the music instrument rental company. He wheeled the xylophone, glockenspiel, marimba, bass marimba, temple blocks, and two large, black containers filled with hand percussion to the rear right corner, next to the guitars. Then he and an assistant unveiled three electronic keyboards and set them up around the piano: a Fender Rhodes electric piano, a Roxichord, and a Clavinette.

The newest *schlepper* arrived to stock the control room and, like all good dreamers, took a moment to stand at the threshold of the recording room, enviously watching Chuck work, hoping to be him one day.

A bull of a man with a handlebar moustache, Bobby Flynn the maintenance guy, burst into the control room, harried as usual. He slammed the alignment tape of tones on the two-inch machine to set it to optimal recording quality.

Nine o'clock marked the arrival of the senior mixer, the star of the technical side of this show, the guy who would be flying this starship to heaven. That would be me. I swaggered in, confident and pumped, dressed in a white jumpsuit, with the words *Elton John-1975 Tour* embroidered on the back in blue, a gift from Bernie Taupin, Elton's first lyricist, when we had worked together on a demo for a singer named Karon Bihari. My red hair was now coiffed late seventies-style, narrow on the sides, high and curly on top. To top the look off, I wore green glasses.

As I watched the pre-session activity, I took in a deep breath. All these people were now working for me. I had made it. I was at the top of my game. I was twenty-three years old. The year was 1979, and by that time, I was most definitely a major cat. I was doing a huge film date. This was the first session for the new musical by the multiple-award-winning choreographer/director Bob Fosse. It was going to be called *All That Jazz*, and I was the recording engineer of record.

I checked out Chuck's work in the studio. He knew what mics and set-up I liked. I straightened some chairs and microphones so they were precisely parallel and evenly spaced. With everything balanced and aligned, I signaled my approval and walked into the control room. Plotnik was hollering down from his perch: "Putz! Could you patch in the audio? I'm gonna come down there and give you a nootzle!"

The maintenance guy bent over the quarter-inch machine, turning a screw, trying to get the needle to hold still at "0 VU." "Fuck off, Plotnik! Why don't you suck my dick!"

I sat at the console. My console, now. I ran my hand along the leather strip at the bottom of the desk. Chuck ran into the control room, and I got out of his way. He placed the strip of masking tape under the row of faders and notated with a black Sharpie which microphone was plugged into which input. I wrote out a track sheet, determining which mics would be assigned to which tracks.

At the board, I pushed up one fader at a time, rotating the preamp to one o'clock, as Chuck walked through the mics, saying "check" into each one.

I patched in the electronic metronome, the click track, so it would play through the cans. Chuck checked to see that every player had a set of headphones and listened to the rhythmic tock to make sure that all the cans were functioning as well. The click track would keep the players at the correct tempo so the arranger's scores matched the film, as he intended.

As we got closer to the downbeat I could feel my adrenaline rise. Then Emile Charlap, the copyist and contractor, came in. Charlap was the classic irascible guy with the heart of gold. He had the posture of someone who spent too many hours at a desk with a calligraphy pen in his hand. His shoulders stooped, and his head hung in front of his body. He spoke from his throat, in an Italian-American accent with a breathy rasp.

In those days, every musical part needed to be written out by hand. That was the job of the copyist. Emile would personally translate the arranger's chicken scratches into a gorgeous master score with the twirl of clefs, the key signatures with their flats and sharps, the notes, rests, and dynamic markings. He hired a number of down-on-their-heels musicians to copy out the rest of the individual musical parts. For a big date like this, with a rhythm section, brass, woodwinds, and percussion, that would be over twenty copying jobs for every cue in the film, some of which were two or three minutes long.

Emile walked around the studio, placing a copied part on the music stand in front of each musician's chair. He took the master score and unfolded it on the conductor's podium.

The final notes of the piano now tuned, Willie took a moment to luxuriate in the sound of the luscious instrument. He played a bit of a Beethoven piano sonata. No one ever paid attention to the poor piano tuner but for this moment we all stopped and listened. We could sense for that moment emanating from within this little, ugly man with the big head and the funny voice the beauty of his soul and the yearning of his heart as his playing rang out from the wondrous Steinway and reverberated against the walls of the grand studio. He closed his eyes as he played, no doubt imagining himself on stage, playing the great repertoire. But then, as if realizing the truth that he would never be the guy on the date, he stopped and sighed. It was his task to prepare the instrument but never to play it for the crowd. And besides, he had more pianos to tune that day. He packed up his wares in his black leather doctor's bag and, as the musicians arrived, waddled inconspicuously out of the studio.

Now the musicians on the gig started wandering in. The room, silent and slumbering just hours before, came to life with sound. Barry Lazarowitz, the young drummer with a floppy moustache, went over to the kit and we kibitzed while I placed the mics in precise positions. I zipped back into the control room to set levels and get sounds as he tuned the tom-toms.

The legendary trumpeter Marky Markowitz sat in the center chair of the horn section. He was booked on this date due to his expertise at playing the rowdy, mid-west, strip-club gutbucket style that was popular in the 1930s and which would be prominently featured on this soundtrack. His cheeks red with the burst capillaries that never healed from spending his life blowing hard on his brass mouthpiece, he had a perpetual grin on his face. He pulled out his horn and mutes, placed his mouthpiece in his axe, and started to warm up with arpeggios.

Soon, the room became a palette of musical colors: the goose-like glissandi calls of the clarinets; the dark farts of the bones; the thud of the kick drum; the wacka-wacka of the electric guitars; the stanky funk of the Clavinette.

I was busy now, getting sounds where I could. A slight fellow with sweet blue eyes and a sprout of white hair and moustache bounded into the control room. He glowed with enthusiasm. It was Ralph Burns, the musical composer and arranger for the film.

Emile pulled Ralph toward me. Emile was not only the copyist. He was also the contractor. That meant that he was responsible for selecting and hiring the appropriate musicians for the date. He also picked the engineer. He had had a long, close relationship with Burns. When Ralph asked Emile to recommend an engineer, he had suggested me. "Berger, this is Ralph Burns. Be nice to him. He's a good guy. Ralph, this is your young hot-shot engineer, Glenn Berger." I shook Ralph's hand. We smiled at each other. I felt an immediate simpatico vibe between us.

Ralph said, "Yeah, man!" and chuckled. "Emile says good things about you, man. I'm looking forward to this!" He crackled with energy.

My heart swelled with excitement and pride, and I exclaimed, "Me, too!" This cat was a legend. He'd been around for decades, writing jazz hits for Woody Herman, playing with Charlie Barnet and Stan Getz, composing for Aretha Franklin, doing string arrangements for Ray Charles, including his classic "Georgia on My Mind." Among lots of other awards, he'd won the Oscar for his score for Fosse's smash hit film, Cabaret.

"Hey, man, let's make sure we catch some of that great Italian food down at Ponte Vecchio in the Village, OK?"

Arrangers were the best, and I dug Ralph right away. He was cool.

It started to hit me that this was going to be good. I loved film and recording and now I had a chance to work on a huge musical movie with a big band and a great arranger. This was my kind of thing. Film dates were demanding. There was no time for dilly-dallying—you had to get stuff down on tape right and fast. The clock was ticking with a lot of union scale out in the room. The pressure would be on, and it was live or die. This was going to be fun!

SCENE TWO:

Meeting Bob Fosse

Everything was checked and double-checked. We were ready to rock. I watched the clock as it moved closer to the ten o'clock downbeat. Now, there was only one person missing.

The door opened to the control room. The energy coming off the guy who entered was so intense it felt like the camera zoomed in for a close up with everyone around him going out of focus.

He was dressed all in black. Black shit-kicker boots, tight jeans, a black button-down shirt, with a few buttons open, and a black vest on top of that. The only objects that broke the black were a silver metal whistle around his neck and a white cigarette dangling off his bottom lip.

There was an immediate hush in the control room. Chuck and I stole a look at each other and nodded. Burns, who was talking details with Charlap, sensed the star entering the room, too. He turned, and said, "Bob! Great to see you!" I could tell Ralph was excited, nervous, eager-to-please, and somewhat in awe. He walked over and they hugged warmly.

"Bob! Let me introduce you to our engineer. This here is Glenn Berger. He is the man right now."

He smiled a beautiful, radiant, sexy smile, and extended a hand for a shake. I knew it right away. I thought, *This is Bob Fosse*. And then, *Wow, this guy is deep*. In that moment, it was like nothing else in the world existed, except for him.

For endless seconds we held eye contact. He was balding, with a golden-brown and greying beard. He had an Irish pixie face, with piercing blue eyes. His winning smile shifted to a pre-occupied seriousness. His lithe body was bent in the shape of a question mark, as if his entire being was asking the question, "Whaddya think?" There was something slightly imploring in his expression. He looked deep in my eyes, scrutinizing me, the way someone would look at his heart surgeon before allowing them to put in the knife. Would I be able to keep him alive? In a soft, high warm voice, he said, "Hi. Nice to meet ya."

This dude was a klieg light of charisma. Through his handshake I was instantly filled with the energy of the universe, what the ancient Chinese called the "floodlike Ch'i."

I didn't really know what it meant to be working with Bob Fosse. I didn't know that he was the only guy at that time to have won an Emmy, Tony, and Oscar, all in the same year. I didn't realize he was the guy who won the Best Director Oscar, beating out Coppola the year he made *The Godfather*. I didn't know that he'd won eight Tonys for choreography and had invented an entire style of dance that would influence that art form for decades to come. But somehow, I knew I was in the presence of brilliance.

I could tell right away that all the music-biz characters I'd met 'til then were small fry — immature kids. A film director was different. Fosse was a towering figure. He was magnificent.

He looked around and quietly said to me, "Where's the screen?"

I pointed out into the studio through the glass, straight across from where we stood — I on one side of the console, he on the other.

Politely, he asked, "Can I have a chair? Anything will do." I walked to his side of the console and grabbed one.

"Right here." He sat down as close to the glass as possible, as close to the screen as he could get, under the giant studio monitors. He clearly wasn't interested in what he would hear; he was singularly focused on what he would see. He lit a cigarette, faced the blank screen, and waited.

As he stared at the screen with a preternatural intensity, I felt this powerful longing for him to approve of me, to notice me, to like me, to — no, I couldn't think it — even love me.

I just wanted to look at him, but I knew I had a gig to do. The clock's big hand hit the twelve. It was ten o'clock: downbeat. Ralph stood on the riser, in front of the conductor's podium, opened up his score, and raised his baton.

The room went quiet. You could feel the anticipation. Ralph said, "OK. Six beats. From the top. Let's go!"

After a few rehearsals, which gave me a chance to balance the entire band, I turned to my assistant. "Roll tape!" Chuck hit the multi, and he also recorded a rough mix on the quarter-inch machine.

I hit the talk back and slated. "Cue one, take one."

I grabbed the intercom and screamed at Plotnik, "Roll film!"

I heard him stomp across the little room above and behind me. "Alright, Berger!"

Then I heard the big motor slowly start to turn and pick up steam with the characteristic thirty-frames-per-second clickety-clack of the film's sprocket holes being grabbed by the machine's gears.

My finger was on the button to start the click machine. Timing was everything now. A black and white clip started to run on the screen. First three white dots, one after the other, and then a double set of white dots. I started to count in my head, *one, two, three.* On the fourth beat, when the double circles came, I hit the click.

Immediately, Ralph counted off. "One, Two, three, four, One AND!" He lowered his baton, and the band hit.

The cats were hot. Great readers, they were precise from the start. My hands flew over the faders, adjusting levels, blending the instruments, getting the headphone mix right. The complex arrangement of horns, winds, rhythm section, and percussion kept me busy. Fosse squinted at the screen, the ash dangling off the end of his cigarette butt. Ralph conducted, keeping the band in sync, with one eye on the screen, making sure that the musical accents hit the right events at the right time in the film. The cue came to an end.

To Plotnik: "Stop film! Rewind to the top!"

To Chuck: "Hold tape!"

Then Ralph, from the studio, "Playback!"

I flipped a switch on the console and flew around to the quarter-inch machine that had the rough mix. I hit rewind and gave the motor a boost, twirling the left reel with my finger. I edged the head-cover toward the tape heads just close enough so I could hear the sound of the tape rewinding over the heads, but not so close that the sound would screech and hurt your ears. When I heard the garbled sound stop, I hit fast-forward to slow the tape down and ran my fingers over the take-up reel, to act as a manual brake. I stopped the tape and hit play. When I got to the top of Ralph's count, I hit stop, and rocked the tape across the heads so that when I hit play it would begin precisely on his first word. We didn't have fast rewind for the film, so we had to wait for Plotnik to get the cue to the top. Ralph came into the control room.

On the intercom, to Plotnik: "Roll as soon as you're ready!"

"Don't pressure me, Berger!"

"Move it, fat man!"

Plotnik hit the start button, and again the film began to play. I watched the white circles, and counted, and on the fourth, hit play. Perfect. Right on cue. The music matched the film like a dream. I was on. The drums popped, the horns were clean. The balance was full and transparent. Ralph turned to me with a smile, and nodded. He turned to Bob. Fosse whispered in his ear.

I heard Ralph say, "Oh, oh, yeah, got it, sure." He went back out into the studio and scribbled some notes on his score and gave directions to the band.

We did another take, the music and performance better. These were the best studio musicians in the world. Their sound was fat, their rhythm was tight, their pitch perfect. And, they could swing.

Playback. I was at the peak of my powers, the flower and the glory of my youth. I was fast and flawless, skilled and experienced, confident, sure, arrogant even. I danced around the control room with my jazz and tap moves, flying through the air, my hands and fingers deft, my timing precisely on the beat. Gliding and twirling to the quarter-inch machine, moving with brilliant speed, landing at the precise mark, I did a *chai'nes,* a pivot step, and a *pas de bourree.'*

I had the giddy feeling of mastery, when everything works because you are sure that it will. I tweaked the balance so you could hear every contrapuntal part with exquisite clarity. I found the magical mix that makes the music dance out of the speakers.

After the playback I beamed at Fosse. He smiled and said, "Nice." I was in.

I felt the camaraderie of being a cat; picked by the best, accepted by the elite corps, it meant I was one of the best. I was the youngest prodigy in town, twenty-three years-old and working on a surefire Oscar-winning hit movie.

The job that was to fill the next year of my life had begun. I knew that I was working on a once-in-a-lifetime project. I had achieved the skill where I could record and mix anything, and this movie stretched every limit, demanded it all.

This would turn out to be the greatest project of my career. But there was a crash to come. Little did I know in that first session that it would also expose my greatest flaw, which would lead to a catastrophe that I would regret for the rest of my life. In those early moments, I glowed with the magnificence that comes before the fall, the glorious innocence (and ignorance) of hubris.

ACT TWO: DANCIN' WITH THE DEVIL

SCENE ONE:

Temptation

Film dates like *All That Jazz* were union gigs, and we had to follow the rules. We cut tracks from ten to one, took a one-hour lunch break, and recorded again from two to five. I didn't have a nighttime session that day, so I got to leave at a decent hour. I took the M-5 uptown bus to my Upper West Side apartment on 80th Street between West End and Riverside. New York was about to become gentrified into a haven for the rich, but it hadn't quite yet. Side by side on this one block you could find middle class apartments, gorgeous townhouses, and welfare hotels.

My girlfriend Ivy and I lived in a renovated townhouse, cut up into apartments. The owner, a failed actor who somehow had managed to put together the dough to purchase the architectural masterpiece, decorated it in a mock medieval style, and supported his acting habit by renting out the upper floors.

I sat at my desk in the living room of our little two-room apartment. Its southern, street-facing wall was dominated by two floor-to-ceiling French doors in the shape of gothic arches with small, wrought-iron lattice panes and balcony railings.

The sun began to descend over the Hudson River, to the right, casting parallelograms of orange light on the room's walls. I placed the album cover of John Lennon's *Walls and Bridges* on the desk. I opened the desk drawer and pulled out a bag of weed and Bambu rolling papers. I shooed our big black cat, Familiar, off the desk. I crumbled some of the sticky, fluffy buds onto the cover and separated out the unusually large white seeds. This was one of the first crops of locally grown cannabis indica. It was the deepest pot I'd ever smoked.

I was finally cool enough to have my very own Greenwich Village pot dealer, known to us only as CJ. His pad on Leroy Street was a coveted hang. His witch girlfriend read some Tarot cards while freaks with long, kinky hair and plushy beards played mandolins and Dobros. Once, while waiting for CJ to weigh my stuff, I absentmindedly stuck my hand in the crevice of the couch and found a bag marked "Panama Red, 1971." Legendary. The shit I was buying was thirty bucks an ounce.

I could roll with the best of 'em. I was practiced. I licked two papers together and placed the crushed leaves into a well I'd made. I spun deftly between thumbs and forefingers, licked the glue, rolled it into a joint, and stuck the whole thing in my mouth to moisten. I sat back, lit a match, squinted my eyes, and inhaled deep.

One hit, and my mind began to expand. My pupils dilated, and the colors got brighter. The doors started opening in my head. I began to lift off the ground. I reveled in the reality that I was working on a major motion picture with one of the top directors in the world. This movie was going to be huge. As the drug passed the brain-barrier, I indulged a very pleasant fantasy. I saw myself on stage at the Academy Awards. I'd thank Bob for the opportunity, and my mom, who would be watching on her TV back in Brooklyn. Yes. I could feel the wanting deep in my belly. Once I had that, I would have it all. Then I had to acknowledge that it would never happen. The guy who recorded the music didn't win those awards. But I'd give anything for that one moment.

Suddenly I felt very high. The previous seven years seemed to descend on me in an instant. I had to lie down, so I stretched out on the Persian rug on the floor.

Sinking into the carpet, a warm feeling filled my belly as I pictured Fosse. Now here was someone I wish I could be like! He was brilliant, won every award, fucked the most gorgeous chicks. It could be fun to be . . . A thought popped into my head that I hadn't dared indulge before. I could be famous. Shit, look at what I'd done by age twenty-three! I wanted it. I could taste it. But how? What would I need to do to make it happen? The answer descended on me. Of course. It was simple. I just needed the guts. That's what I saw around me: artists who were cold enough to stay in the studio all night even if it pissed off their wife; who had no compunction about torturing their fellow man by making them play that part all night long; who had the chutzpah to rip off a good friend's idea and take credit for it.

All I had to do was get the brass cullions to say fuck it to love, my health, damn, my life, to get what I wanted, to get the only thing I really wanted. I felt a flash of embarrassment realizing that I wanted something as shallow as fame. No, that wasn't it. I wanted achievement, success, *greatness*.

But was that all it took? Wasn't there such a thing as talent? Who was to say that I had that? *Maybe I'll just suck, screw up my whole life and end up with nothing. Isn't that what happens to most people?*

Then I heard a voice in my head that I barely dared to listen to. *You've got the magic, Berger! Think about it! You're twenty-three years old and you've made it with Bob Fosse!*

That was too scary. *Bullshit.*

Besides, I wasn't sure if I was willing to make the requisite sacrifices. Was I willing to tell my girlfriend to go fuck herself? I wished I was willing to kill for my work, I knew that was the secret, but sacrificing my love? That was a big price.

But it sure would be nice to win that Academy Award . . .

I could feel a shudder pass through my body. I stood up and walked over to the desk. *I'm not going to relinquish love! All you need is love, that's what John taught me.* I lifted up the album cover, forgetting it was covered with weed, and the leaves flew all over the room. "Shit!"

The room started to spin. I had to lie down again. I couldn't shut up the argument in my head.

You can live a long life of bourgeois, ordinary reality. Kids spitting up on you, maybe a tear at their wedding, if you are lucky and you don't croak like your father, maybe even a grandkid on your knee, that is, if your children don't forsake you. You can have a house in the suburbs, two cars, a nice wife, grow old together, watch each other wrinkle, eventually you start to drool, and it all ends pathetically. You'll struggle and scrimp and save, live honestly, and even feel good about yourself, until you realize you never really fulfilled your potential. But by then, it'll be too late. And you'll have your love. Or you get a few amazing years. You live everything to excess. You live hard. You push yourself to every limit. You go where no one else goes. Yeah, you die young. But you get to suck the marrow out of this bone of a universe. You live an extraordinary life. You fuck more people in those years than most people fuck in lifetimes. Your heart beats more times, you have those moments of superhuman achievement, when you wield a kind of power reserved for just a few mortals. You've got something to say and an obligation to say it! Yes, there will be fear, pain, and humiliation, but there will also be victory, acco-

lades, awards. You will be recognized, you will get the cheers for moving the multitudes. You will bring pleasure to a pain-besotted world, and you will receive the laurels for it. And at the end of it all, you're annihilated. That's all. Just like everyone else.

Wait. I shook my head, like trying to wake myself from the fantasy's spell. *It's all one goddamn lie, this whole show biz thing! It's a lie! Don't get suckered in!*

But what if this is my one chance? What if I say no now, and then I regret it? Then I'll be too old. What if I live a life of regret? Now is my one and only moment to be young, at the peak of my powers. Now is the time to make the commitment, to break through. You get one shot. Blow this one, and it is gone forever. Forever. Grab the world by the balls now, baby, 'cause you'll never be able to again. Don't you realize that so few are chosen? Don't you comprehend the golden opportunity you are getting right now? Don't you see?

I could feel the fear and desire coursing through my being as the huge sun, setting over the Hudson River, burnished the room.

SCENE TWO:
Ivy

I opened my eyes and saw Ivy as she turned on all the lights in the living room. I was still lying on the floor.

"You're home early, aren't you?" she said.

I began to answer, "I, I must've passed out. I had such a weird . . ."

But while I was speaking, I could tell Ivy wasn't listening. She just went on. "What is that strange smell?"

She was right. There was a weird odor. It wasn't just the weed. It was more like burning trash.

"I *hate* this place," she ranted. "This city is so disgusting! The filth… the whole city stinks like garbage…I just got hassled on the street by some asshole. I can't stand it anymore! When are we going to get out of here?"

t me down. Ivy sat down on the
"I don't know what you see in this

nywhere that you can't find here? I
ere in the world, and he chose New

ou don't even know that the rest of

e I knew she was right. "What do
ttle flower in a suburb in Wisconsin.
round writing poetry half the time?"
k her luxurious, dark hair, and
implored me with her huge, sensu-
urope. Just promise me right now

d! OK! I'll go! I'll go!" But deep
cy that led to my grumbling. I had
l and envied Ivy's cultured intelli-

ntensity coming off her so fierce
d, without a hint of sarcasm, and
her face, jumped up, and twirled

d, "Wanna go to the movies?
zz Singer and *Damn Yankees*."
hed by Fosse, was about a guy
a star, and *The Jazz Singer* is a
ake it in show biz. I gulped at

;ot up, smiled wickedly, and
nd best friend.

SION

rough on my

ly blew my
s in such full
grainy black
n the post-
hreadbare
was not how it
nning archi-
ized. As we
n as the City,
ivilizations had

ouw, a white
of a fairy tale.
Concert." Ivy
ite tickets with
.

the magical
ies picknicking
of the floor
d a huge bar-

ACT THREE: THE FATEFUL DECI

SCENE ONE:

The Trip To Europe

I got a break in recording in the spring and, following th
promise, we booked our trip to Europe.

When we got off the plane in London, the city complete
mind. It was true. I was provincial. I was shocked to see it wa
color and bustling. I had been so certain that Europe was in
and white, like I'd seen in such movies as *The Third Man* fron
World War Two era, bombed out, with starving children in
coats rummaging through the rubble in the streets. But that
was at all. It was clean and safe, with stylish graphics and stu
tecture. I didn't think a city could be like this. It was . . . civi
toured the Roman ruins of the earliest part of London know
it penetrated my small mind that entire, highly developed c
existed there for thousands of years.

In Amsterdam, we visited the plaza of the Concertgeb
and gold neo-classical concert hall that seemed straight out
Above the entrance to the hall a prominent sign read "Free
and I could see people handing the door attendant large wl
ornate gold print. I asked the man how one got such ticket

He said, "You want some?"

I nodded. He handed me two and invited us in.

I was entranced and confused as we wandered inside
main hall. There were no seats, just small tables, with fami
and couples dining and drinking Heinekens. In the middl
a crowd of children along with a few grownups surrounde

rel organ. A round man with a moustache that looked like it had been shellacked to his face, in a funny hat, a black and white striped shirt, and suspenders holding up old tuxedo pants, turned the wheel on the mechanical device, causing a carousel-like tune to emanate from the big wooden wheezer. I wandered toward the gathering, appreciating the charming scene. While he rotated the musical contraption, folks around the floor chatted and sipped their coffees and beers.

When the song finished everyone burst into applause. But, all the man had done was turn the wheel; yet, everyone clapped! I collapsed into a seat and started to weep. This place, it was like paradise, no pretense, where music was just a natural part of this world. Here music was so highly regarded and loved that even the hurdy-gurdy man got respect. Everything seemed so familiar, like I was coming home, as if I belonged here.

An orchestra then filled the stage, a conductor appeared, lifted his baton, and the musicians began to play. I could hear musical colors I had never encountered before, shimmering, glistening. Iridescent objects appeared to flit through the air. The music seemed to tumble, swoop, and become purling liquid. I felt something far away, like a distant memory from down a long, dark hallway, a song from another floor in an apartment building on a rainy night. Something stirred, intangible on the tip of my tongue, an ache, a longing for something, but out of reach. I felt as though I was returning from a long journey, not knowing if I'd ever get to my destination.

I thought I had almost found it when suddenly the music ended, and I was left with a feeling of deep loss. The world in the studio now seemed so far away. Everything that had appeared so important there had shrunk to a small image as if on a distant TV screen with muted sound. I dropped into a state of exhaustion seven years overdue, the end result of 20-hour days crashing in on me. I slumped in the chair, my hand over my face.

I could feel the pain in my bones from the abuse I'd endured at the hands of the narcissistic prick artists, who needed to kick me down in order to boost themselves up, the recalcitrance and stupidity of the maintenance guys, who always seemed more interested in obstructing my work than facilitating it, the frustration with the broken-down equipment, which seemed to have a nefarious life of its own, the opposition of management to make it any better, for who knows what reason, the cheap hack clients who just wanted the work done even it if wasn't very good; all of this started screaming in my head that it all wasn't worth it, that there was more to life that I needed to learn, that it was time to get out.

Ivy came over to me, enraptured, and said, "Isn't this place magical?" and then noticed my posture. Concerned, she sat down next to me, put her arm around me, and said, "What's the matter, sweetie?"

I shook my head, unable to speak. She held my hand, patiently, as if she understood. Then she spoke. "Take a look around. This is what I wanted you to see, to feel, to experience. And this is just the doorway. Everywhere you look, if you just know how to see, you can find the wonder of the universe."

I went back to my reverie. *There was something about this music. Maybe it wasn't about being a star. Maybe it was about finding something real, something enduring, something ennobling.*

Besides, if I really wanted to be a star, I'd have to be a producer, and if I wanted to be a producer, I should at least study music theory, right?

What was the name of that music I'd just heard?

SCENE TWO:

What it's all About

Back in the city, I told Emile that I wanted to study music, and he turned me on to one of his minions, a guy named Alex Grimes, who lived in a little apartment overrun with manuscript paper. One day, between music exercises, Alex asked me why I wanted to study harmony when my engineering career was going just fine.

"I'm looking for the magic," I replied. "I want to understand music from the inside. I want to know how it works. Besides, I don't want to be an engineer all my life. I want to produce. I never really studied all the way, and I want to feel like I know what I'm doing. I don't know. Then there's this side of me that just wants to get away from the whole thing. I'm exhausted, and, I figure, maybe I should just take some time off and go back to school."

Alex stopped and looked at me seriously. "I've got an idea. You should visit Maneri. He teaches up in Boston. He's a genius. He'll tell you what to do."

Taking this as a sign, Ivy and I drove up to Boston. She dropped me off at the entrance of a formidable looking beaux-arts building and went off exploring on her own. I walked into the Boston Conservatory of Music. Whereas I felt powerful in the pop world, here I felt small and intimidated as I entered the hallowed hall with the busts of the great composers in scalloped niches along the walls. I hadn't been in a school since high school, and certainly nothing like this. No one here would care about my work with Fosse. I was just the schlepper again.

I found Maneri's class and took a seat as far in the back as I could. My body tight, I watched the other students fooling around. The bell rang, but there was no professor. No one else seemed to notice or mind. I watched the clock hand turn as the minutes passed.

Finally, about fifteen minutes into the period, a rotund guy, with a shaved head and a long white beard like an Italian Santa Claus, burst into the room. He was talking as he opened the door and just kept going. He had a voice that sounded like he had spent the last couple of decades chewing a bag of rocks. Despite his heft, his energy was palpable.

"Let me tell you what it's all about."

I was ready to hear his ideas about modulations, passing tones, and voicings, the stuff I was beginning to grapple with in my studies. But that's not what he got into.

"Every one of you thinks you are going to get into the Boston Symphony. Let me tell ya, not one of you will. And that's not what it's about anyway. I'll tell you what it's all about. Me? I play nursing homes. Yah. The great Maneri. Microtonalist. Composer. Theoretician. That's right. You heard it. Nursing homes. I was in this nursing home on Sunday, see? And I'm playing for the old folks, it's all great. Then I'm done, and I'm leavin', and I see this guy sitting alone in a wheelchair.

"I walk up to this guy, and I start to talk to him, to try to, you know, connect a little bit, when I realize this man is deaf. Deaf." He gesticulated, poking himself in the chest. "Now what is a musician, me, going to be able to do for a deaf guy? I suddenly feel, I don't know, I don't know what to do, helpless."

Joe stopped talking for the first time since he walked in. He took a big breath and blew out the air. He smiled and nodded and walked back and forth across the front of the classroom. He shook his head, stopped, and then shrugged his shoulders. He looked right at me, as with a knowing look, and smiled.

"So what do I do?" he continued, as he scratched his chin. "I look up, I look up to God, and I pray. And I'm moved. I open my case, I've got my clarinet with me, that's what I bring with me to the nursing homes. I open my case, and I take out my axe. I put together my clarinet. I pull out a reed and I suck the reed, you know, to get it ready. And I put the reed in the mouth piece, get it all nice and aligned."

The students are all with him now. The reed players in the room are licking their lips, imagining putting their instruments together and getting ready to play. I'm with him, too.

"I put the instrument in my mouth," Maneri says, "and I look at this guy. I look right into his eyes. Right into his eyes. And I breathe. And I pull all the love I have from my heart, from . . ." and he points with his thumb straight up. "And I start to blow. I'm just trying to blow my love into the clarinet. And the guy looks back at me, and he, and he starts to cry. A tear just rolls down his cheek, and a smile comes on his face. And I continue to blow. And I just play for this guy. I play, and I play, and I play. And when I'm done, he reaches out his hands. I put down the instrument, and he holds my hands in his, and he nods, as if to say, thank you."

The bell rang. The class was over.

Maneri finished, at top volume. "And that is what it is all about."

I went up to him, shaken, and, my voice trembling, I introduced myself.

"Yeah, man! Thanks for coming up. Listen, you've got to meet Berg. He's the guy for you."

I staggered out of the school, confused. I thought I was going for a theory class — what was this? What did it mean?

SCENE THREE:

The Trip to the Woods

Ivy was waiting for me when I got out. I sat in the car, staring out of the window, unable to speak.

"I've got a treat planned for us. I found a place for us to take a hike. Walden Pond."

"Yeah, Walden Pond. What's that?" I said, abstractedly.

"You don't know Walden Pond? You know, where Henry David Thoreau lived."

"Henry . . . who's that?"

Though Ivy was gobsmacked by my ignorance, she tried not to sound condescending. "Thoreau, he was this philosopher, an American. He lived on Walden Pond for a while. Wrote a book about it. He was an amazing guy. Here, I went to a bookstore while you were at the school. I got a copy of the book. I thought you might like it."

I opened the book and read the dedication.

Suck the marrow out of life. Yes, if only. And how? This was why I loved Ivy, for turning me on to shit like this. But somehow, I couldn't quite bring myself to let her know what this meant to me and said nothing.

We hadn't been out of the city in too long, and my little nature-sprite needed to be in the country bad. We found a trail and followed it deep into the woods. Instantly, she became one with the green, frolicking through the trees. When we got to a remote corner of the pond, she ripped off her clothes and leapt in the cool, dappled water. She was in ecstasy. "I'm living Thoreau's dream!" she sang. "Why don't you come in?"

I leaned against a giant tree, cold, feeling nothing. I kept my clothes on. I didn't do skinny-dipping. Nothing got in. I browsed through the book in my hands but couldn't focus on the words. Where had my feeling gone? I looked at the scene around me and tried to see and feel its beauty, but it all seemed flat, meaningless. I began to be overcome by a sense of panic, alarm. Where had it gone? How long had I lived without feeling? Had it always been this way and I had just been unaware of it? I looked at Ivy, with her freedom and verve, as if I was looking at something through a thick glass that was rare, beautiful, and inaccessible.

Then, it was time to go to Berg's. We drove through the bucolic, historic Massachusetts landscape into a little town by the sea with old wooden houses painted different colors. The smell of wood smoke filled the cool, spring evening air. We knocked on the door of one of the creaky domiciles. A guy with wire rimmed glasses and wild black hair answered the door. He wore a thick, maroon, hand-woven sweater and was in stocking feet. His face was radiant with a bright, beaming smile.

"Come in! Come in!" he bellowed. A soft yellow light beckoned from within. "Can I get you a cup of tea?" His house smelled sweet with a wood stove crackling. We sat in his living room on worn old couches with deep, soft cushions and chatted amiably for a few minutes. My stocking feet rubbed against the wide plank floor and the edge of the worn hand woven rug.

Then he said, "Come! Let's go to the piano. Let's see what you have." I offered him the book of rudimentary harmony exercises that I had worked on with Alex. He opened the pages. "Ah! Yes. I see what you are working on, what you are up to." He looked at them, reading the music as if he could hear it in his head, humming, chuckling, and nodding his head with approval. He put the notation notebook on his piano and started to play. He played a few chords. Then, he jumped up enthusiastically. "Listen to that B! Listen! Oh, do you hear? Do you hear? That's beautiful! I love the way you move through the sub-dominant region, and how the alto works against the tenor line. Yes, let me play it again!"

He played a chord, paused, and closed his eyes, like he was sipping a fine wine, taking in the sound, luxuriating in it. "Yes. Yes!"

What was he hearing? What was he feeling? Damn if I knew. I just heard notes in a silly exercise. He seemed to care so much. Why didn't I care? The void inside of me opened up into a dark chasm. The life around me made me painfully aware of the deadness inside of me that felt decades old.

I started to feel this unbearable, heartbreaking longing. I wanted what Ivy and this guy had, but it seemed to be across an ocean, beyond the sea outside our doors, in a faraway land I could only imagine. I wanted freedom from this coldness inside, to break through this barrier, to find the beauty in things, to create beauty. But there was nothing to access. It all felt empty inside. I was consumed with grief, at my own death, which happened mysteriously, out of my sight, who knew when.

In a monotone voice, I asked, "So, if I was to come to work with you, to study, what would we do, what is your method?"

Berg grabbed a book off a shelf. He held it in his hand as if it were a sacred tome from the library at Alexandria. It seemed to glow in his hands.

"This is the book. In German, it is called *Harmonielehre*. In English, *Theory of Harmony*, by my hero, Arnold Schoenberg. His method, ach. I can't even begin. He takes you through the entire history of harmony, he says you must learn the law first before you can break it, but the law is, in the end, for him, love. I learned this from Maneri, who learned from

Schmidt, who learned from the master himself!"

"Schoenberg," I said almost inaudibly. "Great. I'll check it out." I noticed it was dark out. I couldn't stay there any longer. I had to go. I stood up. "Listen, thank you for your time. It really has been great. I'll, I'll . . . get back to you."

As we walked toward the door, Berg said, "I would love to work with you. You really have something here. We could do amazing work! I would love to teach you!"

I looked at him, paused, and looked around, as if, for some reason, there was someone I didn't want to hear what I was about the say. "Maybe I will come. Maybe I will. I promise you'll hear from me." We left, and I felt rattled to the core. Some revelation was peeking through. Not a solution, for sure, but in fact, its opposite, a problem, an unsolvable dilemma. I was stuck, frozen, like in the fairy tales, spellbound.

As we made our way on the highway back toward the city, I was suddenly struck with desperation. I had to get out. I had to get out of New York, away from the studio, away from the drugs, away from the humiliations, the abuse, the endless hours, the narrow life, the studio tan, the boredom, the drudgery.

A snarky voice popped into my head. *Shoeberg, or whatever his name is. What nonsense. We are not living in fin de siècle Vienna! No one cares about modern classical music! Why would you want to get involved in something that no one cares about? You won't be known at all. You'll study, like a good little student, and what will the learning give you? You want immortality? Now Bob Fosse, he is more famous now than Schoenberg ever was or will be. His movies have made millions of dollars! Schoenberg's music is forgotten today. No one knows who he is, and he just died twenty years ago. But 50 years after Fosse is dead, his movies will be adored. Why would you want to give this up for some integrity trip?*

The voice faded as I felt myself getting sucked back into the all-consuming maw of New York. I saw a great big city, filled with people who were dead inside, and I needed to escape, to save myself so I would be the last person to care. Then I became confused. Maybe caring meant staying and sacrificing everything for art. Then back again. No, I had to leave, I knew it was meaningless, I knew there had to be more to life, I knew that I didn't want to be dead inside, and if I stayed, I'd never find myself. A scene from Fosse's *Damn Yankees* sprang to life in my head. In that movie, the devil convinces this old guy that he will turn him into a baseball star, but he has to give up love, his wife, his life, and, of course, his soul. Along the way he and Gwen Verdon, Fosse's real-life wife, the devil's sexy handmaiden, sing "Two Lost Souls."

"We're two lost souls, on the highway of life . . ."

As our rental bumped over the decayed roads of the outer boroughs, it became clear, though I wouldn't say the words out loud. I decided I had to leave. We were just about done with scoring the movie. My work would be finished. As soon as we could, we'd leave the city. I'd find a place to live in Massachusetts. I would study with Berg. It would be a new decade and I would be in a new place, a new life, with my girlfriend. It sounded so much better than the tedium of projects that would never be as good as *All That Jazz.*

If it was going to be real, I had to say it out loud.

I turned to Ivy in the car and said, "Alright. I'm done. We'll leave. *Jazz* will be over soon, and we'll get out of here as soon as it is finished. I'll just quit. We'll move up here. I'll study music with Berg. Whaddya think? We'll get out of this dirty shit hole and I'll be done with all this crap."

She looked at me, her moon-like eyes welling with tears of happiness.

ACT FOUR: THE ACT

SCENE ONE:
The Gig

To just about anyone reading, Bob Fosse's decision, at the last moment, to use the mono version instead of the stereo version of the soundtrack to his film *All That Jazz* would seem inconsequential. But to me, the film's music mixer, it was an utter catastrophe. How could such a minor technical difference be so devastating?

At the end of the summer, when we finished recording the various musical cues, overdubbing the vocal performances for the film's songs, and mixing the music down to six tracks, my part in the process was complete. There was nothing stopping me now from getting out of Dodge. I'd make my girlfriend happy. I could tell myself that *Jazz* had been a great experience. Nothing would top it. I always said that I'd know when to hang up my spikes. I had survived and it was time to move on.

But then something happened that was so uncanny that it made me wonder if there were forces at work beyond my comprehension.

I got a call from Kenneth Utt, the line producer for the film. He was the guy who took care of all the daily details that needed to be seen to in order to get this huge, unwieldy thing called a movie made. He was a lovely, grizzled guy with a spiky salt and pepper crew-cut. He was a pro who knew what he was doing. He asked to meet with me. When we sat down together, he spoke in his even but commanding deep Southern accent and said, "Glenn, you've done a fine job on this film so far. Bob likes your work so much that he wants you to join us on the dubbing stage to do the re-record, handling the music."

I started to bubble inside. This was incredible! After the score was recorded, the final part of the filmmaking process was post-production, where the dialogue, sound effects, and music are mixed together to create the final sound track. This is what Utt was asking me to participate in.

Utt went on. "We had a hard time making this happen, and the guys at Trans Audio, where we are going to do the mix, only agreed to it on the following conditions. You'll get paid a nice hourly rate by the studio, but you can't ask to join the union. This is going to be on background. You'll get credit on the film but not for post-production. That's the deal, my friend. Are you up for it?" He smiled.

"Of course! Yes! I'd love to!"

I was so excited, I didn't give a shit about the small print. Who wanted to be in the union anyway?

It turned out that Ralph Burns put this idea into Fosse's head. The music meant everything to him, of course, and it was a super-important part of the movie. He knew how complex the music mix was going to be and how demanding Fosse could be. Dick Vorisek, the guy who had been hired to do the post-production mix, was not a music guy. Ralph and I had formed a strong bond over the months of recording. We'd shared those meals at Ponte Vecchio. He wanted someone at the final mixing board who got music and represented his interests. He lobbied Fosse to hire me to work alongside of Vorisek. Clearly, Fosse liked the idea.

Mostly, I was pumped to have the opportunity to do this kind of work. I'd never done anything like this. I was up for the challenge. It sounded like the ultimate fun. And, it reinflated that balloon in my head. Ignoring the reality of the deal, that I wouldn't get a post-production credit, I told myself that this was the ticket I had been waiting for. Here was my pathway to stardom. Here was the way I could win that Oscar. Up until then, the movie could win for sound, but my name wouldn't be attached to that. Now I'd be on the dubbing stage. I'd figure out some way to get the goddamn credit.

My excitement and fantasizing slammed into a brick wall of reality: my promise to Ivy.

SCENE TWO:

Claude's

Ivy and I were having breakfast at Claude's, this little French patisserie on West 4th Street in the Village. Claude was an irascible Norman who looked like a french Pillsbury Doughboy. His éclairs were poetry itself. If he didn't like you, he took out what he called his "grandmother's tooth-brush," a large wrench, from behind his counter, and he would wave it at you until you ran out of his shop. But he never did that to us. We were part of the in-crowd at Claude's.

As we luxuriated in our warm *pain au chocolat* and sipped our cappuccini, I screwed up my courage and said, "I got this incredible opportunity yesterday. Bob wants me to do the post-production mix! It's an amazing honor, I mean, I've never done this before, and to do this for *Jazz*, that would be a dream come true."

I could see her tighten. Her already big eyes got larger and started to fill with tears. This was something I experienced all too often, and it drove me nuts. We could never seem to get through a meal at a restaurant without her crying. *Fuck*, I thought to myself, *here it comes*. The last thing that I needed was to have Claude see her blubbering. He'd smack me with the toothbrush. I went on. "Look, I know I said we'd leave, and we will! I mean, this can't go on for that long. The movie has to come out by the end of the year. We'll probably be done in a few weeks. As soon as it's done, we'll leave. I promise."

Her voice trembled with rage. Trying to keep quiet, she seethed, "I don't believe you! This is what this whole thing has been like! You tell me you'll be home by seven and then I don't see you for three days. You say this is the end, but then another 'incredible opportunity' will come along, and the next thing you know, five years will pass. I hate it here!"

I assured her this was the last heist. We'd make a killing on this one, and it would give us the cake to get out in style. "Look, it will be better this way! I'll make so much money, I won't have to work for who knows how long! And you won't have to work. You can just write poetry, like you've always wanted to."

Tears fell onto her pastry.

I couldn't help but react. "Do we really have to? For Christ's sake, don't let Claude see." She just stared at me with a look so cold it was like an ice pick to the heart.

I thought I was fucked, until fate came up with a scheme to get her to go along with the plan.

SCENE THREE:

The Screening

I had now moved into a higher echelon. Bob invited me to an advance screening of a rough cut of the film, to give me an opportunity to see the entire film for the first time so I'd know what we would be working on when we got to the dubbing stage. He told me to bring my girlfriend along. He also invited some of his friends and acquaintances to this showing to get some early feedback.

The first thing I had to deal with was Ivy's resistance to this whole idea. But beyond that, I was nervous about her reaction to the movie. She could be a tough critic. She considered herself a radical feminist. She was a poet with a 4.0 from Yale and could be pretty snobby when it came to art. If anything even smacked the slightest bit of misogyny or female objectification, she felt the obligation to put it down. This included any nuanced or somewhat realistic depiction of human relationships and/or portrayals of beauty and/or sexuality. We had a huge fight on one of our first dates after seeing Woody Allen's breakthrough film *Annie Hall* because she considered the totally beautiful character of Annie to be offensive. There were almost no characterizations of women, especially those created by men, which passed her muster. And I had seen enough clips during recording to know that Fosse didn't shy away from sexualized portrayals of the superior gender.

Nevertheless, when I asked her, despite her attempt to be cool, I could tell she was a little jazzed to be going to a private screening of an as-yet unreleased motion picture. She was as much of a film buff as the rest of us were at that time.

When we arrived at the funky midtown screening room, Bob was there to greet us, and when he turned his klieg lights on her, I saw a change come over her that I did not expect but completely understood, as I had gone through such a *zaubersprüche* myself. My tough German friend became a little fanlet. Bob turned his Eros full force on her, and I could swear she got wet under his gaze. By the time she got to her seat, she was a convert. I began to have hope that maybe she'd come around. But first we'd have to see what the movie was like.

We were blown away. This was a radical film. We didn't quite know what we had seen yet. The cutting was severe, faster than anything we'd encountered. The theme was dark. It was like no musical we'd ever seen. The version was rough, but we could still feel the movie's raw power. We gripped each other's hands during the ride. When it was over, we looked at each other agog, hearts pounding. *Holy shit. I wasn't only working on a major film. I was working on a great one.* Ivy effusively went up to Bob.

He held both of her hands and got close to her face. "You like it?"

"Yes! I LOVE it!"

We floated out of the room to the creaky elevator. A bunch of us crammed into the little box. One man, rather gray, in a floppy hat from the Army and Navy store, spoke somewhat critically. "I thought it would be more finished than that." It was clear he wasn't saying more. It was Woody Allen!

We got out into the street, giddy. New York, 1979. We were peaking. "So, can we stay a few more months so I can get this thing done?" I asked.

"Of course!" she said, her voice vibrating with excitement. We ran through the midtown crush, holding hands, in love, thrilled to be at the height of our New York moment.

SCENE FOUR:

I Quit

Although A&R had built up this extraordinary staff, the times they were a changin': everyone was going "freelance," and working all over town. It seemed to be a good deal; you'd make a higher hourly and get to control your own taxes. Plus, clients might want to work with you, but not at your studio. I was far from the first to make the move.

The first person I went to at A&R to announce my decision to quit was Milton Brooks.

"Brooks, this is it. Fosse has asked me to do the re-record with him over at Trans Audio, and I figured this was as good a time as any to go free-lance."

Brooks squashed out his cigar stump hard. I'd never seen him like this. He'd always seemed to be able to take everything in stride. "I see," he said through his teeth.

"Berger, we invested in you. We put up with you sneaking into the studios on weekends and stealing tape, because we were cultivating an-other hotshot. The only thing on my mind was, who was going to replace Ramone? He wouldn't be around forever. He's spending half his year in Los Angeles these days. And we built you up. Got you in with Charlap, and Burns, and Fosse. And now, just like that, you're out of here? Well, good luck, kid."

"Wait, Brooks, the thing is, the truth is, it's not like I'm going to be working anywhere else. After this project, I'm leaving New York. I'm burnt, man."

"What? Where are you going to go?"

"Ivy and I are going to move up to New England, and I'm going to study music for a while."

"Berger. Do you realize what you have here? Do you know how many people would kill for your slot? You are on the verge of... you're a hot shot! You're going to throw the whole thing away? Are you out of your mind?"

Now I started to get mad. "Do you have any idea of all the shit I've put up with over the last seven years? The crap I've had to take from Sterling? How I've had to beg for a five-dollar raise from Ward when I'm billing hundreds of thousands of dollars? To say nothing of Ramone and Simon and the rest of the freaks around here? I'm sick of this crap! I'm done! I don't owe these people anything! Sure, they've given me opportunities, but I've paid for it all in blood, and they've gotten plenty back!"

Brooks looked at me with pity and understanding. "Alright, Berger. I'm not going to fight with you. I just hope you don't regret this one day."

"What am I going to regret? Look, it's not you. I hope you don't stay mad at me forever. This is just something I gotta do."

By the time I went over to the other side, everyone knew. Sterling, drunk as usual, came up to me and said, "It's about time. I told you you'd never last, you faggot. I coulda told Ramone he was making a big mistake with you. You'll never amount to anything in this business."

I was used to this kind of treatment and just answered it with a fuck you.

Next, I ran into the assistant who was gunning for my chair. "What a great move, man! You are so brave! I wish I had your guts!"

Yeah, right, scumbag. You just want my gigs, that's all.

I went to say goodbye to my mentor Susan Hamilton. She said, "You know, when somebody leaves, I just cross them off my list, like they never existed. People get one shot in my book. When you leave this town, you don't come back."

What do I care?

Bloodied, I went back to the production room to see Plotnik. He sat down with me and smiled. "Berger-queen, I wish you the best of luck. You gotta do what's right for you. I'm sure that whatever you end up doing, you'll be great, you little piece of shit ya!"

I thanked him, and we hugged. I took a long look at the big room and wondered if I'd ever see it again. Then I walked down the back hallway to the freight elevator, maybe for the last time. Inside, Reverend Blalock said, "Well if it isn't the chicken hawk. You catch any chickens lately?" He'd said that to me so many times, and I was still not sure what he meant.

I got out onto the familiar corner at 52nd and 7th. I walked a few steps downtown to look at the plaque that read A&R. I remembered how I had felt on my first day in the studio, full of hope, fear, determination, and clarity of purpose. I still had the fire, raring to move on to my next adventure, but the clarity was gone. I was no longer sure that my answer to everything was "yes."

ACT FIVE: THE NEXT STAGE

SCENE ONE:

Louder! Harder! Bigger!

Once I stepped onto the dubbing stage I entered a different dimension. Now, I was truly on Fosse time. As we got deeper into the re-recording, our days got progressively longer, first eight, then ten, twelve, sixteen hours a day. The days stretched into weeks, weeks into months. I wouldn't say Bob and I were ever friends, but by the end we were spending every waking minute together and so had formed some kind of deep bond.

The control room at Trans Audio was a large box about thirty feet from back to front. The front was covered by a large movie screen, about ten feet high and eighteen feet across, and the mixing console was about three-quarters of the way back toward the rear wall.

Dick Vorisek (the guy who handled the dialogue and sound effects) and I set up the mix around 8:30. Bob showed around nine. He would park himself inches from the screen, at its lower right hand corner. He rarely got up. He was invariably pleasant, professional, focused, and soft-spoken but relentlessly demanding, mostly on himself.

When I'd finish mixing the music for a scene, Fosse would say, "Let's do it one more time. What I asked for was all wrong. I think we can get it better. Let's make the ending bigger."

I never wanted to tell Bob we couldn't do something, so I pushed the meters as hard as I could. Vorisek, a big guy from the Bronx, with a sizable gut from spending too many years behind the console, looked at me and grimaced. Under his breath, he reprimanded me, saying, "You can't do that! The system just won't handle it!"

I'd try to pull back a little, but Fosse would come right back, telling me to push harder on the throttle, taking the plane higher, reaching for the stratosphere, closer to the speed of sound, we'd feel the whole thing rattle, on the verge of falling apart. I started to get the idea that Fosse liked living on the edge, and maybe he'd take us all down with him.

With Fosse in one ear, "Louder! Harder! Bigger!" and Vorisek in the other, "You'll kill us!" I flew that console right to the edge of disaster and destruction, in search of brilliance. This went on relentlessly, detail after detail.

SCENE TWO:

The Optical Track

During a break, Vorisek turned to me with a serious look that telegraphed if you keep going like this you are going to do us all in. "Look, you gotta unnerstand. You just can't cram this kinda volume on a mono optical track."

I didn't know what he was talking about. I didn't want to say: what's an optical track? I was supposed to be an expert. But slowly, I began to gather the information.

In the world of analog that we lived in before the 1980s, every medium of sound reproduction had gross limitations. I knew this from making records and, worse, cassettes. So I knew well the disappointment of not being able to reproduce for the listening audience what we created in the studio. But nothing prepared me for the shock of the mono optical track on movies.

When we transferred a reel of our mixes to optical to hear what the final product would sound like, I was horrified. The sound sucked. That's when I learned that up until that time, sound reproduction had only changed marginally, with a few technical improvements, since the first feature-length talkie came out in 1927. That was another movie with jazz in the title, *The Jazz Singer*, about a Jew who did not want to follow the spiritual path laid out by his forebears but instead wanted to become a show-business star.

There are three basic elements to reproduced sound, and the optical track's technical ability to handle all three of these were from the dark ages. The first was frequency response. The human ear can hear sounds from the low boom of thunder and the thumping bass from your sub-woofer to the sheen of cymbals and the sweet transparency that comes from high frequencies where the air vibrates about 18,000 times a second.

Sound, as it is, exists way above 18k; our ears and brains just can't reproduce it. Cats, dogs, bats, mice, and dolphins can all hear frequencies far higher than humans, for some stretching to 150,000 cycles per second.

This astounding, inspiring capacity of our animal friends stands in contrast to the pathetic range of that movie optical track, which only reproduced frequencies accurately between about 100Hz and 2000Hz. This is basically the sound of an old telephone. No thunder, just a tap on a cardboard box; no tingle down the spine from great highs, just a muffled sound of someone singing through a towel.

The second disappointing attribute of the optical track was that it also had a limited dynamic range. This means that the soundtrack could only get so quiet before being overwhelmed by hiss, or noise, and could only get so loud before the medium could take no more and would distort or simply stop getting louder. Bob's soundtrack, with its wild ups and downs of volume, was like a *blivit* on the optical track; it was like trying to shove ten pounds of shit into a nine-pound bag.

The third aspect of this optical track that made it embarrassing was that it was in mono. All the audio was crammed onto a single track, with all of the stuff coming out of one speaker. I was used to glorious stereo, which turned the musical canvas from a point to a plane, just like a movie screen. If something happened on the left side of the screen, the sound should come out on the left. With stereo, the sound is far more lifelike, rich, and interesting. It is far easier to hear all the different parts, because different sounds are coming to your ear from different locations. Instead of your film soundtrack sounding like it was coming from an enhanced version of Carnegie Hall, with the mono optical it sounded like you were listening to an orchestra playing through a tin can.

I had no idea that this was the case before I started this gig, and I was depressed to find this out. But there was hope for something much better.

SCENE THREE:
The Dolby Disaster

1979 was a turning point in the history of sound in the movies.

In the previous couple of years, a company called Dolby had come out with a process for getting stereo sound onto an optical track with a much wider frequency response and broader dynamic range. You could, theoretically, get a sound that was better than any you could hear at home, because it would be played through huge speakers, at a nice volume, in a big space. The sound would be rich, loud, and large… if it worked.

Making its first appearance in 1975, it had been used on a few big films, like *Star Wars*. The system slowly began to catch on, and a few major theatres started to install the system, but it was far from standard or ubiquitous, and in 1979, for Fosse, it was still exotic.

Fosse was open to the idea of using the Dolby system, but, like all things, it made him nervous. His New York film directing buddy, Sidney Lumet, had used the system on the film version of *The Wiz*, which had been a terrible flop. One reason that the film fared so badly, Sidney told Bob, was that the Dolby system was so fucked up. Afraid that the movie was one bad decision away from failure, Bob, like all show biz people, was superstitious about such things. Nevertheless, Bob agreed to test it out.

We sent a reel of our mixed film to the Dolby labs to make a test copy for us. A group of us, including Bob, went to a movie theatre to listen to the results. I was excited to hear how our film would sound in the theatre with this great, new reproduction system. When we put up the film, there was no picture, and all we heard was a 1000Hz tone, that is, a non-stop, obnoxious-sounding beep. Obvious to my ear, this was a "test tone." I'd heard this sound innumerable times in the studio. It was the standard sound used to align the tape machines. It is not a pleasant sound, and through the loud speakers at the theatre, it hurt!

Whenever something went wrong like this, we all instantly looked over at Bob. By this time I knew that Fosse had had triple bypass just a few years before. He still chain-smoked five packs of cigarettes a day and was taking copious amounts of amphetamines. He told us that he wanted to die on opening day, because he would do anything for a bigger box office. We were just hoping he wouldn't hit the big stop button before then.

We were just waiting for some disaster to strike that would make him keel over and croak, and this, we feared, was that moment. Fosse was a light shade of puce. We tried to reassure him that this was some terrible, inexplicable mistake, and that it could be fixed. He didn't look convinced.

He lit another cigarette and walked out of the theatre slowly, head bowed. He was always expecting the worst, and this seemed to validate his view of the universe.

I left the theatre, too, furious. It turned out that Dolby had sent us a reel of test tones intended for the Army and had sent our reel to an Army post in St. Louis! Bob was ready to throw out the whole idea, but we explained this to him and convinced him to try it again.

We got another test reel, and this one at least had sound and picture, but it sounded like shit. The "intensity" was so off that it was completely distorted. Fosse had no capacity to contextualize. However something was at that particular moment was how it had always been and how it would be forever. Since the sound on the test reel stank, he assumed that was the way the mix would always sound. He was terrified. When things didn't work right, he always blamed himself and went into a panic that it was unfixable. It took a tremendous amount of hand-holding to convince him that this was just the way this one bad copy sounded and had nothing to do with our master mix.

But while we were trying to assuage Bob's panic, I was starting to feel my own. I knew that Fosse was against this Dolby idea, and this latest cock-up on the technician's part would significantly diminish my chances of getting great sound for this movie for Bob, and the awards that would go along with that for me.

My fear was well founded. Fosse bagged the Dolby system.

No one really asked me for an opinion, and I didn't know exactly how to assert one. Once the great director made a decision, there was no way to influence him to change his mind.

Ralph Burns and I commiserated in despair. "Ralph, we've got to do something! There's got to be some way that we can get decent sound on this thing. I mean, mono? Really? And how can we even get what Fosse wants this way? He's always wanting everything bigger, louder!"

"I know. Let me see what I can do."

Burns came back to me with what seemed like good news. "OK. We got Bob to agree to go with a 70mm system for the opening in New York and LA. This is really the best thing out there. It is a four-track system, it'll be in stereo, with better sound than anything."

I felt renewed, hopeful, again. Wow! Maybe we'd have something better than Dolby! The best! 70mm four track! Maybe I still had a shot . . .

SCENE FOUR:
The Burden and the Transcendence

The arduous process ground on, as we mixed the film every day, day and night. Most films take a few days, a week or two at most, to mix. Not this film. Not Fosse. We worked on it for four months.

Not only was sound primitive in those days, but the whole process of working on film was totally analog and painfully slow.

We'd mix a minute of film. Then Bob would quietly ask to have one frame cut out, that is, one thirtieth of a second, and everything would have to be edited by hand to match up. He'd watch again and politely ask to have the frame put back in, and again the film and the sound tracks would be cut with a razor blade, put back together, rethread on the machine, and run again.

Every change took forever, but it didn't matter to Fosse. He just sat at the screen, waiting for playback. We'd finish a scene, and then Bob would watch it the next day, hate it, and ask to do it again. And when we did, it was always better. Small changes in volume between the music and dialogue could deepen the emotion of a scene, tender here, hilarious there.

Fosse, like most of the great artists I worked with, was not super-human, or that different, from you and me, more or less. I never saw him captured by some transporting flight of fancy and inspiration. I never witnessed creativity blossom forth in some miraculous, genius-like way. He was never certain. He never made a decision that couldn't be changed. He was always looking for confirmation from others. This was not the picture of some god-like, all-powerful being who lived in a realm separate from us. He was all too mortal, all too capable of screwing up. What I did see was a guy who showed up every day on time, worked his ass off, and was relentless in demanding more from himself and others. What made Fosse different was that he was willing to die to get something right. That is, the virtue that leads to greatness is thoroughness.

This grueling repetition and obsessiveness was both the burden and the transcendence of the artistic life, which, if you can tolerate it, brings you to a higher state. On one hand, it is torture; on the other, being that deep into a work of art is a path to spiritual revelation. Creating this masterwork became my act of devotion, my *bhakti marga*.

The circular nature of our work, like the enlightenment achieved with the endless repetition of a mantra, brought me to my own state of twisted nirvana. I achieved a kind of trance-like state, Plato's divine madness. The deeper I went, the more I found. Eventually, I became one with the film and could see the workings of the cosmos in it.

And no matter how exhausted I got, no matter how spent, Fosse would be there for it all, never flagging. Of course, the speed must have helped.

ACT SIX: THE MOVIE

SCENE ONE:

Exegesis

Now, my education into art, music, film, and the psyche of Bob Fosse was about to really begin. Watching each scene endlessly, I felt as though every frame had become seared into my nervous system. I plumbed ever deeper strata till I was certain I had penetrated the film to its core. Layers of symbolism and meaning glowed transparently. I came to believe that I not only knew what the movie was all about, but what Fosse was about, what all the crazy artists I worked with were about, and maybe even a little bit about myself.

In the film, the lead character Joe Gideon is a choreographer/director who is creating a movie and a Broadway show. He is a workaholic, alcoholic, drug addict, and sex addict. His addictions are killing him. His compulsivity is beyond control, and he is incapable of stopping his inexorable slide toward death. He hurts everyone around him, especially those closest to him: his wife, his girlfriend, and his daughter. But the pain he causes has no impact on him. It is this inability to feel the suffering of those around him that prevents him from doing anything to change his behavior. He lives a perversion of the golden rule. He does treat others as he treats himself; he is willing to hurt himself, and he is willing to hurt others. He does this in answer to a higher god, the god of "show biz." His morality is of a different sort: boredom is the only sin.

When the film came out, everyone asked if Gideon was Fosse. He would always say no, but of course, in many ways, he was.

During the course of the film, in between sexy dance numbers, Gideon has a heart attack — just as Fosse suffered when he was directing the show *Chicago* and the movie, *Lenny*. But unlike the real Bob Fosse, after hearing a bad review of the movie he had been making, Gideon dies. The final scene of the film is an epic thirteen-minute production number of Gideon's funeral.

SCENE TWO:

The Final Scene

By the time we started working on the final number three months into the re-record, I was completely wrecked, broken, out of my gourd.

Fosse, sitting an inch from the screen, smoking thousands of cigarettes, endlessly fussed over syllables of dialogue, door creaks and footsteps, frames of film, and the balance of trumpets to trombones. The nuances became infinitesimal, microscopic, quantum.

I hadn't slept more than four hours a night for seven years. Every part of my body and psyche throbbed. I was past the limit of my endurance. I had hit the wall and gone through it to an alternate reality. I was becoming Gideon. I was completely nuts. My entire consciousness was possessed by this movie.

The editor and Fosse's right-hand man, Alan Heim, also lived on the Upper West Side of Manhattan. Going home at the end of another four-teen-hour day, we stood on the bus repeating the same sentences over and over again, ventilating our anxiety. "Do you think Bob likes it? Do you think we got the scene today? How the hell are we ever going to get this thing done on time? Do you think Bob likes it?"

I stumbled into my apartment. It was after midnight. I was anxiously craving the few hours of sleep I could get before it was show time again. Ivy was curled up in a chair in the living room, smoking a pipe, reading Anaïs Nin. I could tell from the way she thumbed through the corner of the pages of the book that she was not happy. Her intellectual eccentricity mixed with a bit of hippie is what attracted me to her in the first place, but with her bad vibe it didn't seem quite as charming, now. I felt the psoas muscle in the center of my body tighten. I tried to ignore the signal and pretend that nothing was going on.

"Hey. How was your day?" I asked.

"Fine. How about you?"

I couldn't help myself. It was too late, and I had no filter. "All right. What's wrong?"

"Nothing," she said, tightly.

"OK. I'm going to bed."

"I haven't seen you in months."

"I know. I'm sorry. We're almost there. You have no idea how intense this is." *I wish I could get some support around this, instead of shit,* I thought.

"Whatever you say. It's always your way. You always do what you want. And I just have to go along with it."

I had nothing left. "You know what? Why don't you just go? If I'm that horrible just leave! You know what else? This is the way it is going to be. Maybe I won't leave at all. You don't seem to give a shit that I'm actually working every day, on something important. What the hell are you doing every day? What the hell do you do? You don't work, and it doesn't seem like you are writing very much poetry. Maybe if you did something you wouldn't be so miserable!"

I'd struck the jugular, and Ivy looked at me with those saucer-like assassinating daggers, huge and brimming with the ever-available tears. With malice in her voice, she said, "You are such a self-involved prick."

She was right of course, but I couldn't admit it. "Oh. Now here they come! The tears! I am so sick of this! I'm all wrong, always wrong. I don't have time for this. I've got to be back in the studio in a few hours."

As I walked into the bedroom, I heard her wailing. I laid down in bed, hallucinating in the dark from the lack of sleep and the endless projection on the screen. I began to see all the scenes in the film where Gideon fucks around on his wife and girlfriend. It started to seem like a very attractive idea. I could feel myself getting infected with his disease, like I'd been bit by a vampire. I wasn't all the way there yet, and maybe I could still escape, but it was starting to twist in my blood. I entertained the idea of just dumping Ivy and going all in with this show biz thing after all.

The next thing I knew, the alarm went off.

Practically sleepwalking, I somehow made it back to the mixing stage. It was time for Joe Gideon to die. Fosse, who was convinced that he would die any second, was going to go out with the biggest production number of his life, an extravaganza where he got to direct his own funeral. This number was clearly his swan song, the finale of the great finale of his life, his last chance to go out with the ultimate big finish.

But, by my lights, it was Fosse's ironic destiny that in the final moment, his pathology got the best of him. Instead of his death producing his most beautiful song, he bombed. In some strange way, it was as if he had to, in the penultimate scene of his life, punish himself, finally, by failing artistically. As far as I was concerned, his last scene was the biggest mistake of his career, and, as it turned out in the end, mine.

What I mean is, he picked the wrong song.

From the opening count-off that began the movie; to the incessant Vivaldi which mocked the hamster wheel of Gideon's speed-addled life; to the pop songs whose lyrics illuminated the show biz life; to Burns' over the top burlesque music that provided a counterpoint to Gideon's self-destructive behavior; to the corny old stuff, done in gleeful arrangements to undercut the seriousness of the messages attached to them; all of his musical choices were spot on, the perfect ironic touches to his dark vision.

But the last song was, well, thin. He decided on a parody version of the old Everly Brothers hit, "Bye Bye Love," changing the lyrics to "Bye Bye *Life*." It's a slight song to begin with, lacking the resonance of the other choices. At the moment when he needed his greatest inspiration, out of all the melodic and lyrical combinations available in the universe, he chose a turkey. The song had no intrinsic build, no motivic power, no emotion to pull on, no depth of perspective. This was the moment when we should have had something original, written by a genius. We needed an ironic anthem of death, a perfect distillation of razzle dazzle, with the hugest, most remarkable, stupendous finish. And this song was not it. When it really counted, Fosse choked.

He tried to make the most of this chintzy song. He came up with every variation of the arrangement to build this epic production piece, and Burns copped these styles well. But even these arrangement ideas fell flat, as they were too obviously ripped off from tacky sources like Chuck Mangione and Billy Joel.

I tried to soothe myself by telling myself that he was right and I was wrong. After all, he was Fosse, the genius. Then I found a copy of an early shooting script, and I read the following,

NOTE: THE FOLLOWING NUMBER, "BYE BYE LOVE," IS WRITTEN BY FELICHE AND BOUDLEAUS BRYANT, RECORDED BY SIMON AND GARFUNKEL ON THE ALBUM "BRIDGE OVER TROUBLED WATER." WE HOPE THAT A NEW SONG CAN AND WILL BE WRITTEN THAT WILL SERVE THE SAME PURPOSE IN THEME AND ENTERTAINMENT VALUE. CONSIDER THIS, THEN, A DUMMY.

Fosse knew it! He'd known it! Why didn't he get that great new song written? I'll never know.

But of course, I couldn't say anything. The movie was done, the choice had been made. As a good soldier, it wasn't for me to question why, just for me to do or die. The flimsiness of this lightweight choice frightened me, because I knew what kind of emotional impact he wanted the scene to have, and the responsibility to make it work now landed on me. Now, I was in it all the way. There was no turning back, and I was stuck with the material presented to me. I had nothing to do with getting us here, but here I was with no choice but to try to kill this whale with a toothpick.

I threw my whole being into the number. Over the course of a month, we worked on it second by second. I crammed every piece of magnetism onto that pathetically inadequate piece of oxide that I could. If every other scene had its wild dynamic swings, this was the biggest, roller-coaster moment of all.

Finally, we got down to the last scene of the last scene. Gideon was dead, the crowd gone home. Gideon stood in his black sequin jacket, make-up perfect, hair coiffed, a gentle smile. He'd had his big celebration, and now it was time to finally embrace Lady Death.

I faded out the music and applause to silence. I watched a tracking shot of Gideon moving down a corridor, stunningly decorated with black-and-silver mirrored paper by the film's Oscar-winning production designer, Philip Rosenberg. At the end of the path was a white light, just like those who have been there and back say it is going to be. But no one says that along with the white light you are greeted by the gorgeous Jessica Lange, who plays the angel of death in the movie, and who, by the way, Fosse reputedly fucked, of course.

As Gideon moved toward the light, I faded up the music. I got the pace and timing just right, increasing the volume as Gideon glided down the corridor: louder, louder, louder, LOUDER! When Gideon got to the end, I built to the loudest possible volume. At the peak, there was a sharp cut to silence, then a zipper sound effect to mark the closing of the body bag, with Gideon's dead body in it. Perfect. At least, so I thought.

Bob turned to me from the screen, squinting, the ubiquitous cigarette dangling. In his typical, serious, gentle voice, "Could we do it again, please, and make the end a little bigger?"

I turned to Vorisek, looking for some help, having been through this a thousand times. He grimaced, as if to say, *You know you can't. You've already gone way past the limit of what the medium can handle. If we keep going after this goddamn whale we are going to get eaten.*

But I had sworn my fealty. It was December, and the sun had set many hours ago. It was cold outside, but it didn't matter. We hadn't seen daylight in weeks. We'd skipped Thanksgiving, and now Christmas was drawing nigh. Pushing through my exhaustion, I told myself that I just had to make it through this one last part.

There had to be a way that I could do the impossible. Make it louder, make it seem louder, while not driving Vorisek, or the gear, nuts. Make it louder, and not louder, at the same time.

"Sure. Let's do it again."

I hit the play button, and all the cranky mechanical dubbing machines linked to the film started to roll. I punched into record at the cut to the scene. I pulled the faders as close to the bottom as I could, with barely a trickle of sound. I was into the groove, meshed to the movement of the camera. We had been through the scene so many times, I knew just how long it would be before we reached the climax. I knew just what pressure to use as I pushed up the volume controls. Just a gentle lick at first, then harder, harder, louder, louder, deeper, deeper, more pressure, I watched the needles, I held it back as much as I could, the longer I could hold back, the bigger the explosion would be when it finally came at the end. I put all of myself into it as I thrust the knobs beneath my fingers upwards, this was the big finish, the big finish of the big finish, this was the happy ending, the ultimate rub and tug, the electric piano, the *flugelhorn*, the strings, I pushed the strings, that pull of tension, I could feel it down to my balls. First the thrust, then, the release, the final blast, the spurting electric guitar, O'Connor Flood's ecstatic scream. Right in the middle of the scream, silence. Zipper.

I waited. I hit stop. I could hear the machines slow to an exhausted halt behind me. My breath was heavy. I had a sheen of sweat. I looked at the clock. It was three a.m. We'd started at nine that morning, as we had been for weeks. Another sixteen-hour day. I was fried. I just wanted to get out, to go home. All I craved was for the pain, and the tedium, and the repetition, to stop. I had nothing left to give. I couldn't possibly get it up again. I prayed that Fosse wouldn't ask for one more time. There was no more I could do.

Fosse came over to the console and leaned on it. "That was great. Is there any way that you can make the ending any louder?"

My stomach burned. I never wanted to say no to this guy. I loved him that much.

Vorisek spoke quickly. "No, Bob. It's already too loud. We'll never get this on the optical, as it is."

Fosse paused and lit another cigarette. "Terrific."

I thought, great. *We get to go home. I can get a few hours sleep before we start again tomorrow. We are almost there.* I felt this overwhelming relief and exhaustion descend through my body. I was about to get up and get my coat to leave, when Bob spoke.

SCENE THREE:

The Last Playback

"OK. Let's do a playback of the whole number."

Fuck. I knew this was wrong. We'd worked on this mother for a month. It was the scene that was going to make or break this film. And when Fosse asked for the playback, I knew listening to it at that moment would be a gigantic mistake. At the end of a sixteen-hour day, your top end is all gone. Everything sounds like mush. I knew my ears were shot, and so everyone else's had to be as well. This was not the way to premiere this all-important piece of work.

I had never resisted a request, but now I had to. "Bob, I really don't think that's a good idea. I'm sure we're all fried. Let's come in first thing in the morning after we've gotten some rest, and our ears will be back, and listen then."

Fosse ignored me. "Let's give it a listen."

I tried to insist. "Bob, really, you know I never say no, I really don't think this is a good idea."

"One time from the top."

I looked at Heim, and he shrugged his shoulders. I looked toward Vorisek. He wouldn't make eye contact with me. I looked at Burns. "It'll be alright," he said, unconvincingly.

It took forever to rewind the mammoth scene.

"Bob, at least sit here, in the sweet spot," I said.

Bob sat behind the console, in the middle of the speakers. Without anyone noticing, I notched up the monitor volume one tick, just to give it all an extra oomph.

I sat behind Bob. My legs twitched with terror. I had that fetid taste in my mouth from having gone too long without dreaming or seeing the sun. I felt that familiar hollowness. I was drained.

I couldn't do it, so Dick hit the play button. We watched the scene. I had no idea if it was any good. It sounded like someone had thrown a blanket over the whole thing. It was small and soulless.

When the playback finished, Bob turned to us with a look of grotesque panic on his face. I'd seen that look a few times before, like when the distorted test reel came back from Dolby. I was afraid of his reaction and afraid that he would die on the spot. My own heart pounded, as I was obsessively aware of my own heartbeat, having watched this movie about a heart attack too many times.

Bob paused, crushed out his stub with his boot, and said, "It's a disaster. I don't know what we're going to do."

The room started to melt and swirl like chocolate stirring in cake batter. Everything got fuzzy around the edges. I felt nauseous and dizzy.

I walked out of the room, defeated, empty, despondent, despairing. I stumbled over to the coffee machine. There were plastic rings with handles. You'd put a hot cup in the ring, so you had a handle to hold the cup. I held the ring, and completely spaced on the cup. I didn't need to be drinking the rot gut that was in the pot at three in the morning, anyway. We would be going home, and theoretically going to sleep, but I wasn't thinking. I had just needed an excuse to get out of that infernal room. I poured the hot mud through the ring, and stood there watching the black bitter goo stream over my shoe, causing it to smoke. I was devastated.

I staggered out of the studio, wrapped in my winter coat, cold in the early morning air. I shared a cab with Heim, but this time neither of us said a word. We each gazed vacantly out the window. Once back at my apartment, I crawled into bed with Ivy asleep and oblivious and stared in agony at the ceiling for the rest of the night. I began to feel some weird feeling in my chest. Was it heartburn from the rotgut coffee or a heart attack? I'd watched Gideon's heart attack so many times, how could I not be having one? I couldn't take this anymore. I didn't care what happened. I just needed out. Fuck the goddamn kudos.

SCENE FOUR:

Bye Bye Life

I went in the next day a zombie. I hadn't slept for a second. I sat at the board. We were all funereal. I asked the tech guy if he'd cleaned the heads, aligned the machines, made sure playback was perfect. He promised to give the heads an extra swab and check the test tape twice, so all the needles would read zero. That way, what we recorded would be played back exactly as we'd created it. Fosse came in last, as always, and without emotion, said, "Let's play it back." Again, I attempted to usher him to the best seat in the house. He resisted, heading for his spot in the front, next to the screen, saying, "No, no, that's fine. You sit there." For once, I got a look on my face of defiance. He'd never seen me look that way. He stopped and said, "OK," and sat in the seat I wanted for him.

What would Fosse think? Would we live, or like the end of a Shakespeare tragedy, would the stage be littered with corpses? With the air of inevitability, like a guy getting to flip his own switch sitting in the electric chair, I pushed the button.

The epic, thirteen-minute death number began.

A gentle music track begins, with harp and electric piano. This cross fades into a building fanfare with horns and rhythm section.

Ben Vereen, playing a character named O'Connor Flood, a parody of show biz clichés like Sammy Davis Jr., introduces Joe Gideon, as he is about to perform his funeral song. He tells us that Gideon was adored but not loved. He was successful in show biz, but flopped in life and relationships. Twisted by drugs, sex, narcissism, cynicism, and self-loathing, he came to believe that everything, his whole life, even his success, all that jazz, was bullshit. Then the only thing real for him was death.

Flood invites Gideon to the stage where he is met by thunderous applause.

Thirteen minutes later, after the biggest act of self-parody in any movie ever made, death as a huge production number, Gideon finishes it off by singing, "Bye bye, my life . . . goodbye."

Huge rock band finish, crashing drums, pounding bass, screaming guitars, crowd going wild . . . fade out.

Cross fade to the trip down the white tunnel, from silence to top volume.

Cut to silence.

Zipper.

I waited. I was beyond fear, numb. I couldn't care anymore. Acceptance.

Bob turned to us and said, "It's terrific. Sounds great. I guess I shouldn't have listened last night. My ears must have been shot. Let's move on. Let's do the final credits."

That was it. Without a word, everyone danced their steps, did their choreography, prepared for the last detail. There was no whoop of glory, no audible sigh of relief, no acknowledgment, high fives, doing a jig. No. It was just back to work, serious, concentrated, focused, no bullshit, no jazz, no razzle fucking dazzle, just work. We made shit for everyone to scream over, while us we nihilumpen toiled away in the bowels of the earth, sullen, resigned to our fates. The fun was not for us.

We had one last cue. As the final credits rolled across the screen, Ethel Merman sang the ultimate ironic song for this film, and my life, "There's No Business like Show Business."

ACT SEVEN: THE SCREW

SCENE ONE:

The Scratch

Roll the final credits. Long after the Merman song was done, by the time everyone would have left the theatre, right before the copyright and MPAA and IATSE logos, in white letters on a black background, for all of six seconds, my name scrolled by on the big screen. Fade to black, film runs out. Someone hits the stop button. And then the whole thing was done. Well, almost.

Now, we weren't repeatedly watching one scene, we were watching the entire film again, and again, and again. The tedium was bone-crushing.

20th Century in California sent us a test four-track transfer. It was a nightmare. It sounded like shit. It was dull and hissy. My optimism for the 70mm was shaken. This method wasn't so great, after all.

This meant more work. All I could think about was the day I'd get out of this Sing Sing. But it was not to be, not yet. There was one more time, one more time.

20th Century made us a new transfer. Yet again, we watched the whole friggin' movie. We opted to use one part of the Dolby system, called noise reduction, to get rid of the hiss. The techies had fixed the dullness problem, so the new transfer sounded good, but there was still something odd about the sound. I figured out that the third track was out of phase. I had the maintenance guy at Trans Audio reverse the phase on that channel, and now the soundtrack was quiet, clean, bright, and virtually identical to our master. Maybe there was cause for hope.

This left me with one last thing to do: get the sound systems right in the theatres for the premiere. The film would be opening at Cinema One, the second-most prestigious movie theater in New York at that time (after the Ziegfeld), and the Avco in Los Angeles.

Fosse asked if I would fly out to help set up the theater in LA after we got things right in New York. Working on this big-budget movie, I'd get the star treatment. I'd travel first-class, get picked up by a limo, all that jazz. Not only that, he invited me to the premiere.

Hollywood! I was going to a Hollywood premiere! I could see it now — the black and white news reel, crowds in front of the theatre, klieg lights, flash bulbs, the stars of the film being interviewed, Hollywood royalty coming to be seen, Bette Davis, Cary Grant, Henry Fonda, Jimmy Stewart, Katherine Hepburn, Ingrid Bergman. And I would be there!

The release date of December 20th was fast approaching. When I went to Cinema One, I discovered the system was antiquated and in terrible shape. We convinced 20th Century to pay for a new sound system in the theatre. This meant new projectors, pre-amps, equalizers, power amps, and speakers. I was told that they'd be sending a technical wizard named Rich Woodcock who worked with the Dolby Company to install and tweak the new sound systems in both theaters. This would cost over $15,000, a shit-load of money in 1979. I was thrilled. I was now convinced the movie would play spectacularly for the audience. The fantasies started getting inflamed again: I'd get the nomination, no, I'd get the Oscar. The pain would be worth it.

The first important screening was set for December 13th. Kenny Utt hustled a ticket for Woodcock to fly into New York on December 6th. When the date came, he didn't show. Every minute that passed cranked up my anxiety. We needed as much time as we could to set up the system, and we were losing precious hours. Despite our panicked phone calls, he didn't show till the evening of the 9th, leaving three days before our first screening.

When Woodcock finally appeared, I could tell right away what kind of guy he was. He was that classic techie prick that had been the bane of my existence since I entered the biz. These know-nothing losers hated the mixers, because we got to hang with the stars and get the credit while they did the shit work. They thought they knew it all because they understood, theoretically, the technical side, while we mixers were just pushing a few knobs around. Woodcock was a minor functionary snob who barely deigned to acknowledge my existence.

On the 10th, the cocksucker started putting in the system, promising we would be able to hear something on the 12th. That would give us one day to make sure it all worked right. Given Murphy's Law, which stated that if something could go wrong it would at the worst possible moment, this was a bad plan.

The 12th came, and Woodcock informed us he was not ready. He would have to work late into the night.

I told Woodcock to call me when he was done, so I could give it a listen, or if he needed help, because I knew how the film was supposed to sound. I waited to hear from him, but he never called. At some point, I must have fallen asleep.

When I woke up a few hours later, I called Utt. He told me that Woodcock had left a message at 3:30 in the morning saying the installation was done and the system was ready. We were to meet him at the theater at nine to check out the film. This was the morning of the first screening.

When we got there, Woodcock was nowhere to be found. The only person present was an eighty-year-old projectionist, who had never seen a 70mm film before. He didn't know how to thread the four-track onto the new projector. Utt tracked down Woodcock, who refused to come. He said the projectionist could handle everything from here on out, and that his work was done and perfect.

The show had to go on. The projectionist threaded up the film, as Fosse, Alan Heim, Utt, Ralph Burns, I, and a few other guys from the team sat scattered throughout the otherwise empty movie theatre.

We told the guy to roll film. As we watched the title sequence, a nightmare rolled before our eyes. We watched in horror at the sight of a black line getting scratched down the middle of the pristine, $7,000 copy. We sat in stunned shock, as this lame old fart destroyed our beautiful creation. It was like helplessly witnessing the disembowelment of your favorite puppy — you could just feel the knife going down the midline. Time distorted, like what happens during any catastrophe. As if in slo-mo, we all turned in panic toward Bob. I was sure this was it for him. His wish to die right before the film opened was certain to come true now. He blanched, as we expected, but his recalibrated, if somewhat bionic, and most certainly cold-as-amphetamine heart continued to tick and tock.

With Fosse not keeling over, we all turned toward the projection booth in the back of the theatre, and screamed, "STOP!" But the film kept running, and the gash kept cutting, and the black line kept ruining the first several hundred feet of film. I ran as fast as I could, through what felt like molasses, my legs unable to move fast enough, to the back of the theater, and up the stairs, and shook the oblivious projectionist from his hypnotic slumber.

"What the hell are you doing?" I screamed.

Alan was right there with me and yelled, "Stop the film!" as he leapt across the room, tackling the projector like a caught criminal. The light flickered out, the engine stopped its hum, the clickety-clack of the spokes in the sprocket holes silenced.

We walked down the steps and back out into the theater, shaken to our bones. "Don't do anything," Bob said, trembling.

We sat silently in the theatre, resounding from the shock, unable to incorporate what was going on. Utt was off frantically trying to score us another Reel Number One.

Fosse sat alone, frozen. Finally, Ernie, one of the techs from Trans Audio, showed up. An ally, I thought, someone I could vaguely rely on. At least, I hoped so. A new reel arrived. Ernie, Alan, and the music editor hovered with the projectionist, and made sure the film was threaded correctly this time.

In our state of post-traumatic stress, we flinched as the projectionist started up the film again. As we watched the new reel, I noticed all kinds of problems. The stuff that was supposed to sound like it was coming out of the center was all diffuse and weird sounding. That third channel was out of phase again. One speaker was distorting badly, the side channels were low in volume compared to the center channel, and the equalization was all wrong. Everything sounded tinny.

When we got to reel six, the film broke. The projectionist pulled the movie out of the projector, and spliced the film back together, cutting out a piece of a musical number, mauling Fosse's delicate, precise editing and complex vision. Fosse was still breathing, I don't know how. He got up and left, clearly distraught, telling us to fix the problems.

SCENE TWO:

The Murder

There was still no Woodcock, so Ernie and I set to work. We replaced a speaker, fixing the distortion, and reversed a wire so the phase problem was undone. With the moments shrinking, and the audience clamoring to come in, we had two more huge problems: the imbalance of the channels and the EQ.

I said to Ernie, "OK, let's get going on the balance of the channels. Let's get up the alignment tape."

"Oh, no I can't do that. That's the Dolby stuff. I'm not allowed to touch that," Ernie said, anxiously.

"What? Come on! I mean, these guys promised everything was OK, and clearly it wasn't, and now the guy is nowhere to be found! Let's just put up the alignment tape and get this thing fixed! We've got a screening coming up in a matter of hours!"

"No can do, friend. We'll just have to get Woodcock down here."

I was so out of it. The blaring burlesque music from the film pounded in my head. I told myself I just needed a break, some sleep, and hoped to God I wasn't going crazy. I took a deep breath. But then I had this strange feeling of guilt. No, that was crazy. Just because I was planning on leaving when this was all done, that couldn't possibly have anything to do with this nightmare . . .

"Well, get that shmuck Woodcock down here, now!" I bellowed.

Utt looked at me, shaking his head. "I'm doing everything I can to get him here."

Ernie had to leave. I was alone in this, now. As the minutes passed I became increasingly livid. The steel doors were closing. Everything sounded horrible. My chance at stardom was getting sucked into the vortex of irretrievable time. And it wasn't all about me. It was all about *Jazz*. It was this movie, our work, our glory. It was our art. It was our meaning, our purpose, our identity, our heart, our soul. We poured everything into this, and now it could all be ruined by one asshole who wasn't showing up at the very last minute.

I sat there, helpless, waiting, unable to fix anything.

Rich finally showed up at 4 p.m. The show was set to go on in three hours. I explained to him what I was hearing: the side channels were low in volume. Rich had a sullen attitude as he reluctantly put up the reference tones from our master mix. Channel one read -4VU; channel two read 0VU; channel three was also -4VU. This proved my ears were correct. To accurately reproduce the balances we created between dialogue, music, and sound effects, and within the musical instrumentation itself, the three channels were supposed to read 0VU. That would mean that what we put in, we'd get out. No wonder the side channels sounded low; they were down four dB. But it was OK. This was a relief. This was a problem that was easy to repair.

I pointed to the meters and said, "See? Just like I said, the side channels are down. Bring them up to zero, and everything should be cool."

Rich shook his head.

"My machines are aligned correctly, to our specs. If the tracks are off, it is because your film is wrong."

Everything started to vibrate in front of my eyes. I looked at the clock. It was getting closer to five. "What difference does it make if your machine is calibrated correctly or not? The whole point of reference tones is so you can set up this equipment to match our equipment, so the audience will be able to hear what we created in the mix. Just turn the screw to make it match!"

"I'm not doing it, man. I spent hours getting this right. We don't do that. We don't adjust the alignment. Our alignment is the right one."

I could feel my muscles shake. Trying to stop myself from exploding, I lowered my voice, in desperation. I walked right up to Rich and looked him in the eyes. I decided to grovel.

"Rich, you are right, I'm sure. (Even though I knew he wasn't.) I'm sure your set up is perfect. I'm sure you are right that our reels are wrong. The movie is wrong. All wrong." Now my voice became more beseeching. "But you've got to help me out here. We've got a premiere in days, a first screening in hours! I don't care who is right and who is wrong, we just have to make it right NOW! You've got to help me fix — my fuckup!"

"Look, I don't know what to tell you. I set up the equipment to standard. I won't adjust my system."

I could feel myself losing it. "You won't change it. You won't turn the screw, and make the needle read zero. You won't do it?"

Rich shook his head.

I fell down the vortex. Everything broke inside me. All semblance of self-control disintegrated. I started to scream. "Give me the screwdriver! Give me the goddamn mother fucking screwdriver! You fucking asshole!"

Woodcock looked at me with contempt and turned away.

I couldn't take it anymore. I couldn't take one more thing. My rage was beyond human capacity. I wailed, just screaming an inchoate, primeval sound. I raised my arms. I lunged for Rich Woodcock. He lifted his arms to ward off my attack, but I was possessed with superhuman strength. I put my hands around his throat and started to squeeze. He tried to push my hands away, as I banged him up against a wall, screaming and squeezing. He had a look of terror in his eyes, as I stared into them. Spit flew from my mouth as I yelled, "I'm going to kill you! You goddamn motherfucking piece of shit, if you don't turn that goddamn screw I'm going to kill you!"

I felt big, strong arms grab me from behind. I tried to push them away but couldn't as I tried desperately to squeeze harder. It was Kenny Utt, pulling me from behind in a bear hug. I couldn't hold onto the neck any longer. As he pulled me back, I screamed, "I'm gonna kill that mother-fucker!" As he lifted me off the ground, my feet windmilled in the air.

Kenny spoke as he held me tight. "Whoa. Let's slow it down. Let's slow it down. What the hell is going on here?"

"This low life piece of shit won't turn one goddamn screw to make the stereo sound right. All he has to do is turn one screw and everything will be fine and he won't do it!"

Kenny turned to Rich. "What about it?"

Woodcock pushed back a strand of dark, wet hair. His face was red. He panted, "It's not my responsibility! If you turn that screw I won't be responsible for what happens."

I interrupted before he could finish. "Nothing bad is going to happen! He's just being an asshole! He just wants to fuck this thing up because he works for Dolby and we decided not to go with the Dolby system! He just doesn't want this to work!"

"Hey, hey Berger, let's not go that far," Kenny interjected. "Is there anyone else we can get an opinion from here?"

"Yes! Call any technical guy! They'll all tell you the same thing! Zero is supposed to equal zero! That's what the screw is for! Call Ernie at Trans Audio, he'll tell you!"

Kenny looked at Rich.

"Go ahead, call him, but don't expect me to do one more thing for this piece of garbage movie! And you," Rich growled, pointing at me, "I'm gonna sue your mother fucking ass! You are dead in this business!"

We got Ernie on the phone, and he said that it was fine to turn the screw. Rich wouldn't let me touch the screwdriver. He adjusted the meters so they looked right.

Then I said, "Great. Now we've got to work on the equalization."

Rich turned to us and said, "Are you out of your mind? I wasn't kidding. I'm done with you people. Here, you do it. Go ahead, do whatever you want to the EQ. I don't give a shit."

It was now after six o'clock. Kenny held me at arm's length and looked at me as if to say, are you going to be a grown up, now? I nodded. Then he said, "We're going to have to go with the mono tonight. We can't go with the stereo without Bob hearing it first."

This was the first stab wound, not fatal, but it hurt. I held my breath and nodded. I understood. He was the general, I followed orders. "OK. But let me come back in the morning and get things right. Make sure Woodcock is here."

Kenny agreed. I couldn't watch the film one more time, and I certainly couldn't stand listening to the mono, so I split.

I was up as the sun rose and got to the empty theatre early. I only had a few hours left to try to save my life's work. The last screening was in a few hours. The next day I'd be leaving for Los Angeles, to check out the system at the Avco. Kenny told me Woodcock wasn't coming back. They sent another guy from the movie studio named Doc. He let me tweak the EQ. Things sounded damn good. Maybe we'd get away with this.

Fosse only had time to listen to a few reels. He asked for a small change, as usual, which I made, and as we played the test reel, he seemed to be satisfied. Then something went wrong. The left channel got extremely loud. Doc went behind the gear. After a minute or two, everything sounded fine again. There was nothing more I could do here. Doc had to split. Hopefully, everything would be OK. Next was Los Angeles.

I just wanted to go home, smoke a joint, have sex with Ivy, and pack for Los Angeles. The final screening was tonight, the movie would open soon after. I certainly wasn't going to stay for this screening. I couldn't watch it again. I couldn't stomach the open heart surgery scene. I never got used to that. I couldn't stand being banged over the head with all of the mistakes I'd made in the recording and mix. Everything in my being screamed for me to get out of there. I remembered my first minute in the studio, when I had hung out in the control room during a James Brown session, and it was so loud I couldn't stand it and just wanted to run. I couldn't handle the tedium, the repetition, "It's show time, folks!"

But then a voice inside me said that I should stay, stay all night if I have to. That would be the right thing to do, that was what I should do. That is what my training told me to do.

But I couldn't find the care. I told myself it would be ok, I didn't have to stay, this was one thing I didn't have to do. It was done, it was fine, I'd done all I could.

A vague, distant echo played in my head. I knew I should stay. I should stay. The real heavies wouldn't leave. If I was a real heavy, I wouldn't leave.

I couldn't fight anymore. I couldn't think. I couldn't make decisions. I got up and walked out of the theater.

It is always weird to leave a movie theater in the middle of the day, into the sunshine. There I was, on the Upper East Side of Manhattan, across the street from Bloomingdale's. All of the '70s upper-middle-crust babes cruised along the avenue in their stone-washed jeans and dyed-blonde Farrah hairdos. Everyone was oblivious to what was going on in Cinema One. I looked at the marquee and saw the words, "All That Jazz Opening December 20th."

I wandered across town, through Central Park, on the cold, bright day.

I smoked some dope, did a few lines, and spun into a euphoric fuzz. I had prevailed. The movie would premiere in 70mm four track. It would sound amazing. I'd do the same in Los Angeles. The nominating committee would hear the movie in glorious sound. We'd win. I could relax, at least for the next sixteen hours. I packed my bags with summery clothing for Hollywood.

SCENE THREE:
86 the Ereo-Stay

As I waited for the car to take me to the airport the next morning, I got a call from Kenny.

"I've got some bad news, son. The screening was a disaster."

I saw the dark tunnel before me. "What happened?" I didn't want to know.

"All kinds of problems. The volume levels kept changing, and the sound was horrible."

"What about Woodcock?"

"I tried to get in touch with him, but he followed through on his threat. The man split and there were no other techs around to deal with it."

Then I asked the question I didn't want to ask. "What does this mean?"

"Well you know that Bob is leaving today for LA and there is no time to fix anything. So . . ." Utt hesitated. He knew what this would mean to me. "I'm sorry, kid. Fosse had to make a decision. He's canning the stereo version."

"No stereo version in New York?"

"Nope."

"LA?"

"Nowhere."

No one would get to hear it, anywhere, ever.

The final blow, the zipper on the bag, no big finish. I was dumbstruck, sucker-punched, fucked, kaput, 86'd, ix-nay on the erio-stay. I couldn't access my brain. My voice was small, almost inaudible. "Kenny, it can't be. We . . . I . . ."

"I know you're disappointed. We just couldn't take the chance. Bob couldn't take the chance."

I nodded to no one in particular and hung up the phone. It was done. My one chance at stardom, at the big award, the accolades, gone, dead, never to return. My one chance, over. The shock began to surge, like a distant tsunami rushing toward land, first just a rumble, and then a roar, then ear-busting thunder. The anger blasted out of me. Woodcock! That fucking asshole! How could these goddamn mother fucking tech guys do this to me? Then it really hit. Seven years of work ruined in one turn of a screw! I collapsed and put my hands on my head. Pain seared through my body. "Bob! How could you do this to me when I gave everything to you? How could you panic at the last minute and ruin our beautiful movie without even giving me a chance . . . how could you hurt me this way?"

Then the burn set in. The burn of regret and shame. *Goddamn it, why didn't I stay for the screening? Maybe if I would've been there, I could've figured it out, maybe I could've done something. Maybe I could've turned the right screw. Why did I go home? I could've begged, stayed up all night, found someone to help. Couldn't I have just stayed awake one more night? Hadn't I taken it this far? Did I have to drop the fucking ball on the one-inch yard line? Why didn't I stay with Woodcock every second he was here? Why didn't I stay up for those seventy-two hours and make sure this went right? What was it in me that just wanted to blow the whole thing to smithereens? I wasn't the guy. I just didn't have it. How could I have been such an idiot?*

My whole career, the whole past seven years, all the pain, all the struggle, all that fucking jazz, gone, blown, dead.

SCENE FOUR:

The Premiere

The next day, numb and glassy-eyed, I took a cab to the airport. I sat in first class, the first time in my life that I got to experience that luxury. It was late morning, and the stewardess brought me a glass of champagne. But I had nothing to celebrate. All I felt was bitter. Ironic. This was supposed to be my supreme moment. The Hollywood premiere of the greatest movie of the decade and my name on the credits. I would stand on the red carpet. Now, it was all just a hollow shell. An empty joke. A cruel finale. I got off the plane, and there was a black limo waiting for me. I got in, and gazed in the mirror provided for chopping coke. I looked like such a babe in the woods. Out the window, I watched the blue sky, palm trees, and swirl of cars on the 405 and 105. Hollywood, the cosmic sphincter of show biz. Here I was: disaffected, pissed, disillusioned. Of course. That's show biz. I got to the pink and classic Beverly Hills Hotel in one hell of a crappy mood, and checked in. All these things that should have been so much fun, just a set, just a façade, just bullshit, just jazz. I sat in my room, alone, despondent, and waited. Alan Heim picked me up in his rental car. As a New Yorker, he seemed particularly uncomfortable driving.

We went to the theatre, and they played the film for us. Again, I had to sit through the whole thing, this time, in tortuous, horrific mono. On certain drum hits, it sounded like the speakers just couldn't handle the volume and splattered. Nothing was going to work. We fucked with the equipment as much as we could, but everything sounded like shit to me, anyway. It was all one gross, painful embarrassment. Mono optical all over the world. I ruined everything.

That night it was time for the premiere. I put on my monkey suit. I stood on the carpet. There was one guy who was there to meet the celebs, a guy named Cesar Romero, a second-rate actor who had been relegated to regular guest appearances on game shows. An old guy, who once was good looking, a definite hack.

No one else showed up.

This second rate actor, at a tacky theatre in Hollywood, with a microphone in his hand, and the only person there who cared was the uncredited, non-union, *schleppedickeh* music guy who had fucked the whole thing up anyway. So much for Nicholson, Bogart, and Joan Crawford.

The champagne tasted flat on the jet ride back to New York.

SCENE FIVE:

Bye Bye ?????

Ivy and I took one last look at our empty apartment, got into a U-Haul, and drove up to Marblehead, Massachusetts. Our big black cat vomited all the way.

When we arrived, a perfect white Volkswagen bug, purchased by my composer friend Mason Daring who lived up there, was waiting for us in the driveway of our cute new home.

Ivy jumped out of the truck and did a pirouette. I opened the cat carrier, but the big black thing slunk back into a corner. I stood warily by. Ivy skipped up and threw her arms around me. I felt a strange blend of emotions. There was relief that I had escaped being eaten by one leviathan, but there was also some vague anxiety that I risked getting devoured by something insensate and insatiable that lived within me. She kissed me passionately. Whatever. I let myself go and fell into the love. I was out of my element. All I could do was surrender. In that moment we were both innocent to the lurking infection that was incubating within me from my New York days and time with Fosse which would eventually lead me to screwing up horrifically and causing unforgivable pain.

But for now, I was done with New York, A&R, and all those rock stars who wouldn't take no for an answer. The dream was over.

*

On November 7, 1980 I received a typewritten letter from Bob Fosse on his letterhead. He wrote that the film might be re-released in several major cities across the country, and that he'd had an opportunity to listen to the stereophonic version at the Ziegfeld Theatre in New York. He wanted me to know that it sounded "terrific," and that while he'd had his reasons for not releasing the stereo version originally, he now knew this decision had been a mistake. He wanted to assure me — because of all the hard work I had done on the stereo version — that "finally it would be appreciated." The letter was signed "sincerely, Bob."

The re-release never happened.

CODA

All That Jazz was nominated for nine academy awards, tying *Kramer vs. Kramer* for the most nominations that year. *Kramer vs. Kramer* took home the top awards for best picture and director, but *ATJ* still won four. Ralph Burns won for adapted score, and Alan Heim won for editing. It did not get nominated for sound.

The film won the Palme D'Or at Cannes.

It was nominated in the BAFTA awards for best sound. My name was not included in the nominees. It lost to *Fame*.

Bob Fosse died on September 23, 1987 of a heart attack. Ralph Burns died on November 21, 2001. Kenny Utt died on January 19, 1994. Roy Scheider, who played Joe Gideon, died on February 10, 2008. Joe Maneri died on August 24, 2009.

I found Alan Heim on Facebook, and wrote:

Hey Alan, I don't know if you remember me, but we worked on All That Jazz together. I'm writing a memoir about my days in the biz, and I'm working on my Fosse chapter. I'm wondering if you would be up for answering a few questions, just to make sure my memory serves me well. I hope you are well, and look forward to hearing from you soon.

He wrote back and said,

Hi Glenn,

I remember and I'd love to speak with you. My cell is 323 677 4035 but my reception at my office is iffy. Try me and leave your # and I'll call you back.

FOX has restored All That Jazz with our wonderful stereo mix and will release it on blu ray soon. I'm hoping to see it in a screening room on the lot. The folks at Fox are very excited about it.

Alan

To hear those words, "our beautiful stereo mix," made my obsession over my tiny, little, insignificant piece of the universal puzzle suddenly seem important. Someone else, from all those years ago, remembered and understood. The thing I couldn't explain to you, dear reader, that I feared no one would ever get, that would be laughed at, was taken seriously.

I called him at that number and got his voice mail. I left a message.

He never called me back.

I never heard from him again.

Ah, I love show biz.

TRACK FOURTEEN

How Paul Shaffer Almost Got Me Killed

New York's best horn players, the cats from the Blues Brothers Band — that is, Alan Rubin on trumpet, Blue Lou Marini on sax, and Tom Bones Malone on the trombone — passed a doobie and laughed among themselves. The rest of the band hovered around their instruments. Paul Shaffer was on keys, Steve Cropper and Sid McGinnis on guitar, Duck Dunn on bass, Anton Fig on drums. A crowd of onlookers hung in the control room of studio R-1 at 322. The tape was rolling.

"One, two, three!"

Without missing a beat, the horn section blasted a chord.

A screaming voice, "One, two, three, yeah!"

Another horn blast.

The rhythm section kicked in.

"You gotta know how to pony, like Boney Maroney!"

It was Wilson Pickett, the wicked Mr. Pickett, singing one of his biggest hits, "Land of 1000 Dances."

We were cutting the track live, everyone playing at once, the way it would have been done in the old days. I was probably one of the last cats around who could engineer such a thing. The year was 1988, and I was back in New York working on the last movie soundtrack of my career. We were recording a couple of songs for the film, *The Great Outdoors,* a comedy starring John Candy and Dan Aykroyd.

The audience in the control room was astounded we could do it this way. Real musicians playing in a room together was becoming an increasing rarity, and certainly doing live dates, where everyone, including the singer, recorded at the same time, had become almost extinct.

For me, this was a peak moment. The whole reason I got into this crazy biz was to do just this kind of thing. When I was a little kid, it was records just like this one, "Land of 1000 Dances," that gave me the bug, that made me think, I want to make one of those when I grow up. And to be in this room with one of my rock and roll heroes, Steve Cropper, made this last moment all the more special.

Ending up doing this gig was an unexpected treat. In the late '80s I'd returned to New York after a two-year trip around the world. Having been out of the scene for several years, I had to claw my way back in. I ended up helping this cat Weinstock set up a studio in Soho called Krypton. Everyone was opening their own rooms at the time as the price of the gear came down, and you didn't need as much real estate as you did in the halcyon days. It wasn't a top-tier or fancy room, but I wasn't in a position to be choosy, since I had burned a few bridges on my way out and had dropped a few thousand feet in catdom.

My old friend Paul Shaffer came in to this downtown hole-in-the-wall to record what was ostensibly a demo for his upcoming album, *Coast to Coast.* The concept behind the record was for him to travel across the country, hook up with regional masters, write songs with them in their signature styles, and collaborate with them on recording tracks for the album. The track he was coming in to record with me was called, "What is Soul," and was supposed to do honor to the '60s Stax sound of Memphis, Tennessee. He co-wrote the song, and would co-produce it with Cropper, who had written such eternal hits as "Dock of the Bay," and Don Covay, who wrote the super-funky Aretha hit, "Chain of Fools."

The band they were using was the World's Most Dangerous Band, the cats that Shaffer was playing with on the David Letterman show. I knew all these studio musicians from the old days. They were the best in the biz and, to top it off, nothing could beat being in the presence of Cropper. He not only wrote some of the greatest songs ever, but he had been the guitarist in Booker T. & The MGs. That legendary rhythm section had made many of my favorite records from the classic age.

We cut the basic track real easy, and that was that. I would have liked to have worked on the rest of the overdubs and stuff, but Shaffer was cagey about it, and I didn't push. Weeks passed. I figured that was it. Then Shaffer booked time to come back into Krypton.

What happened was this. Shaffer and his crew tried to recut the song at a real studio, but the thing they cut at the Hit Factory, or wherever, just didn't have the down-home, natural, funky spunk of the track I'd cut in that humble basement room. Truth was, this little ol' *schlepper* might've had a little bit of something you couldn't buy with more money. I may not have been in NYC for a while, but that didn't mean I'd completely lost it. And an old school soul track was right in my pocket. So Shaffer, Cropper and Covay had come to their senses and decided to do the rest of the song with me.

Covay was this cool, nutty black dude who sounded a lot like Mick Jagger. In fact, the Stones recorded his song, "Mercy, Mercy," in 1965. Actually, it may have been that Jagger had modeled his sound on Covay.

Covay would come into the studio, put his hands on my shoulders, look me in the eyes, and say, "Glenn? Are we gonna make history today?"

And I'd say, "We're gonna make history!"

And Don would say, "All right! Let's make a hit reckit!"

Now, that is the way I like to start every day.

Despite Cropper's legendary status, being more of a sideman than a star, he was totally cool — open, friendly, laid-back. Listening to him reminisce the legendary tales in his warm Southern tone was heaven.

Shaffer and I went way back. We'd worked together on one of his early New York recording gigs, the soundtrack for a hit Broadway show called *The Magic Show*, written by Stephen Schwartz, who was famous for *Godspell* and *Pippin* and has subsequently won a zillion awards for things like his music for *Wicked*. Shaffer is an amazing musician, which is why he always ends up as bandleader. He has an encyclopedic knowledge of every pop song ever done, and can cop the groove no prob. He is also a leader because he is so easy to like. As two bald Jews with a love of the hits he and I had an easy vibe between us. Sure, he is a bit ironic, and maybe was a touch high on the weed back in those days, but he is always the real deal.

The three cats had bigger ambitions for this tune than to just cop a style. As mentioned, in the early 1960s, Atlantic Records had been making the hottest soul records in the nation. A group of the extraordinary singing and writing talents from that label got together in 1968 and cut one single. They called themselves the Soul Clan. Circumstances led to the almost immediate dissolution of this Holy Grail of supergroups. Aficionados of soul tried for decades to reunite these players to no avail.

Shaffer, Cropper and Covay had almost managed to do it. On this one record they got nearly all the original surviving members to sing. There was Covay, Ben E. King of "Stand By Me" fame, the aforementioned Wilson Pickett who, with Cropper had written, and had a hit with, "In the Midnight Hour," among other timeless tunes, and Bobby Womack, who wrote the first Stones hit single "It's All Over Now."

King was smooth when he came in to do his vocal and did his verse one-two-three.

Covay, on the other hand, was a different story. He strangely kept putting off recording his vocal. Finally, Shaffer corralled him into going out to the studio to sing his part. I set him up as I would any singer. I checked his mic and had a sweet mix in his cans for inspiration. I escorted him into the recording room and adjusted the mic in front of him. I went back into the control room and, over the talkback, asked if he was ready. He sang melismatically to us that he was. The tape was cued a few bars before his entrance. I hit the red button.

At his cue, Covay began to twist and turn his body, and his mouth opened wide as if he was singing his ass off. But the needle didn't move. It looked like he was singing, but I couldn't hear anything. I was sure I had just checked the mike. This was weird. Shaffer and Cropper looked at me, as if I was doing something wrong. I twisted my nose and perused the board to see if I had forgotten anything, but it all looked right to me. I turned to the two producers and shrugged my shoulders, as if to say, I have no fucking idea what is going on.

Now if Covay would have been singing, and the mic would not have been working, he would not have heard himself in the headphones, and he would've stopped and complained. So, I looked closely. I could see that Covay was shuckin' and jivin'. He was movin' and groovin' but nothing was coming out of his mouth! The guy was acting like he was singing, but he wasn't!

The three of us sat there stunned, not having the least clue what to do. The verse came to an end, and I hit the stop button. Shaffer hit the talk-back, and said, in his nasal, Canadian show-biz twang, "Uhhhhhhh . . ." and then, like all producers everywhere since the beginning of recorded time, "That was great, Don. Let's do one more and see if we can top it."

It was certainly the greatest vocal performance I'd ever not heard.

When Pickett came in to sing, that was another thing entirely. Pickett's nickname of the "wicked Mr. Pickett" was no joke. Rumor had it that one time he didn't like something his bass player had said and plucked his eyeball out with a fireplace poker. Eesh!

He did a take or two, and then Shaffer got on the talkback and said, "Wilson, that was really good, but, I think we can get a better performance on the second line, so we'll punch in, ok?"

Pickett wasn't the kind of performer who had a lot of patience for working a part over and over. He threw down his headphones and stormed into the control room, his entire body shaking. He ran right up to me and grabbed me by the shirt. I noticed his skin had this plastic sheen. These stars always had an artificial look to them – probably too much Botox to make them look eternally young. His sparkly curls glistened in my face. His eyes were bulging out of their sockets. His lips quivered. His nostrils flared. His gums were purple. He screamed, in that rough soul voice that had sold a billion records, "You pluckin' now! You chicken pluckin'!"

I realized he had mistaken this balding Jewish engineer for that balding Jewish producer. Seeing my life pass before my eyes, without a thought, I quickly threw Shaffer under the bus. I pointed to Shaffer and said, "It wasn't me, Wilson! That's Paul Shaffer! I'm just the engineer! He's the one who told you to do it again! It sounded just fine to me!"

Wilson let go of my shirt and glared at Shaffer like King Kong. Shaffer quickly said, tremblingly, "That's fine, Wilson, I'm sure what we have is just fine. You don't have to sing anymore."

We got Pickett out of there as quickly as we could. And it did sound just fine.

Now, all that was missing was a guy named Solomon Burke. (Otis Redding, who sang "Dock of the Bay," and Joe Tex, of "Skinny Legs and All" fame, were dead.)

I had the blessed fortune of having worked with King Solomon Haile Selassie Burke, as he was formally known in 1983, remixing a live album of his for Rounder Records in Cambridge, Mass. where I worked for a short while after I'd left New York. The disc was called *Soul Alive*. Of all the unique characters I got to work with in my years in the biz, Mr. Burke was one of my favorites. Solomon told me that he had a Cadillac, a girlfriend, a child, and a church in every city of America. He would land at the airport in, say, Chattanooga, Tennessee, and his long tall Sally and a longer car would be waiting for him.

Solomon's gigs were made up of endless medleys interspersed with his personal brand of sermon. The King's philosophy, at its heart, could be summed up in one word. He told us that the word love was overused these days, as he purred in his rich baritone, "I love you. I love you. I LOVE you." You could feel the women in the audience perspire. But though the King truly walked his talk by siring at least 21 children, he was something of a feminist.

"And if he doesn't love the child you had with another man, don't give him none!" he would shout to the hot squeals of the women in the audience. "You don't need a man to sign your welfare check for you!"

The big guy and I had lots of fun together in the studio. He had a great sense of humor. But I learned on this Shaffer gig that it was not a good idea to mess with the King.

Shaffer got Burke on the phone. We were psyched. But after the call, Shaffer came back in the control room downtrodden. Burke told Paul that not only would he not sing on the song, but that he had written it, (He hadn't. Shaffer, Cropper, and Covay had.) and if Shaffer insisted on putting it out, he would sue! The reunion of these icons, second only to the Beatles', was not to be.

The moral of the story is, you can't go back. In Cropper's day, you'd write a song in a few hours at night, cut the A side from ten in the morning till lunch, take a break, do a little blues jam for a B side that might turn into "Green Onions," press the record, stick a $20 dollar bill in the sleeve, bring it over to the local radio station, and in twenty-four hours you'd know if you had a hit.

Things were different by 1988. Shaffer's record was ruined by the taste-deaf record company execs who kept demanding changes to make it "marketable." Over-produced, we worked on it way past the expiration date. After cutting all the parts, I didn't get to mix the record, because they wanted some hot shot at the Hit Factory to make it sound "current." Chicken pluckin' indeed. The track, and the album, bombed.

You can't go back. Isn't that what the sweet pain in art is all about? The King is dead (Solomon Burke died on October 10, 2010) and the soul clan will never be reunited. This moment in American musical history is no more.

For me, having made that momentary connection with Cropper and Shaffer, I then got to record "Land of 1000 Dances" live when they got the gig to contribute to the movie. Covay came to my thirty-fifth birthday party, and we had a great time getting drunk together. You can't go back, but I get to hold onto these memories.

And King Solomon Burke, with songs like "Everybody Needs Somebody to Love" (and in Solomon's case, it should have had the subtitle, "And I'm Available") and his 21 children, 90 grandchildren and 19 great-grandchildren, truly leaves behind a legacy that will long endure.

The Time Mick Jagger Sang "Honky Tonk Women" Just for Me

I waited for my friend Duke on 7th Avenue, outside Madison Square Garden. A throng, astir with mounting anticipation, flowed into the arena to await the arrival of the Rolling Stones. It was September 13, 2005.

Duke had been my best friend from the time were both in an experimental high school together in Brooklyn 35 years before. Back then, he had a crazy Jew-fro, wore blue work-shirts and reeked of patchouli oil, and bounded into a room like he owned the place. The first time I saw him in our 11th grade class, with his clever energy and social élan, I knew he was the friend I had been searching for. I wanted to spend every day with him.

Now, we only saw each other once a year. He was on the road 300 days a year traveling to places like Tajikistan to help people with the treatment and prevention of AIDS. I lived in the suburbs with my wife and kids. Each day, I commuted in my Façonnable suit to my psychotherapy office on Park Avenue. We got together near our birthdays to celebrate the ridiculousness of how long we'd known each other.

In the last few years, our meetings had taken on a strange, melancholy distance. Things hadn't been the same since AIDS hit. He seemed to have retreated unreachably into his gay world. Maybe he was depressed. I imagined that Duke judged me harshly. He certainly had witnessed my worst choices through life. Angry at the world during my late teens, I treated him like shit. Perhaps he had never forgiven me. His urbane cynicism still led me to long for his approval, which I felt I never received. So, I was thrilled that he came up with this idea to celebrate our 50th birthdays together by seeing the Stones.

The Stones meant something special to us. I was indifferent to the band until Duke had dragged me to see them at this same venue of Madison Square Garden in 1972, when we were sixteen.

When we were kids together, going to concerts was our reason for living. We'd gotten tickets for that classic '72 show from Binky Phillips, the absolutely coolest person we knew. Later, Binky realized his legendary status by fronting a punk band called The Planets and running a record store called Sounds in the East Village. I still have the ticket stubs from that concert, and the envelope with Binky's writing on it.

In those days, apotheosis came by getting as close to the stage as we could. The $4.50 seats placed us about halfway up the Garden's side. Duke, my girlfriend Debbie, and I knew how to get past the guards. Implacably, we pushed our way down to the floor and advanced up to the front. We ended up in the fourth row center. I stood on the back of seats held up by the moshing crowd for the entire show.

The band, at the peak of their powers, held me enraptured, filling my body with the energy of the cosmos. No dervish ever had an ecstatic experience to match mine. The image of the young god-like Mick in his white studded jumpsuit, on his knees, whipping the stage with his belt to the crash of Charlie and Keith during "Midnight Rambler," will be forever cherished as a singular golden memory.

Now, three decades on, those memories playing vaguely in the back of my mind, Duke approached me on the New York street with his same old crooked smile. For the first time in our lives, we were showing signs of age. His skin had begun to puff and sag. My hair was long gone, and my beard was turning white.

As we walked inside, the din increased, and the passel of fans, a little worse for the wear-and-tear, swirled around me. As we got nearer to our seats, like feeling the shock wave of an explosion before seeing the fireball, I began to weep deeply; uncontrollably. The emotion welled from some inscrutable depth.

When Duke saw my tears, he appeared alarmed. Having become a shrink, I'd become more touchy-feely than he was over the last years. I told him I was fine. The tears actually felt good, but I had no idea what they were about.

The Stones always knew just how long to keep the audience waiting, building the tension and excitement to an almost unbearable peak. After obediently taking our assigned seats, in time-honored tradition, Duke produced a joint. I wasn't smoking these days, but I wouldn't pass up a hit or two for the Stones. The pot wasn't so great, nor were the seats. I had seen the band a few years before with my wife Sharon. At that show, I scored better weed and seats than Duke had been able to procure. My old friend, who I had always held in such estimable regard when it came to such things, seemed to shrink a bit into humanness.

As we waited for the band, the pot hitting, my mind began to expand and I hurtled backward through time.

*

In my mind's eye, I was sitting in the control room of studio R-2. It was September of 1974. I had not yet reached my 19th birthday.

The King Biscuit Flower Hour, a syndicated radio program that broadcast live recordings of the greatest bands of the time, booked studio time with Phil to remix tapes of the Rolling Stones recorded in Brussels during their '73 European tour. Mick was coming in to supervise the remix. We'd be spending the next several days together.

Waiting for Mick Jagger to arrive at the studio was agonizing. Having become apprenticed to my master almost a year before, I had already worked with a number of famous people, but none that I loved. My heart beat with tremulous excitement.

Like a true star, in the same way that the Stones would build excitement by getting on stage at the last possible moment, Jagger waited in the wings till we were all assembled in the control room so he could make his grand entrance.

The 31-year-old Jagger, in a billowy green silk shirt, a blue ascot with yellow polka-dots, tight black pants and low, black leather boots, blew into the room, affecting shyness. In his deliciously crusty Mockney baritone, he asked, "Am I in the right place?"

The question was ironic. How could Mick Jagger ever be in the wrong place?

For once, the reality beat the fantasy. He could shine his charm on a room of 4 or 5 as brilliantly as he could light up a stadium of 50,000. With his moppy hair, crinkly eyes, and toothy smile, he was radiant, spectacular, gorgeous.

We were all deferential to the future Sir. Even Ramone, whose first record was the Grammy-winning "Girl From Ipanema," who later recorded Procol Harum's "Whiter Shade of Pale," and had worked with the scariest artists from Streisand to Paul Simon to McCartney, seemed a little humbled in Jagger's presence. Usually, Phil was fiercely possessive of his console. But for some unknown reason, without his client saying a word, he yielded the mixing seat to Mick, who sat down and placed his fingers on the red faders. These were the sliding volume controls for the various instruments: Bill's steady bass, Charlie's propulsive kick, snare, toms and cymbals, Mick Taylor's crying lead guitar, Keith's indomitable, archetypal guitar riffs, assorted horns, keys, and background vocals, and Mick's own manically-inspired lead vocals.

We listened to the first song, "Brown Sugar." Mick adjusted the balance between the instruments, trying to get a blend that would bring you into the middle of the concert.

*

I was pulled back to 2005, my reverie disturbed by the explosions, fanfare, and the crowd's ritual cheer that greeted the band when they finally emerged on stage. It was like seeing some more old friends, also noticeably aged, but still having it. Duke and I sat on the right, Keith's side. As the memory of Charlie pounding the tom-toms and Keith's syncopated guitar chops on "Brown Sugar" morphed into the real live opening chords of "Start Me Up," I was lifted out of my seat and filled with joy. If I didn't have the same endurance I had in '72, I had a deeper appreciation of the music. I knew every note by heart now. As I had discovered the limits of my own talent through the years, I knew how impossibly magical it was to create such a transcendent spell.

When Mick pointed his finger in the air and pulled the mike toward him, his weathered face dissolved, replaced by the one I had seen so many years ago. As I watched the band in front of me, I saw other, older pictures in my mind.

*

I sat inches from young Mick, at his side, by the console, watching his hands on the red faders. Usually, when a mix was in process, the mixer would become quite precious about the placement of these faders. Balancing the instruments could be a delicate affair, and when you got something you liked you were very careful to keep the slider in a very precise place. Before the advent of digital recording, it was my job to notate exactly where every knob in the studio was placed, so we could always get the magic back.

But Jagger, after playing with the mix for a while, got frustrated and knocked all the faders down to zero, ruining all that he had just built up. He got out of his seat, growling, "Ahh!" and signaled Ramone to take over.

Ramone, without hesitation, leapt behind the board to ride the faders like he was running a thoroughbred, swooning and tapping his foot, bringing his mystic vibe into the proceedings. But as amazing as he could be, this wasn't his thing. He was more a jazz, folk and pop man, not a rocker.

As Ramone tweaked the timbre of Keith's guitar, Mick looked at me, and without Phil seeing, he rolled his eyes and crinkled his nose, signaling he wasn't happy with the sound Ramone was getting. Nodding back at Mick, I intuited that he wanted something tougher than the clean sound Phil was going for. Mick tilted his head, encouraging me to crank it. He wanted me to sharpen the tone, using what we called an "outboard equalizer" which sat behind and out of Ramone's view. Behind Phil's back, I twisted the "EQ" knob all the way up to boost the midrange, so Keith's guitar would rub in your face. Jagger nodded his approval and smiled at me. I swooned. I never told Ramone that little secret; it was just between me and Mick.

This memory suffused me with a warm glow, as I watched Jagger on the stage circa 2005, his voice as strong as ever, albeit somewhat thicker with the decades. My smile broadened, as I remembered how, after the EQ moment, he had seemed to take a liking to me. Or maybe he was just a sweet guy who was nice to all the assistant engineers. He'd come into the studio and walk straight to me, gently punch me a few times, rub my long, curly red hair and say, "How ya doin' Gin-jah?"

With that, I ascended to a realm somewhere between heaven and nirvana. I'm straight, but if he would've asked, I would've said yes to spilling some beans all night long.

It had been a crazy couple of weeks at the studio. When Mick had come in, we were finishing up Dylan's *Blood on the Tracks*. At the end of our first day of working together, we told him that Dylan was going to be in the other studio. He asked to be brought over. Ramone gave me the assignment to make that happen. I was happy to be the go-between. They'd apparently met before but were not fast friends.

These two titans in the rock pantheon couldn't have been more different. If Jagger was the most charming man on the planet, then Dylan, it seemed to me at the time, was the exact opposite. The two hung out together for a short while, but it was awkward, and their meeting ended with a thud.

*

These pictures played out in my mind as the current Stones moved through their set, hitting one peak and then taking it higher. During "Miss You," I saw that my wife Sharon had left me a message on my cell phone. There was only one reason she could have been contacting me. Maybe this was why I'd been having such a deep emotional reaction.

The infant boy we were planning to adopt was being born right then in Wichita, Kansas. He would be entering this world just as the Stones were playing the final song of their main set, "Jumpin' Jack Flash."

I knew that the next day my life would be fundamentally trans-formed. But now there was nothing to do but watch the Stones do their encore.

When they finished, Duke and I waved goodbye to Mick and Keith, sweaty and exhausted, and followed the crowd out of the stadium onto Seventh Avenue. We hugged each other good night, knowing this was the last time we'd ever see the Stones together, and also sensing that our relationship was growing so distant that it could disappear as easily as the Stones leaving the stage and driving off in their respective limos. We lingered an extra moment. I didn't tell him about the call I had received from Sharon. I was excited and scared in a way that I couldn't put into words and didn't think he'd understand anyway. So we parted silently.

As I sat in a cab on my way to Grand Central to catch a late commuter train to my suburban home, I returned yet again to 1974.

*

On our second day of mixing, Mick must have needed some inspiration. He called his dealer to deliver some stuff. An hour or two later, in walked Mick's candyman, who turned out to be John Phillips.

John had found fame with The Mamas and the Papas. They recorded hits like "California Dreamin'," which Phillips wrote along with some other classic songs, including "San Francisco (Be Sure to Wear Flowers in Your Hair)" and the song that was played more often than any other by the Grateful Dead, "Me and My Uncle."

Trouble was, by this time, Phillips had become a severe drug addict. Though Jagger was ready to promote Phillip's solo album on the Rolling Stones Records label, he wasn't above using Phillips as his dealer.

From that time in the '70s, Phillips continued to spiral down. The solo project never manifested, and he was eventually convicted of trafficking in 1981. Most ignominiously, his daughter, Mackenzie, herself famous from having starred in the TV show "One Day at a Time," claimed on "Oprah" that, after injecting her with heroin and coke, her father embarked with her upon a ten-year incestuous relationship.

But Phillips seemed pleasant enough to me at the time. In a big brown envelope, he delivered two large film canisters, one filled with pot, the other with cocaine.

Jagger had me roll a joint for him. This was part of the assistant's job, and one I could do well. From what I could tell, Mick wasn't much of a druggie; maybe he'd take a hit or two off the joint, then stamp the oversized roach out in the ashtray. Or a pinky fingernail's-worth of coke up his nose once or twice, and that was about it.

Phillips hung out. He and Mick appeared to enjoy one another. Along with the hooch, he'd also brought along some tabloids with scurrilous reportage on the Glimmer Twin. Mick loved reading about himself and laughed. He said, "I remember what Elizabeth Taylor told me: 'I don't care what they write about me as long as it isn't true!'"

With Jagger having barely touched the stuff, at the end of our mixing day the two containers were virtually full. Mick gave me his hug and tousle goodbye and, pointing at the canisters, said, "That's for you, Ginger!"

*

I was jostled from my memories as the Metro-North conductor announced our arrival at my Westchester station. Having arrived home late from the concert, I knew I'd only be getting a few hours of sleep. I crawled into bed next to my blissfully sleeping wife, and kissed her delicately on the forehead so as not to wake her. Having adopted a child before, I knew what we were about to get into. Sharon would need all the rest she could get.

The next morning we moved into action. There are odd differences between adoption and biological birth. You don't hop in the car and go to the hospital. Instead, we quickly packed our stuff and took a limo to the airport. We arranged to drop off our two-and-a-half year old daughter with Sharon's sister in St. Louis and we were in Kansas before the ringing from the previous night's concert went out of my ears.

My wife and I had developed a relationship with the birth mother over the previous several months and we had been following the pregnancy, so we were surprised when we got the news. The boy had been born three weeks early. We were told that the baby was in the hospital, but that everything was fine. When we arrived at the Wesley Medical Center, we were relieved to discover that the boy wasn't in the NICU, the Neonatal Intensive Care Unit. They had just wanted to keep him there for a day or two to make sure he was eating sufficiently to gain weight.

Still, we were understandably anxious. One of the great lessons one gains from parenthood, whether biological or adoptive, is learning about the things you can and cannot control. So many things could go wrong with a birth. Suddenly, life felt so fragile. We prayed that our new son was going to be OK.

Once inside the hospital, having sufficiently killed all possible bacteria by scrubbing our hands, we walked into a room that held a few tiny beds. A nurse pointed to one holding the boy that would be ours. We padded over silently and looked at this *vantz* (as my Jewish mother would have called this "little thing") smaller than a puppy. I squinted my eyes, moved in close, and scrutinized him like you would a used car, checking to see that all his parts were intact. He looked perfect, and, like all newborns, he had the glow of someone who had just shed his wings. You could still hear the heavenly choir in the background. He was very cute as his tiny chest moved up and down with each delicious breath.

I should've been relieved, and seeing his sweet little body did help. But my concern over his health and well-being was replaced with a new anxiety. Like the sadness I felt vaguely outside The Garden after the Stones concert the night before, this, too, was unexpected. I instantly felt a pang of love for our new son, but something made me clench inside. An awesome weight descended on me, a doubt that rose in my mind: he was fine — but what about me? Would I be the kind of father this beautiful boy deserved?

As I looked over at my wife, her blissful smile signaled that she was unburdened by such doubts. Of course there was the oxytocin factor, the natural love hormone that all mothers secrete in the presence of their baby. I could see that she was falling into that narcotic euphoria of infant motherhood. This anxiety was something I was suffering alone.

As we sat in the hospital by that little bed, Sharon saw the preoccupied expression on my face.

She asked, "What's wrong? Our boy is healthy and beautiful."

"It's weird. I didn't expect to feel this way," I answered.

I could see her getting nervous. "What do you mean?"

"I just don't know if I can do it."

Now she started to show alarm. "Do what?"

"Be the great dad that I want to be for this guy."

She visibly relaxed, and shook her head. "Don't be silly. Of course you will be. You're a great dad to your daughter."

"Yeah, but this is different. She's a . . . she's a girl. He's a boy. That's different."

"What do you mean?"

"Well, you know. My dad died when I was young, and he wasn't much of a father even when he was around. He didn't teach me how to catch or throw a ball, fish, or defend myself in battle."

"So what? That stuff isn't so important. You're a different kind of man, a better kind of man."

"I know, but a boy needs that — I needed that — and I didn't get it. It's bigger than that. I want so much to be the kind of father to this kid that I never had. But if I never had it, how can I do it?"

"Honey," she said solicitously, "you're the best. I love you so much for worrying about this. And I get that you'd be nervous. But, hey, I'll teach him how to play basketball. You'll be fine."

Looking deeply into my eyes, Sharon reached over and kissed me, and I remembered why I married her. But somehow, this didn't soothe me. It only worried me more.

Soon enough, within a few days, we would sign the papers that would make this newborn our son forever. By the time he would be ready to leave the hospital, it would all be done. I felt like I had to find some wellspring of power within me, and fast.

Having had a long day, and with the infant resting peacefully on her chest, Sharon fell asleep. As I sat there in the quiet room, the songs from the previous night faded up in my mind's ear. It was as if someone was turning up the inner volume knob in my brain. Again, I traveled back to the '70s.

*

My friends felt an intolerable envy that I was spending the week with "ol' rubber lips." When I told them that I couldn't get them into the studio, at first, no one would speak to me. Then I put out the word that I had two film canisters filled with Mick's drugs. Within hours, we were in Duke's basement, all blasted to smithereens. Everyone loved me again.

Feeling profound under the chemical influence, my friend Messer had a revelation. He got in my face and pushed his long, stringy, blond hair behind one ear. "Berger! You're hanging with fuckin' Mick Jagger! You've GOT to talk to this guy, I mean, this could be your one and only chance in the history of the universe to have a one-on-one with Mick fucking Jagger!"

I squeezed my lips together. "You're right, man, I know, I really should, but it's just not the protocol. My job is to be invisible. And besides, what am I going to say? Why would he be interested in talking to me?"

Now everyone joined in. This was a critical moment for our entire group.

In his officious tone, Noel said, "Well, if what you said is true, the guy digs you. I mean, he calls you Ginger, for Christ's sake! Of course he'd be open to talk to you."

Duke chimed in, "Who cares if it's not allowed? You've got to do it." And then, opening his eyes imploringly, "You've got to do it — for us."

I stewed in conflict as inspiration and trepidation battled inside of me. "OK, OK. But, I mean, what do I say?"

"Say anything!" Noel offered.

As he snorted another line, Messer got thoughtful. Then he began to pace. "No, you've got to be strategic. You'll have Jagger's ear. He wants you to talk to him. He wants you to ask him a question. If you could ask Mick Jagger one question — one question in the whole world — what would you ask?"

I thought carefully. The words that formed in my head scared the shit out of me.

Duke could see there was something behind my eyes. "What?"

Everyone sat in front of me, waiting for the words. "If I could say anything, anything at all, to Mick Jagger, if I could ask him one thing, I'd ask him . . ." I hesitated. "I'd ask him if he would take me on the road, with The Stones."

Messer slammed his hand on the waterbed he was sitting on. "Yes! That is exactly the question you must ask!"

The fateful rightness of the question descended over the entire group. They all looked at me as if I was the hero who had been given the task of capturing the Golden Fleece. This was my destiny. I was the only one who could do it.

The import of the mission overwhelmed me. I sat there, nodding my head, all of us silent, feeling the moment.

*

In those first days in Wichita, waiting for the baby to get out of the hospital, as I struggled with my crisis of confidence, I discovered something surprising. I liked this little Midwestern city. Its people were nice. My blue-state, New York prejudices had led me to expect a congregation of gun and NASCAR loving, abortion-and-gay-hating fundamentalists. I was surprised to see copies of *The Nation* and *The New Yorker* in the hospital waiting room. The nurses were kind, open-minded, and seriously dedicated to doing good work and to getting food on their family's table.

The city was a small grid. It was clean and easy to navigate. We were able to find healthy food and the best children's museum I'd ever been to. In the middle of the next afternoon, I left the hospital to pick up some supplies. While I was out, I decided to explore our surroundings. I took a drive by myself to the edge of town, ten minutes from anywhere in the city. The grid ended abruptly. Suddenly, I found myself facing a flat prairie that went on for about a thousand miles till you hit the Rocky Mountains. I drove a few miles into Wizard of Oz country with only the occasional silo on the horizon. I felt a rising tension in my stomach. I stopped the car and got out.

The stillness was ominous. I found myself gripped with an existential terror. I was sure that I was plunging head first into the endless void. In a panic, I jumped back in the car, turned it around, and drove at eighty miles an hour back to civilization.

Our local adoption attorney came in to visit. I envied how he picked up the boy with a joyous verve and beamed. He stated unequivocally that this guy was as precious and love-worthy as he appeared and we were blessed to have each other. Though this lawyer always liked to say that he operated from an "abundance of caution," this apparent certainty did not convince me. Sure, we were blessed to have him, but him, me? Everyone else seemed to know something about me that I wasn't privy to.

*

Returning to A&R that Friday, burdened with the charge from my posse, I waited for my chance to pop the question.

Mick had planned to do an interview that would be part of the radio show. He thought it would be fun if Peter Cook moderated.

Peter Cook was a brilliant English comedian. He was an extremely influential figure in British comedy in the 1960s. The actor and comedian Stephen Fry called him "the funniest man who ever drew breath." For a while, he was famous for teaming up with Dudley Moore, another pretty funny guy who ended up a movie star.

Dixon Van Winkle — the aforementioned strange and brilliant engineer — Mick and I crammed our bodies in a cab with our remote recording gear to tape the interview at the Pierre Hotel. Though I touched thighs with Jagger, with Dixon there, I couldn't complete my mission. The timing was not yet right.

We hung out in a suite at this posh New York hotel by Central Park with Mick and Peter, but nothing really came of the recording. Peter drank some of the hard stuff. We left after some chuckles, but with nothing usable on tape.

That night, Mick had nothing better to do, so he asked if there were any good restaurants nearby and would we like to have dinner. We went to our go-to place, Pierre Au Tunnel, the French restaurant on 48th Street between 8th and 9th Avenue, right down the block from the studio.

It was Mick, Phil, Bob Meyrowitz from King Biscuit, and myself. Mick was impressively cultured and sophisticated, especially to this provincial boy from Sheepshead Bay, Brooklyn.

He swallowed his garlicky escargot and sipped on a nice little Bordeaux. In his rich, resonant tones, he entertained us. "When we were in Fraaahnce, you know, doing *Exile*, we had this brilliant sommelier who provided us with these stellar Lafites. That's when I really learned what good wine was all about." Then, after rolling the juice in his mouth, "This one's not bad."

I saw Duke's imploring eyes in my mind, but, clearly, this also, was not the moment. I simply wanted to get through the dinner without anyone figuring out that I was in so over my head that I felt in a constant state of drowning. I might have pulled it off better if I'd kept the adoring, goofy grin off my face.

My plan went especially awry when I made the mistake of ordering the french dessert called a Napoleon. For those of you who don't know, a Napoleon is made of endless layers of very thin puff pastry, alternating with vanilla cream. There's no way to eat a Napoleon gracefully. When you try to cut through the layers, the cream squirts out the sides. As I tried to negotiate this sweet lasagna, I watched in horror as my hands took on the shape and skill of awkward clam claws. I suddenly couldn't remember how to hold a fork and knife, as I spastically tried to cut the oozing morsel. Cream shot across the table. Mick glanced at the awkward performance but had the grace to ignore it, barely raising an eyebrow, and chatted on.

*

The final night before we would sign the papers and take the boy back to our hotel, Sharon and I whiled away the hours in the hospital. She seemed serene, holding the baby in her lap. I felt too ashamed to reveal that I was still plagued with doubts and insecurities. My mind anxiously raced through the "what ifs." As a therapist, I often ask, "What is the worst that could happen?" as a way of helping my client gain perspective of what is most often an unreasonable fear. In this case, the answer was, I could fail this child miserably, and he would be forced to endure the scars of my ineptitude for a lifetime. The worst, in this case, was really bad.

As I bit my fingernails, a very large woman with a mid-western buzz cut and big square glasses slowly strode toward us with a warm smile on her face and an outstretched hand. She introduced herself as Dr. Marcy, our birth-mother's doctor. It was she who had delivered the child.

She plopped herself down into a chair. It seemed like she was planning on staying for a while. I was used to doctors coming in late and leaving early. Glove on, cough, glove off, watch your pressure, see you next year. But this woman had a different vibe. She asked us questions about ourselves, and we found ourselves opening up to her, telling her how we fell in love, about our longing for a child, our struggles with infertility, the joy of adopting our daughter, and how we came to be here tonight.

Dr. Marcy spoke of her family. She told us about her journey of becoming a doctor, how she left the profession and returned back to it again. She shared the story of the discovery that her daughter had a hole in her heart, the way the girl survived this life-threatening condition with a dangerous operation, and how this forever changed her husband's perspective on life.

One of the nurses came by to attend to the twin bananas in the hamster-cage-sized incubator that was next to our little boy's bed. These three-pounders were safe enough to have been moved out of the intensive care unit but they were still pretty tiny. I was astonished at how she handled them with delicacy and ease. She joined in our conversation and told us about her own troubles, and what she went through taking care of her husband's kids.

I mentioned how astounding it was to see these premature babies alive and how much I admired the work that these doctors and nurses were doing. Dr. Marcy told us that given the big empty spaces around us, this was the central hospital for many miles, and so it had the biggest and best neonatal intensive care unit in this part of the country. The nurse asked if we'd like to see it.

We disinfected again, and Doc and the nurse took my wife and me into a vast room lined with rows and rows of incubators. Each one held a tiny, fragile human life. Some had just been born, right on the edge of viability, maybe little more than a pound. They were hooked to tubes and machines and looked like thumbs. Their actual thumbs were smaller than pencil erasers. Others were getting closer to moving on into the great, big world. They had gained weight and grown outside their mother's bodies where they should have been. The technology was extraordinary, but it was through the ministrations of these devoted women that these preemies lived and took in life and turned that love into brains and bones, muscle, flesh, and heart.

They had little hands that one day would hold someone else's hand; mouths that would one day smile. They had eyes that would one day look into a mother's eyes. Through seeing themselves reflected in that love they would come to know that they existed, that they deserved to be loved, and would love others themselves. They would have the chance to do this beautiful thing called life.

We left the unit and went back to our station. We all looked at our little fella snoring contentedly. He suddenly looked huge. Not wanting to wake him, my wife and I silently smiled to each other, our hands together held tight.

*

Mick would be coming in on Saturday so we could finish up. As the assistant engineer, I always came into the studio first and, having cleaned up after the party, left last. It was my job to get everything ready so the big boys could play. This quiet weekend morning, the midtown streets were strewn with garbage and a few straggling late-working hookers. Every storefront was covered with metal grates.

I was thrilled to open up the studio, the only one there.

It was a sacred ritual to unbox the thick, warm, multi-track tapes with their iron-oxide filings dancing so pretty. I slid the big two-inch reel over the large shaft on the bulky tape machine. I threaded the tape through the metal guides and over the tape heads and swiftly twirled the end of the tape to catch hold on the take-up reel. I hit the rewind button, and the tape swooshed across the heads until it emptied one reel and filled the other. I hit the fast-forward button to put a break on the speeding tape, and the machine slowed to a near halt when I hit stop.

I walked over to the console and hit play on the multitrack's remote. I started to set some basic levels. I was just getting into the track when Mick walked in. I hit the stop button and stood up.

Mick and I alone, Saturday morning, 1974, New York City. Yes! Here was my chance to have that real conversation with the Midnight Rambler. I heard my friend's voices in my head. This would be the only moment in my life that this would happen. What to say? I couldn't just leap into my question. I puttered around the control room, patching in limiters, as we talked.

We talked about the lyrics to the song, "Dancin' with Mr. D" from the Stones latest album, *Goat's Head Soup*. We talked about how weird we thought Dylan was. I could feel our connection building, but I wanted to see if I could impress him in some way before I popped the big one.

I had an inspiration.

I thought of my endless nights at New York's repertory film houses, The Elgin, Bleecker Street, Thalia, or Theatre 80 where I had repeatedly watched that movie *Performance* that starred my new friend Mick Jagger as a washed-up pop star.

Watching that movie a dozen times when I was sixteen years old taught me how to really see films. Nicholas Roeg, the cinematographer and the guy who supervised the editing, had a radical approach to cutting: playing with time, place, and point-of-view in non-linear ways. Unless you knew how to really focus, you couldn't follow what was going on. It was the first time I was motivated to really concentrate, which was to help me later on in making art and making love.

My friends and I were passionate about this wild film. It was hot, with great nude sex scenes with the voluptuous Anita Pallenberg, Keith's real-life girlfriend; androgynous Mick; a child-like French actress named Michèle Breton; and kinky-masculine James Fox, who played a sadistic gangster. It had a super-tasty soundtrack by Jack Nietzsche that peaked with a Jagger composition called "Memo from Turner," performed by Mick in slicked-back hair and a suit. The story was full of drug-laced allusions to hip literature and other esoteric cultural references. Its plot and dialogue, centered on the tension and love in the relationship of the gangster and the rocker, were stoned-cool.

In an era when movies were just starting to break out of the orchestral, straight mold, it was a groundbreaking, pioneer rock and roll movie. I'd studied the movie frame-by-frame and knew all the great lines and its subtle nuances.

I also knew the film had been a flop. I figured this was my way in.

"You know, I think *Performance* is an amazing film."

Mick seemed genuinely pleased.

"I've thought about this movie a lot." I was digging deep. I mentioned an obscure moment in the film. "The book. It is Borges, isn't it?"

"Right . . ." I had grabbed his attention. I could see his feathers fluff.

"The thing about Turner losing his 'demon,'" I went on, "it's like genius is the freedom to say yes to yourself, and that requires a lack of self-consciousness. If you looked in the mirror, that is, if you became self-aware, it was gone. And Chaz had that lack of self-consciousness which allowed him to be the best at what he does, even though it was pure evil. And that's what Turner wanted from him. But the irony was, Chaz had lost it too. It's like when Moody says, 'He's an old fashioned boy,' and then Harry Flowers, 'An out-of-date boy.' Chaz symbolizes the world before the '60s, which can't work anymore. Maybe what the film is trying to say is that there's no room for that un-self-conscious genius in the world anymore. No one can do anything, because we know too much, and that leaves us filled with paralyzing self-doubt."

I felt a flush of embarrassment. Had I sounded like a pretentious idiot?

"Brilliant!" Mick said, his eyes bright with surprise. "Yeah. I never thought of it that way. It's nice to know that someone got it." Then the feathers went down. His face grew dark. "I was just really disappointed that it was so misunderstood. The critics ripped it apart. After that debacle, no one wants to put me in a movie."

"That's crazy! You were amazing!"

Mick shrugged, almost humbly.

Oh my God, I thought, I did it. I'm having a real conversation with Mick Jagger, alone, and I've got him! The time was fast approaching. Was it now? The words were in my head.

But before I could speak, Mick asked, "What track do you have up?" Shit. I missed the opening.

*

Dr. Marcy eased herself back into the chair and looked at us as if we had known each other since she had delivered us herself. She'd been hanging out with us now for four hours. Not your typical New York doctor's appointment. I never revealed my fears, but by her presence I was beginning to sense the vague outlines of the message that I was desperate to receive. I started feeling weak, as we had not had much to eat that day and it was now approaching 10 p.m. I asked her if there was a place to eat nearby. She told us the best burger joint in town was right across the street. She said that she needed to see a few other patients, but she'd probably still be at the hospital when we got back.

We stumbled out into the warm Kansas air, crossed the road, and sat outdoors at Billy's Burgers, which looked like something right out of *American Graffiti*.

We had been through so much on this adoption journey. The pain and disappointment of infertility, the miracle of our daughter, the extraordinary gift we were receiving right now.

Sitting at this plastic table on the patio, as we ordered our burgers, fries, and shakes, I felt like I was on the lip of something profound. Hanging with Dr. Marcy and the nurses, I knew I'd learned something of immense importance but it had not yet turned into words. The stars in the sky glittered with numinous brightness.

Old rock and soul songs played through the restaurant speakers. I knew that I was in an altered state, as each title seemed to be sending me a personal message. First, "Do You Believe in Magic" by The Lovin' Spoonful. Then "It's Alright" by Curtis Mayfield and The Impressions.

And then, the miracle occurred. The next hit on the radio was by the Rolling Stones. I heard the signature cowbell intro, and then the unforgettable beat, presaging one of their biggest hit singles, circa 1969. A song everyone alive at the time knew. Like Dorothy picked up by the tornado, I instantly swirled backwards through time, landing in a magical land.

*

I told Mick that I had "Honky Tonk Women" as the next song on our list to mix. He asked me to play it for him. He sat next to me while I rode the levels and put myself into making it sound as hot as I could. He listened seriously.

"Ach, I don't like the vocal. Let's do a new one. Set up an SM-57 for me, will ya?"

As I walked out into the studio, the realization of what was about to happen suddenly dawned on me. Mick Jagger was going to perform "Honky Tonk Women" and I would be the only person in the audience! I set up the mike and walked into the control room.

I turned the mike on, adjusted the preamp level, turned up the attenuator, and clicked the talk back to make sure it was working. I placed a set of headphones on my ears and set up a mix for the cans. I ran back into the studio to make sure the headphones worked, dashed back into the control room and told him we were ready. We ambled out into the studio together. He said he wanted to hold the mike, so I took it out of its stand and handed it to him. Then I flew back to the control room.

We stood about eight feet apart, separated by a thick piece of glass. I pressed play and "record" on the massive multi-track.

The song began with Keith's rhythm guitar: Baaah-dep. Bah-bah dee-dep; Charlie's drums: Boom, pow. Boom, boom, pow; then the signature guitar lick that told us Mick's vocal was about to enter.

And then, looking straight into my eyes, with a glorious, Dionysian smile on his face, the greatest rock and roll singer the world has ever known or ever will know opened the most famous mouth alive and sang the lyrics of this quintessential Rolling Stones hit single — the very song that would be playing all those years later at Billy's Burgers.

Mick's dancer's body writhed in his signature style, his hair falling on his face, his arm slithering like a snake, his finger pointing in the air as the entire band burst into the chorus. And he, pouring his heart out, growled the notorious refrain of this signature hit.

I looked straight back at him, while making sure the vocal was going down on tape at the right level. I breathed and tried to take it in, almost knocked over by the intensity of the feeling but staying upright, knowing this was, and would forever remain, the glory of my short but precious life.

He sang the second verse, then the second chorus hit, with Mick Taylor wailing on his fluid axe. The band rollicked through Keith's solo, then Mick kicked it over the top on the balls-out final chorus.

I prayed that the track would never end, but all too quickly, at just over three minutes, the coda hit, and it did. The crowd of thousands burst into rapturous cheers and applause. I wanted to join them.

I hit stop on the multi. I pressed the talkback button and said, "Great!"

Mick, out in the studio, took a small bow, looked up, pointed his finger at me, and wailed, "That one's for you, Gin-jah!"

Mick Jagger had just performed "Honky Tonk Women" for me!

With his vocal done, he slowly walked into the control room for a playback. With every cell in my body vibrating, it took all of my will to act nonchalant, cool. He sat next to me as we listened back.

He was satisfied. So was I.

This was it. Now was the time. I tried to summon the courage to ask the question. I dug deep. My heart hurt, my breath was short. I hesitated. I looked at the superstar next to me. Seconds passed. I told myself to say the words, but they wouldn't emerge.

Then the door opened and Phil and Meyrowitz burst in and began chatting it up with Mick. It was over. I had lost my chance.

*

As Sharon and I sat at Billy's Burgers that warm September night, my heart filled with emotion, the final chords of "Honky Tonk Women" ringing through the air, the memory of my missed opportunity stinging still, it all became clear.

I could hear the command of the universe blaring in my head. I remembered my favorite adoption story, "What Men Live By," by Leo Tolstoy. In this story, he tells us that it is not given to us to know what is good for ourselves. Instead, what is given to us is to know what is good for each other. In this way, the universe insures that we are bound by care. We do not live by bread alone, we live by love.

I looked at Sharon, radiant in the light of the soft Kansas night. I said, "I've been thinking about all this the wrong way. It's not about whether I can do this, you know, be a great dad for our son; it's about whether I will do it. It's not a question of whether I am capable. It's about, do I have the courage?"

She said, "I know. Taking on this responsibility is huge. I feel the enormity of it, too. But there is nobody else in the world that I would rather do this with than you. I know you can do this, I know we can do this, together."

I looked off into the distant horizon, to the end of Wichita, the edge of the world, and felt certainty pervade my being. Everything I had learned, everything I had struggled with, all the work I had done on myself, cohered. The same message rang out everywhere.

Whether we follow the dictum of "living according to God's will" as Christians might put it, or find the "central harmony" by aligning to the Tao, as the Confucians would say, all wisdom traditions tell us that we find our greatest fulfillment by surrendering to something bigger than ourselves. It comes from using our will to become willing. It comes from learning how to say yes to life and what it demands of us at each moment, whatever the personal consequences. It comes from asking the question: What does the universe want from me now, rather than what do I want from the universe?

To "live" by avoiding the demands of our nature may be temporarily more comfortable, but we do so at our peril. Jonah ends up in the belly of the whale until he follows God's dictates.

There are a few lucky moments in life when we are truly put to the test, when we are selected for a unique and important task. Parenthood is one of those times. For me, this was such a moment. Everything, including the music on the jukebox, was telling me that this was not my choice. Instead, I had been chosen.

"I get it. It's not about me throwing a ball or fixing cars. It's about me being a good person. It's about me doing the right thing, no matter what. That's what I couldn't do before you came into my life. You've shown me that I can trust myself."

Now, I knew what the tears were about at Madison Square Garden. Time passes, and it doesn't come back. My friendship with Duke had faded. I couldn't take back the times I was cruel to him when we were kids. I couldn't take back all the mistakes I made in life because I was afraid. I would never be sixteen again, seated in the fourth row at a Stones concert in 1972. I'd never be nineteen, with Mick singing solo to me again. I'd never get a chance to go out on the road with the Stones. When it comes to time, there are no second chances. If you miss the moment, it's gone forever. To quote from another famous song of theirs, time waits for no one.

I did not heed the call with Mick, and there is always a price to be paid when we avoid the directives of the cosmos. Back with him, I was still a boy. At that young age, I'd shown some damn good gumption by pushing my way into that room to be with him in the first place, but I didn't have what it took to close the deal. Remorse was the toll exacted on me.

I could not undo my past mistakes, but I could find redemption in what I would do right now, in this present moment. Now, I was a man. The radio at Billy's told me so. I knew exactly what I had to do.

I smiled at Sharon, and as I looked in her eyes and saw the love that was there, I felt she knew everything that was in my heart. I said, "I've always been looking for a father 'out there.' With all the men in my life, whether it was Phil, or the stars I worked with, I was always asking myself, Are you my father? Are you my father? But none of them were, and I was always hurt and disappointed. Then I'd run away, thinking I was punishing them, but I was only hurting myself. I'd achieve some success, but then I'd sabotage that, ruining things in the end."

Sharon listened intently and sympathetically. "I get that. I understand now. But if you hadn't have gone through all that, you wouldn't be right here, right now."

"You're right! I had to go through all of that to be here, with you, doing this. I was never going to find that father, because I couldn't go back and have the father I needed as a child. But now, I've been able to find something so much bigger. I've been able to find the husband, the father, the man, where I should have been looking." I pointed at my heart. "I'm ready. Let's go get our son."

*

That Saturday would be the last day that I would get to hang with the lead singer of the Rolling Stones. We finished up the mixes. Mick complained about the recorded performances, saying the band rushed, that they played too fast. It was ok for a radio broadcast, he figured, but they were too embarrassing for anything else. Listening to those mixes now, with the wabi sabi that comes with age, the frantic tempos just sound like blistering enthusiasm. Though I assumed our mixes would only be heard once on the radio, since then they have become legendary. They are the only top-quality mixes of the Stones from a time period that many consider to be the ultimate live moment for the greatest rock band in history. This was guitarist Mick Taylor's last tour with the band, and many believe that the Stones were never as good after he left. This recording also occurred before the band was dragged down for a number of years by Keith's heroin addiction.

These mixes have found their way onto multiple bootleg releases and are generally known as "Bedspring Symphony."

When we faded out the final applause, with the concert and our week in the studio together done, Mick stood up to say goodbye and purposefully walked to my end of the control room to give me one last punch and tousle. He said, "See ya, Gin-jah!"

I took one last look, paused, and said, "Goodbye, Mick."

As those world-famous hips sauntered out of the studio, and his narrow frame receded into the distance, with a lump in my throat, my voice caught. I cringed, envisioning Duke's disappointed, judging, eye-roll. In my head were the words, "Hey, if you ever need someone to help out on the road . . ."

*

Now, about forty years later, sitting in my minivan, my son and daughter clipped in their car seats in the back, Sharon looking so hot behind the wheel, I press the button on my smart device. "Brown Sugar" blasts through our JBL Surround-Sound system. My son grooves to the beat. Whenever I can, I play-wrestle with him and give his hair a rub. He's perfect in his imperfect human way. He loves dogs, Legos, and his mom, and when I woke him up the other day, the first thing he said was, "I love you, Dad."

Riding down the highway, I hear Mick's voice in my head, saying, *This one's for you, Gin-jah!* and I know that my job is to get these kids as close to ecstasy as I, or anyone, can bear. When the end of the song comes, in my best Mockney accent, I shout out to my family, "I can't hear you!" and we all join in with my old pal Mick, singing at the very top of our lungs, "Yeah, yeah, yeah, WOOOOOOOOOOOOO!"

I wonder if my revelation about the universe was true. But whether there is a grand master plan, or if the only meaning in a meaningless world is the meaning we give to it, the answer is still the same. You can hear it in Keith's guitar. He plays it, holding nothing back, just so he can ring that cosmic bell again and again. Because this is his only chance in a very long eternity to do so. Because that's the way the universe sings.

POSTLUDE:

It Was All Them

I left the tape recorder and the box of tapes downstairs through the days, weeks, months, and years, as I recalled, and wrote down these stories. I'd been changed by the process, and I'd learned a great deal along the way, but there was still something essential that eluded me about the emotions I experienced on the day when I listened to Aretha with my client. My wife complained about the clutter, but until I could find that missing piece, I didn't know what to do with all that old jazz.

I worried that I would never find what I was looking for. I came to realize that there was no way to fully grasp the complexity of experience, shaped by meaning, and transmuted by time and memory. Whatever I wrote about these events, and my place in them, there was always something I left out, a new way of seeing it all, after I called the story finished. But that didn't keep me from my pursuit. I went back to the box one more time to see if I could find something, anything, in it, that would clarify and resolve this confusion of feelings.

Once more I listened to Paul Simon's "American Tune," with its rhymes of "mistaken," "confused," "forsaken," and "misused."

Again, this triggered associations. Neurons connected to neurons. Patterns that hadn't lit up in decades illuminated my brain. I floated back to a time when I was particularly incensed at what I considered to be some unconscionable behavior on Paul's part.

I ran up to the second floor and stormed into Max's office, throwing up my arms. "You will not believe what just happened!" I said indignantly.

Max nodded knowingly with mock-sympathy, closing his eyes. He said, "Tell me."

I went into the story, which was some variation of the theme, "This guy Simon is a total prick!"

Max opened his blue eyes wide and said with great exaggeration, "But Glenn, of course he is!" Then he paused for effect. "So?"

Having the intended impact, I replied with incredulity, "So? So? He . . . he . . . can't do that!"

Max leaned back in his chair and let out a giant throaty laugh.

"I don't see what's so funny!"

I didn't then. I was a kid who was looking for heroes and villains, a story that made sense, a drama where I could be on the right side, if I could only find those on the wrong side.

Max stopped laughing. He looked at me with affection, understanding, and the wisdom that can only come from the perspective of having been young once, and now no longer being so.

As I remembered that moment, and I imagined how he looked at me, I could suddenly see through Max's eyes, as he sat there with me, all those years ago. I saw myself sitting in Max's chair, as old as I am today, looking across that desk, at the young boy I was back then.

In Max's skin, I understood that the studio world we lived in — with all the craziness, drama, egos, disasters, pricks, triumphs, and astounding accomplishments — was precious.

From Max's point of view, having escaped Minneapolis to come to the Great White Way, where he was living the exact life he was meant to live, what could be better than this? After all, we were in show biz. Sure it hurt, and Paul could be mean, and Phil acted like a nut, but it beat selling handkerchiefs.

I now understood what he knew then: this was a passing moment, our one short spin on the turntable. These artists would fade, the studio would one day be gone, the scene would end, all too soon. For that one speck of eternity — midtown Manhattan in the 1970s — we were living at the center of the universe. And Max knew how to savor every loony moment of it. He accepted it all: black, white, and gray, like a Hindu sage.

"Enjoy it kid," I heard him say to me, "one day it'll make a great book."

But back then, I had no idea what he was talking about. "Max, you don't understand!"

"Look, Berger, it's getting late. You doing anything right now? Let's go get a bite at The Tunnel."

It was Friday night, and our work was done for the week. I agreed to join him. Pierre au Tunnel was the French restaurant that was our hang right down the block from "322." When we entered the old-fashioned French restaurant, Jean Claude, the gallant proprietor, greeted us warmly. The room was suffused in a golden glow with a gentle aroma of wine and garlic.

The usual crowd was there. There was Tony, going from table to table, schmoozing with the stars. Plotnik was there, avoiding going home to his wife, joking around with Holley. The receptionist was at the bar, passing a bag to the latest up-and-coming *schlepper*. Sterling was three sheets to the wind. A couple of horn players sipped their Remy Martin VSOP, trying to take the edge off the blow.

Emile Charlap walked in right behind Milton, and the three of us hung at the banquette near the bar. I spent a minute or two kibitzing with these two old-timers.

Max said, "Emile, you should know this kid. He's a firecracker. He's coming up. He's our next hot shot."

"Good to know, good to know," Charlap acknowledged.

I didn't get, or appreciate, that Max was doing a *shidduch*. He was making a match between me and Emile. He knew that if I played it right,

Emile could book me on a lot of dates.

Instead, I was distracted by a sexy, wannabe girl-singer, who was hustling me for free studio time. Maybe, I thought, if I promised to get her into R-1 this weekend, I'd get laid. Without a thought, I blew off Max and Emile.

As I cavalierly walked to the door of the place with my arm around the girl, I suddenly remembered Max and turned around to say goodbye. He looked at me, and I thought I heard him say, "Take it in. Take it all in. Now. Before . . ." And then I couldn't hear him anymore.

The neuronal pattern in my brain, and along with it my memory, dissipated, and everyone was gone. The restaurant was dark and empty. I looked to my side, and the hot chick had also disappeared. What did she look like? Oh yeah, she was the one who blew me off for Steve Jordan . . .

I found myself, like in a dream, transported to the studio at "799." The halls were quiet now. There was no red light lit above the studio saying "closed session." There were no messengers sleeping on the couch. No one running down the hall with a fire extinguisher. No smell of brass and wood, no sound of bass and electric guitars. The old gear, the Pultecs and the Fairchilds, the MM-1000s, and the Macintoshs, all were dusty relics, unused. The studios were empty. There was no more music. Just silence.

I felt the same pang that I had when sitting with my client and listening to Aretha sing Paul's masterwork.

Then it hit me.

I didn't recognize, or appreciate, the gifts that were being handed to me by a benevolent universe. I didn't see what Max was doing that night when he was creating a singular opportunity for me by hooking me up with the great Emile Charlap. I didn't appreciate the open-hearted generosity of all the people I had worked with, who had welcomed me into this amazing world of music, and gave me the chance to witness and participate in this fantastic creative adventure. I was so focused on what I didn't get, that I didn't take in the value, the love — what I did get from this extraordinary group of people. My attention elsewhere, only thinking of pussy, I didn't linger with Max and Emile.

I didn't recognize that the dad I was looking for wasn't the glamorous star, who not only didn't want the gig but was incapable of it, anyway. The guy who fit the bill was the man in the dandruff-covered suit. The closest thing I got to the dad I never had was Mr. Milton Brooks, better known as Broadway Max.

Then the regret hit. I never, never properly said thank you. It was worse. I had been cruel and callous. Not only had I been unappreciative, but in my anger, I had left in a rejecting way. I never said I'm sorry.

The regret morphed into longing.

I remembered those rare moments, a long time ago, when I really had it, when I was at my peak, when the cosmic wind blew through me. It was like the entire universe thrummed around me and everybody stood up and cheered. But each time it happened I got scared. I wasn't ready. It was too big. I couldn't handle it. I remembered that place, that feeling, and I wanted it back. I'd know how to deal with it now, I told myself. I want to feel it again before I die.

But I had to face it. It was too late. Not just my moment, but the whole thing was gone forever.

And then the longing became sadness. Whenever anybody asked if I missed the biz, I always said no. And I believed it when I said that. But it wasn't true. It took all of this to find that the answer to my quest was a simple one. I never wanted to admit it, but those days in the studio were important to me. I guess I just never wanted to feel the loss.

It was all gone, and I missed it in the painful core of my eternal being. My tears were tears of grief. One good reason I cried with my client was because I missed my days when I was the *schlep* with Phil and Paul at A&R Recording.

That feeling of *duende* — the Spanish word for the awareness of death, that I got remembering the Sinatra story — I really got it now: I'm getting old, youth has passed, and the moment will never, ever come back.

I was feeling it. It hurt, but strangely, I felt so alive.

Suddenly, something cracked inside of me. Light started pouring through. Pain. But wait a minute. It wasn't only my pain. What about . . . their pain?

In that one moment, everything changed. It was like someone knocked the stopper off the bottle, and I could feel all this anger just draining out of me. Everybody, Phil, Paul, Fosse, Dylan, they were all in so much pain! That's what was going on. We were all in pain! How could I have not seen that? It's so obvious now!

I wanted to contact Ramone right then and there and say . . . but I didn't, because I received a text telling me that he had died.

Phil. My mentor, my sensei, my guru, my rabbi — dead. Phil gave me the greatest of gifts, which has earned him a permanent esteemed place in my inner world. I dreamt of him just last night. What he birthed in me was a standard of excellence. This vision of quality was, and remains, the meaning and purpose of my life. This is the part of him that lives in me in every waking moment, whether it is in the work I do now as a psychotherapist, in my marriage, as a father, or in the creative work I do. It is that aspiration to magic (with a little less of the craziness, I hope) that I aim to pass on to my own children.

In the way Phil treated me, and in what he demanded of me, I experienced a lot of pain. But what I learned from him was that life and art demands that we rise above our own comfort to fulfill a cause greater than ourselves. And when I followed Ramone into that breach, I lived life to the fullest.

All of us who worked at A&R under Phil's tutelage share an ineffable bond. When we get together now, from our experience of having lived in the Great One's presence, we know something that no one else in the world knows. We each and every one of us will say that our years at A & R, under Phil's leadership, no matter how hard, no matter how insane, were the most thrilling and unforgettable of our lives.

That was what you got with Ramone. The lunacy, the pain, the glory, and the pride. We were the best, and we got to be a part of history. And as crazy as he drove me, none of this would have existed without Phil.

What I would have said, if only I'd had the chance, was,

"Look, I get it now. I get what it's all about. I know your suffering was something I can only begin to imagine. But the beautiful thing is, you made my life meaningful. You made all of our lives meaningful. You were our mad captain. You had a mortal wound that inspired you to fight nature itself, and we all knew that you were doomed to fail at the end. But we were all ready to go down with you. And you know why? Because, in work, in art, in life itself, we rarely, if ever, get to take something all the way, to do our absolute best, to be able to say, this is what I am made of, this is what is in my heart. But you made it possible for me to do that. You pushed me past my limit and gave me the opportunity to find the best within myself. You fought the good fight so I could be great. And I will always love you for that. I love you."

I sighed and hit the rewind button on the old tape machine one last time. The tired motors, close to a half-century old, tugged at the tape that I had found tucked among the outtakes in the bowels of the basement at "799," of Paul razzing Artie, but the reels didn't move. I had to give the machine an assist, twirling the reel with my finger, until the tape was back in its home. I put the relic back in its box, and unplugged the recorder. The machine sighed, too. I thought it would be happy to be in use again, but now it was tired and just wanted to get some rest.

As I put the cover on the reel-to-reel, and coiled the power cord, I felt sad for my dad, who never got to experience the moments of glory, meaning, and purpose that I have had the blessing to have in my life. He was one of those poor souls who had been so badly wounded that he didn't believe in the possibilities of life and died a broken and unfulfilled man. I felt sad that he didn't get to live long enough to see that his son did do something with his life, not merely by making some good records back in the day but by the work I do now as a therapist. Maybe that would have eased his pain a little.

I felt sad for all the therapy clients that I work with who are wasting their precious few moments of their lives because of fear, because they live with the conviction that they somehow aren't good enough, because they have never imagined that they can get what they want out of life. If they just paid attention . . . the way I wish I had paid attention . . .

And then, for some crazy reason, Maneri, the guy I visited at the Boston Conservatory, popped into my head.

After I left New York, I followed Maneri's path. I studied Schoenberg's method and learned all about harmony. But I couldn't abandon the biz completely. I eventually came back to New York. I was producing this girl act called Little Diva. Three girls, around twelve years old. All with killer voices. After recording and rehearsing, we had our first gig. It was in Atlantic City. We thought it was going to be at a dance club. When we got there, we discovered that Atlantic City was a nightmare — pathetic, desperate loners spending the few pennies they have on a dream they always lose. It was noisy, ugly, crude, vulgar. The girls were a little freaked. Then we went into the place where the gig was, and there was a convention for kids with disabilities. The audience was just a row of kids in wheel chairs. This was not the glamorous show biz moment they were envisioning. I could see their disappointment and fear. They didn't want to do the gig.

Backstage before we went on, we stood in a circle holding hands, all the girls looking at me. I told them the story about Maneri, about the time he played in the nursing home for the deaf guy. And when I finished the story, I said, "You all think that you're gonna end up playing in stadiums and making a million dollars. And whether that happens or not, that's not what it is about anyway. Those kids, in the wheelchairs out front, that's what it's about."

I could see the light bulb go off, the look of understanding, on their faces. They relaxed, looked at each other, and smiled. One of the girls said, "Let's rock!" They ran out on stage and sang their hearts out.

Everything was quiet for a minute. Then I looked over at my book shelf, and one book stared back at me. It was *What Makes Sammy Run?*, the book Milton Brooks gave me when I first started at A&R, now forty years before. I'd always wondered what his intention was in giving me this book about a guy who destroyed everyone on his way up the ladder and ends up destroying himself. I had thought that Brooks wanted me to make it in the biz, but the book seemed to say that Sammy's way of making it, the only way to really make it, was, well, hell. I could never figure it out. Was it intended as an instruction manual, or a cautionary tale? Now that became clear. It was meant for me to ask that question. I could go either way. I had both parts, everything, within me. I was the *schlepper* and the superstar. That choice would determine my life. And when I thought of that moment in Atlantic City, I realized I had made my choice.

I had just a few seconds to savor this reverie before my kids came in, "Dad, let's do something else!"

I carried the tapes and the machine back up to the attic.

As I put the stuff into a corner, I thought of an old phrase we'd use when evaluating whether a particular recording was good enough: "close enough for rock 'n roll." But that phrase was mostly used ironically. Everyone involved in the crafting of a recording took their task absolutely seriously, whether it was the producer, the studio musician, the engineer, the piano tuner, the arranger, the artist, or, even me, the *schlepper*.

Despite the power and exuberance of the hot, tight, funky tracks we cut, there was a deadly earnestness to the process. In our twentieth hour, weary to our bones, we'd cut a track. When it was done, the troops would march into the control room. During the playback, the cats would stand around the control room silently, listening intently for the slightest, most imperceptible, flaw in a performance. At the end of the take, there'd be no burst of applause. Usually, rather, there was a sullen acknowledgment that it could be better. The producer would say, "That's great. Let's try it one more time." And then, all the musical soldiers would march out to the studio to do it again.

I wish that we could do life that way. I wish we could do a playback, listen closely, reverently, self-critically, consider the mistakes, and, like good soldiers, stolidly return to our lives, to get another chance and try again.

As a kid it was so important for me to present myself as being cool. I didn't want to ask questions or admit that I didn't know something. I couldn't be humble and ask for help or advice. Out of my own narcissistic insecurity, I had to appear the know-it-all.

If I could have another take, that's what I'd do differently. I'd soak up everything I could from all the great women and men who had so generously taught me. I'd gather together all the people from those days: the folks from the beginning, like Susan Hamilton and Buddy Edel, who took an interest in this cocky little kid and made things possible for me. I'd thank Plotnik for his love and craziness, and Tony for his eternal lessons, and the assistants for their friendship. I'd thank the engineers, the musicians, the producers, and the arrangers for showing me how to make a really, really good record.

These wonderful human beings, who all worked hard to be the best in their field and, beyond the confines of our musical world were often unsung, were even more special because their goodness, generosity, and egolessness were rare in a culture that feted jerks. I'd tell them all how amazing they were and say thanks.

I'd even thank the jerks. Confucius said we can learn something from everyone, either what to be or what not to be. To the jerks, I can say thanks because without you this book, and a great deal of great art, wouldn't exist.

And Mr. Simon, I'll admit it. The truth was, it was all you.

I am honored to have known you all, both the mensches and the schmucks. I will cherish forever the times we shared.

Thank you. And, I'm sorry.

As I folded up the attic ladder, I smiled. I remembered an old joke. Two friends meet on a street and plan to get together one day after work. The first guy says to the second, "I work in the circus. Come meet me at the menagerie."

The second guy gets to the menagerie and finds his friend shoveling elephant shit. He says, "Man, this is the most disgusting job in the world! How can you do it?"

And the first guy says, "What, and get outta show biz?"

I closed the attic door, and stood in the hallway where my one gold record hung, and I looked at my life as it was right at that moment: the house I lived in, my spectacular wife and children, my career, and all the beautiful, struggling people who are, and have been, my therapy clients. But given the strange way that memory and imagination works, I also saw my past and my future. I knew where I had been, more or less. The future was less certain, except for the final outcome. As I looked around, seeing it all, I understood the true import of the A&R way, the first lesson that Tony had taught me all those years ago. It wasn't enough to say the words. You had to mean them. Nothing was close enough for rock and roll. You had to care. You had to care to the depths of your soul, no matter the cost, no matter the pain, no matter the outcome. You couldn't do things half-assed. You had to do it again and again, until you got it right.

I looked at the life I had led, the life I was leading, and the life to come, and I heard Tony's dictum resounding in my head. My entire being reverberated with love. This *schlepper* was ready to get to work. Give me my hand-truck. As if I was Aretha, I sang, at the top of my lungs, *yes*.

THE END

Acknowledgments

would like to thank my teachers in the craft of recording; the making of art; the workings of the psyche; the ways of the word; and how to love.

Thanks to my first teachers, the folks who helped get me into the biz: Willie Edel, Herman Edel, Buddy Edel, and the great Susan Hamilton.

At the top of the list of my teachers in recording is my mentor Phil Ramone.

Next are the world-class engineers Don Hahn, Eliot Scheiner, Dixon Van Winkle, and Rich Blakin. I thank all of the assistants who generously welcomed me into their world, including Brad Davis, Randy Masser, Dave Masson, Gary Roth, and Major Little. I would like to thank my assistants Ollie Cotton, Chaz Clifton, Georgi Offrell, and Anne Pope. I thank my studio compatriots Nick DiMinno, Dave Smith, Nancy Sorkow, Leanne Ungar, Vicki Fabry. Brad Leigh, Laura Doty, and Helene Stansky.

Thanks to all the generous producers, arrangers, contractors, and musicians who taught me about music and what it means to be a professional. I cannot mention you all, but I want to give a special shout out to Emile Charlap, Michael Small, Pat Williams, Ralph Burns, Arif Mardin, Steve Burgh, John Simon, Paul Shaffer, Will Lee, Eliot Randall, David Spinozza, Don Grolnick, Steve Gadd, Tony Levin, Rick Marotta, Warren Bernhardt, Ralph MacDonald, Tom Bones Malone, Alan Rubin, Blue Lou Marini, Kenny White, Murray Weinstock, Ken Bichel, and Mason Daring. Thanks to studio owners Bob and Janet Lawson.

Thanks to all the great artists I worked with who do not get mentioned in this book, from whom I learned how to make great art, including Ray Charles, Michael Franks, Steve Forbert, Susan Osborn, Bill Staines,

Jeanie Stahl, Fiddle Fever, Rory Block, Ashford and Simpson, Leiber and Stoller, Paul Anka, Kate and Anna McGarrigle, The Starland Vocal Band, The Holmes Brothers, and Bobby Scott. Thanks to all the great singers and musicians who made me look good when I worked in the jingle world. Thanks to Marc Blatte and Jeanne Neary for their belief in me and their sage advice.

Thanks to my teachers in the arts of psychotherapy including David Yarosh, the staff at the Gestalt Associates for Psychotherapy, Harville Hendrix, and all of my clients who must remain nameless.

On top of the list of those who taught me how to write, I would like to express profound gratitude to my wonderful publisher and editor, Tim Schaffner, whose genius allowed me to realize my vision.

I would also like to express thanks to the wordsmiths and publishing gurus Tom Staudter, Helen Eisenbach, Ruth Greenstein, Irene Reichsbach, Michael Pietsch, Jill Cohen, and Tracy Behar.

A special thanks to Robert Couteau for his time, effort, modeling, support, and wisdom.

A very special thank you to Don Shewey for his overwhelming generosity, invaluable brilliance, unstinting moral support, and impeccable standards. This book wouldn't be what it is without him.

Thanks to friends Chuck Granata, Denise O'Connor, Joe Magnetico, Neeta Ragoowansi, Michael Cohen, Mary Murphy, Lisa Fragner, and Jason Eaton for their encouragement, wisdom, and life lessons.

Thanks to my publicists Scott Manning and Abigail Welhouse for their enthusiasm, belief, patience, and being cool people.

Thanks to my book and cover designer, James Kiehle, for his great sense of style.

Thanks to Ebet Roberts for taking great photographs.

Thanks to my distributors at IPG and all the sales reps who are championing this book.

Finally, there are no words to capture my gratitude and love to my teachers in love: my wife Sharon, my kids Maya and Ethan, and my pets Ollie and Bruno. Without you, none of this would matter a whit.

Glenn Berger: A Select Discography

1974

Paul Simon, *Live Rhymin'*; assistant engineer
Urubamba, *Urubamba*; assistant engineer
Terry and Maggie Roche, *Seductive Reasoning*; assistant engineer
Mood Jga Jga, *Mood Jga Jga*; assistant engineer
Phoebe Snow, *Phoebe Snow*; assistant engineer
The Magic Show, *Original Cast Recording*; assistant engineer
Gilbert O'Sullivan, *A Stranger In My Own Back Yard;* assistant engineer
The Harlots of 42nd Street, "Cool Dude & Foxy Lady/Spray Paint Bandit"
(single); engineer
The New York Dolls, *Too Much Too Soon*; assistant engineer, engineer
Bo Diddley, *Big Bad Bo*; assistant engineer

1975

Bob Dylan, *Blood on the Tracks*; assistant engineer
The Rolling Stones, *Bedspring Symphony*; assistant engineer
Judy Collins, *Judith*; assistant engineer, engineer
Paul Simon, *Still Crazy After All These Years*; assistant engineer
The Dynamic Superiors, *Pure Pleasure*; assistant engineer
Felix Cavaliere, *Destiny*; assistant engineer

1976

New York Tuba Quartet, *Tubby's Revenge*; engineer
Steely Dan, *The Royal Scam*; assistant engineer
Phoebe Snow, *Second Childhood*; engineer
Judy Collins, *Bread and Roses*; engineer
Ashford & Simpson, *Come As You Are*; assistant engineer
Starland Vocal Band, *Afternoon Delight*; assistant engineer
Bobby Scott, *From Eden to Canaan*; engineer
Paul Anka, *The Painter*; engineer

1977

The Jimmy Carter Inaugural Album; engineer
The Arbors, *The Arbors*; engineer
Judy Collins, *So Early in the Spring*; engineer
John Handy, *Carnival*; engineer
Joe Thomas, *Here I Come*; engineer

Jimmy McGriff, *Tailgunner*; engineer
Kate & Anna McGarrigle, *Dancer with Bruised Knees*; engineer
Film Soundtrack, *The Turning Point*; engineer

1978
Phoebe Snow, *Against the Grain*; engineer
Ray Simpson, *Tiger Love*; engineer
Steve Forbert, *Alive on Arrival*; engineer
Film Soundtrack, *Superman – The Movie*; engineer
Ray Charles, *United Negro College Fund*; engineer

1979
Toledo, *Crime Doesn't Pay*; engineer
Michael Franks, *Tiger in the Rain*; engineer, mixing
Carolyne Mas, *Carolyne Mas*; engineer
Mikio Masuda, *Goin' Away*; engineer
Television Soundtrack, "Jack Frost"; engineer
Film Soundtrack, *All That Jazz*; engineer, producer

1980
Gary McMahan, *Colorado Blue*; engineer

1981
Bill Staines, *Rodeo Rose*; engineer, producer

1982
Hypertension, *Got This Feelin'*; engineer
Bill Staines, *Sandstone Cathedrals*; engineer, producer
J.B. Hutto & The New Hawks, *Slideslinger*; engineer

1983
Jeanie Stahl, *I'm Just Foolin' Myself*; engineer, producer
Paul Winter, *Sunsinger*; engineer, mixing
Film Soundtrack, *Lianna*; engineer, producer
J.B. Hutto & The New Hawks, *Rock With Me Tonight*; engineer, mixing
Rory Block, *Rhinestones and Steel Strings*; engineer
David Mallet, *Open Doors & Windows*; producer, engineer
Hazel Dickens, *By The Sweat of My Brow*; mixing
Russ Barenberg, *Behind the Melodies*; engineer, mixing

1984

Solomon Burke, *Soul Alive!*; engineer, mixing, editing

Various Artists, *They'll Never Keep Us Down: Women's Coal Mining Songs*;
engineer

The Kentucky Colonels, *On Stage*; mastering

Johnny Adams, *From the Heart*; mixing

1985

Buckwheat Zydeco, *Turning Point*; engineer

Paul Winter Consort, *Concert for the Earth*; engineer, mixing

Carpenters, *Lovelines*; engineer

1986

Paul Winter, *Whales Alive*; engineer

Susan Osborn, *Susan*; engineer, producer

Paul Winter, *Wintersong*; engineer, mixing

Mike Metheny, *Day In, Night Out*; engineer

Paul Winter, *Living Music Collection '86*; engineer

1987

Oscar Castro Neves, *Oscar*; engineer, mixing

Paul Sullivan, *Sketches of Maine*; consultant

Buckwheat Zydeco, *Buckwheat's Zydeco Party*; engineer, mixing

1988

Rory Block, *Best Blues and Originals*; engineer

Various Artists, *Downtown NYC: A Compilation of the Best NYC Artists*;
engineer, producer

Hazel Dickens, *A Few Old Memories*; engineer, mixing

Paul Winter, *Wolf Eyes: A Retrospective*; engineer

John Fahey, *Popular Songs of Christmas & New Year's*; mastering

1989

Paul Shaffer (featuring Steve Cropper, Don Covay, Ben E. King, Wilson
Pickett, Bobby Womack, Mavis Staples, Darlene Love, and Ellie Greenwich),
Coast to Coast; engineer

Bill Staines, *The First Million Miles*; producer, mixing

1990

The Holmes Brothers, *In The Spirit*; engineer
Music From The Original Soundtrack, The Civil War, "Ashokan Farewell";
engineer, producer
Clarence "Gatemouth" Brown, *The Original Peacock Recordings*; mastering

1991

Michael Bolton, "A Dream Is a Wish Your Heart Makes," *Simply Mad About the Mouse*; engineer

1993

David Darling, *Eight-String Religion*; engineer

1997

Delia Bell and Bill Grant, *Dreaming*; engineer

2002

J.B. Hutto, *Slidin' the Blues*; engineer

About the Author

Glenn Berger, Ph.D. was for many years through the 1970s and '80s a recording assistant and later engineer/producer for A&R Studios where he first apprenticed under the legendary Phil Ramone at the age of seventeen. After twenty years in the music business, Glenn became a psychotherapist and currently practices in New York City and around the world by Skype. He is the inventor of a series of psychology iPhone apps called "Shrinky," and blogs about relationships, success, and creativity at www.glennberger. net. He is also the author of a children's book, *Princess Chantik and the Outside World*. Excerpts from this memoir have been published in *Esquire*, *Rolling Stone*, and *SOS* online.

Glenn Berger as a young schlepper *circa 1974 at A&R Studios (left);*
and as he is today at MSR Studios.